TIM GUNN'S
FASHION
BIBLE

TIM GUNN'S FASHION BIBLE

THE FASCINATING HISTORY OF EVERYTHING IN YOUR CLOSET

Tim Gunn

WITH ADA CALHOUN

GALLERY BOOKS
New York London Toronto Sydney New Delhi

Gallery Books
A Division of Simon & Schuster, Inc.
1230 Avenue of the Americas
New York, NY 10020

First Gallery Books paperback edition September 2013

GALLERY BOOKS and colophon are registered trademarks of Simon & Schuster, Inc.

For information about special discounts for bulk purchases, please contact Simon & Schuster Special Sales at 1-866-506-1949 or business@simonandschuster.com.

The Simon & Schuster Speakers Bureau can bring authors to your live event. For more information or to book an event contact the Simon & Schuster Speakers Bureau at 1-866-248-3049 or visit our website at www.simonspeakers.com.

Designed by Kris Tobiassen

Manufactured in the United States of America

10 9 8 7 6 5 4 3 2

The Library of Congress has cataloged the hardcover edition as follows:
Gunn, Tim.
  Tim Gunn's fashion bible : the fascinating history of everything in your closet / Tim Gunn.
      p.   cm.
  Includes bibliographical references.
  1. Fashion design—History. 2. Clothing and dress—History. 3. Fashion—History. I. Title.
II. Title fashion bible.
  TT507.G863 2012
  746.9'2—dc23
                            2012010786

ISBN 978-1-4516-4385-5
ISBN 978-1-4516-4386-2 (pbk)
ISBN 978-1-4516-4387-9 (ebook)

*Dedicated to fashion lovers
past, present, and future*

CONTENTS

Introduction......1

**WHY A HISTORY OF
WESTERN FASHION?**

1. *Underwear*......9

SECURITY VS. FREEDOM

Panties, bras, lingerie . . . *In defense of
the corset*

2. *T-Shirts*......23

**FROM UNDERWEAR TO
EVERYWHERE**

Graphic tees, tank tops, V-necks . . . *Why a
white T-shirt signals sexual availability*

3. *Jeans*......37

**THE ITALIAN, FRENCH, GERMAN,
ENGLISH, INDIAN, ALL-AMERICAN
GARMENT**

Low-rise, boot-cut, skinny . . . *Jeans, the great
American wardrobe staple*

4. *Dresses*......49

**FROM THE TOGA TO THE
WRAP DRESS**

Cocktails, shifts, sheaths . . . *Are you
a Cleopatra or a Helen?*

5. *Capri Pants and Shorts*......89

THE PLAGUE ON OUR NATION

Bermudas, Daisy Dukes, hot pants . . . *From the
battlefield to the beach party*

6. *Skirts*......99

MINI, MIDI, MAXI, AND MORE

Pencils, hobbles, poufs . . . *The shorter the skirt,
the younger—not necessarily the sexier—the look*

7. *Belts*......109

FRIEND TO SOLDIERS AND VIXENS

Cinches, aprons, tool belts . . . *Giving shape to
the shapeless for thousands of years*

8. *Dress Shirts*......119

PRUDERY AND PUFFERY

Collar stays, secretary blouses, French cuffs . . .
*Are you button-down casual or buttoned-up
dressy?*

9. *Ties and Scarves*......129

COLOR ME BEAUTIFUL, **HERMÈS,
AND OTHER CULTS**

Neckties, bandanas, pashminas . . . *Men in the
nineteenth century knew dozens of ways to tie a
tie; every man today should know at least one.*

10. *Vests*......143

TAKE THAT, FRANCE!

Tweeds, silks, waistcoats . . . *Why vests are fashion's freedom fries*

11. *Suits*......151

ALL HAIL BEAU BRUMMELL!

Business wear, zoots, tuxedos . . . *Are you a single-notch or shawl-collar man?*

12. *Pants*......169

THE TRUTH ABOUT DRESS REFORM

Khakis, trousers, cargoes . . . *No, leggings are not pants—jeggings either!*

13. *Hosiery*......179

FROM THE *MAYFLOWER* TO THE BEDROOM FLOOR

Socks, stockings, panty hose . . . *Tights should look like tights.*

14. *Shoes*......189

THE WORLD AT YOUR FEET

Heels, boots, slippers . . . *The more impractical the shoe, the richer the look*

15. *Athletic Wear*......205

ATTACK OF THE PLAYCLOTHES

Sweat suits, swimwear, hoodies . . . *Get thee behind me, yoga pants!*

16. *Sweaters*......223

KNIGHTS, FISHERMEN, AND SWEATER GIRLS

Jerseys, knits, crochets . . . *The cavalry has arrived—wearing cardigans.*

17. *Coats and Jackets*......241

FROM CAVEMEN TO *REAL HOUSEWIVES*

Pelisses, trenches, peacoats . . . *Why fur belongs in the dustbin of history*

18. *Hats*......251

CROWNING GLORY

Baseball caps, fedoras, berets . . . *The lost etiquette surrounding hats indoors*

19. *Gloves*......263

THE LONG-LOST LOVE TOKEN

Mittens, gauntlets, fingerless . . . *Why gloves went the way of the crinoline*

20. *Handbags*......271

ENEMY OF THE POCKET

Purses, clutches, messengers . . . *Size matters!*

Conclusion......279

HOW TO SHOP WITH THE PAST, PRESENT, AND FUTURE IN MIND

Appendix......289

YOUR CLOSET WORK SHEET

Notes......297

Bibliography......305

Acknowledgments......311

WHY A HISTORY OF WESTERN FASHION?

WE ALL HAVE an intuitive sense of what clothes mean. When you walk into a room or down the street, even without thinking about it, you immediately take note of clothing clues and judge the wearers accordingly. You can usually tell at a glance whether a person is rich, poor, or somewhere in the middle. Often, you can even guess what someone does for a living—the messenger with his pants legs rolled up, the businessman in his suit.

And yet, it's rare that people think about what their own clothes signify about their place in the world or their priorities. Clothes are self-expression. If you have a limited range of outfits—say, only capri pants and T-shirts—it's as though you have a limited range of words in your vocabulary.

While many historians concern themselves with the dress of indigenous civilizations, the work of certain designers, or with very specific periods in fashion, I am most interested in the clothes we wear right here and now and how various looks came into vogue. My focus in this book is on Western fashion, with a particular emphasis on America. I will look, piece by piece, at the items most Americans have in their closets and ask, "Do you know where this garment comes from—before Old Navy?"

This old thing?, you may think.

My answer is yes. Even that ratty band T-shirt has a fascinating history that goes back far before the Steel Wheels tour. While American fashion is often vilified as sloppy or as the poor relation of Parisian couture, I find it full of surprises, beauty, and history. And I love

exploring the ways in which and the reasons why clothing changes over time.

Before writing this book, I considered myself to be something of a fashion expert. I was an educator for twenty-nine years, during which I loved learning as much as I loved teaching. And yet, while working on this book, my learning curve has so profoundly accelerated and my body of knowledge has so increased that I feel as though I've gone through graduate school again! The research required was simultaneously daunting and exhilarating. Every day brought exclamations of surprise and wonder.

For example, I have always maintained that fashion is all about context—societal, cultural, historic, economic, and political. But even I was shocked by what a massive fashion shift occurred during the French Revolution. The sumptuous gowns during the reigns of Louis XIV, XV, and XVI became so dazzlingly vast and the wigs and headdresses so loftily high that architecture, interiors, and furniture all had to be reimagined. Then, in a moment, these dramatic silhouettes suddenly

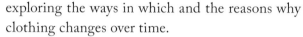

Marie Antoinette, wife of Louis the XVI, in a gown that typified the excess of the French court.

vanished, along with the royal court. In their place were dresses so basic that they resembled the simplest of nightgowns. These unbleached cotton garments had no infrastructure and no embellishments. It just goes to show: fashion and history are inextricably linked!

Why is it, you may ask, that the lion's share of fashion history books examine fashion in the Western world? The answer is simple: for centuries clothing in the Western world has changed and evolved, while clothing in the East has remained unchanged. The Indian sari; the Chinese cheongsam, or qipao; the Korean *hanbok;* the Japanese kimono have all stayed the same for thousands of years. Their evolution is in the textile. The kimono, for example, is belted with an obi that must be 12 inches wide and 4.38 yards long. How's that for prescriptive?

In the 1920s, the drapiness of the ancient toga returned for the first time in centuries (although not usually as explicitly as in this 1920 photograph!).

There are many examples of beautiful clothes in these parts of the world, and their histories are also fascinating, but there isn't the same level of evolution. For this same reason, I'll also put aside discussion of the European folk tradition. Regional peasant clothing is remarkable in its consistency. There is a Bronze Age clay figurine found in Romania of a woman whose costume bears an uncanny resemblance to a Bulgarian folk costume worn in the early twentieth century. That's thirty-five hundred years in which the dress barely changed![1] But it's a dead end for us if we're talking about how fashion evolved to where we are today.

When you think, by contrast, about what happened to the toga, it's pretty mind-blowing. The toga was just a piece of cloth that you draped around your body to preserve your modesty. The original toga was floor-length, and it was the apparel of the aristocracy. Wealthy Greeks and Romans wore it when gliding around rooms.

Outside, the ground was filthy, so the toga became shorter once Romans started to wear it beyond their marble-floored villas. Then, of course, people noticed that the bottom half of the garment became dirtier more quickly than the top, so the toga eventually evolved into separates . . . and today into both modern sportswear and the wrap dress.

When I take students to the Metropolitan Museum of Art, I love to lead them through the museum chronologically, because that way they come to understand the evolution of ideas. Even more exciting: they start to anticipate what may come next. Everything comes from somewhere, for some purpose. That's why I love Renaissance painting. Every element has meaning, from a sparrow to a lily. And that's true of fashion, too.

In this book I will guide you age by age through fashion's evolution from cavemen's animal hides to the latest runway collections. Just as my students cheer when paintings with perspective emerge in the Met's collection, I hope this book's readers will gasp as they see how Saxon underwear begat the cargo capri pant (and why that's the worst fashion trend in America today), or how the traditional Roman sandal, strapped up the leg to stay on in the heat of battle, evolved into the flip-flop worn by nearly every twenty-first-century college student.

High, narrow heels, by contrast, have always signified wealth—there's no need to walk anywhere if you're of such a high class

Jayne Mansfield shows off her high heels. A craze for clear shoes brought about the invention of sandal-foot—or sheer-toe and heel—panty hose.

that you are carried around in a sedan chair or—in modern times—a car. You can wear Jimmy Choos when you're just stepping out of the back of a limo and onto a red carpet and don't need to worry about getting your heel stuck in sidewalk gratings or cracks. In the 1990s, we had chunky heels, partly because it was not as fashionable to be rich during the grunge era.

Things happen for a reason and only have staying power for a reason. Some fashion historians argue that every change in fashion reflects a focus on a new erogenous zone and that changes in necklines and hemlines stem from a desire to stave off sexual boredom.

Fashion innovations vanish quickly if they aren't sustainable—some garments return, some die out completely, and some never seem to leave at all. As I write this, some of the hippest young people in Brooklyn are running around in little tunic rompers nearly identical to those worn by soldiers in ancient Greece. Both groups value the freedom of movement such a garment provides, even if one is running on a battlefield and the other is scampering off to an indie rock show.

And yet, most people are unaware of our nation's political history—much less its fashion legacy. We're living in a woefully a-historical age. Often when I asked my students at

Claire McCardell is one of the all-time great American designers.

Parsons to tell me when World War II was, no one could. It's especially galling that so few young designers know about American fashion history because there aren't even very many years to learn about! Until World War II, we were a nation of copiers. During the war, we couldn't copy from Europe, because the couture houses had closed. Along came American innovators like Claire McCardell and Norman Norell, representing two different aesthetics—sportswear and evening wear, respectively—and American creativity in fashion was born. The 1940s weren't that long ago, but even fashion students at some of the best schools are ignorant of what a huge shift occurred in the field during that era.

Meanwhile, I could frequently tell which students had no historical sense simply by looking at how derivative their designs were. They kept thinking they were inventing the wheel with every new design because they hadn't bothered to inform themselves that the wheel already had a long and happy history. This situation always reminds me of the Phoenicians. They made reproductions of Egyptian and Greek art, but they couldn't read hieroglyphs, so the writing they reproduced was all gibberish. They'd never seen a chariot in real life, so the scenes they depicted on vases showed someone standing in a little cart without the horses attached. Borrowing from cultures without understanding the fundamentals can yield some pretty weird and wholly illogical perversions.

I am especially concerned that American fashion not be forgotten. Once, I met the head of a hot design school in the Netherlands, and she expressed nothing but contempt for American design—an attitude I find very offensive when espoused by Europeans and downright tragic when held by Americans. When I look through *Project Runway* applications, I am always struck by how few American designers are cited in the influences section. Invariably, the only designers they name are Alexander McQueen, Christian Dior, and Coco Chanel—often misspelled "Channel." You only rarely see American designers listed. If you do, it's usually Donna Karan. (I don't understand why people don't write Michael Kors—even just in their own political self-interest.)

When it comes to fashion, we clearly need to become more patriotic and defend our own country's tradition as a worthy extension of Western fashion history. I always wonder how these people who are trying to be the "next great American fashion designer" can fail to appreciate any of the historically great American designers. I'm thinking of Pauline Trigère, Claire McCardell, Norman Norell, Bill Blass, Rudi Gernreich, Bonnie Cashin, Larry Aldrich, Geoffrey Beene. . . . The list goes on and on! Instead, many young designers I meet idolize the Antwerp Six, early-eighties graduates of the Royal Academy of Fine Arts, including Dries van Noten and Ann Demeulemeester—and if people can't spell "Chanel," they *really* cannot spell "Demeulemeester."

While I'm naming names, a quick note on terminology: there has been an assault in certain academic circles on the word "fashion." I am unsettled by people's dislike of the word—it's not the other F-word! Some TV executives once suggested I use "style" instead, because "fashion" is elitist. But the elite don't always like the word, either. A certain prestigious art school in the Northeast uses the phrase "apparel design" instead of "fashion design." I was once on campus as part of an external review committee. In our exit interview, I told the president: "I believe the reason the program eschews the term 'fashion' is because this curriculum has nothing to do with fashion. It doesn't address the marketplace. It doesn't teach fashion history. It's basically a dressmaking school. I was bored out of my skull. No one here is interested in innovation. Don't you want your graduates to change the world?" (And that, dear readers, is one way to exempt yourself from future external review committees.)

I love the word "fashion." That's why I'm using it in the title of this book. Fashion is about change and about creating clothes within a historical context. To me, dismissing fashion as silly or unimportant seems like a denial of history and frequently a show of sexism—as if something that's traditionally a concern of women isn't valid as a field of academic inquiry. When the Parsons fashion department was founded in 1906, it was called "costume design," because fashion was then a verb: to fashion. But the word "fashion" has evolved to mean something much more profound, and those who resist it seem to me to be on the wrong side of history.

American fashion designers are doing so much in spite of severe disadvantages in the global fashion world. First of all, they have always needed to make money from their work. They're not subsidized by the textile mills, as the French are. And they haven't enjoyed any of the design piracy protections that exist in Europe. It's hard to be a designer in America! It takes a lot of courage and feistiness. In short: up with America; up with fashion. If I never get invited back to Europe, or to another conference on structural garment design, I can live with that.

Lastly, before I am deluged, inevitably, with mail from academics complaining that I didn't mention a particular neckline or didn't pay proper attention to doublet construction: this isn't meant to be a textbook or exhaustive. Entire books have been written about what in this book are mere paragraphs. I have done my best to make sure the facts are straight, but minutiae have been eliminated. Unless you've read other histories of fashion, you wouldn't believe the degree of complex detail with which authors write about the transition of a collar width from 1750 to 1753. Do we really care? Well, yes, but not that much.

I encourage anyone whose interest in fashion history is sparked by this book to educate themselves further with more-academic sources. For now, I hope you'll enjoy this sweeping and selective look at my favorite parts of fashion history and that it will help drive home how much fun fashion, and historical inquiry, can be.

The primary purpose of this book is to give your clothes more significance. I've found that many people are afraid of taking a hard look at what's in their closets, because fashion is scary to many people. It shouldn't be. Fashion is fun and thrilling—and it's something that concerns everyone who gets dressed in the morning, not just an elite crew in Manhattan.

I hope this fashion bible will encourage you to study your clothing and appreciate its fascinating origins. Every article means something—usually a lot of things. By exploring the meaning and history of our clothes, I hope this book will magically transform your cluttered closet into a world of wonders! To that end, I have included a work sheet at the back of the book as a guide if you'd like some suggestions for what to look for and what questions to ask. This kind of closet inventory can teach us a lot about fashion, and a lot about ourselves.

So, let's climb into our time machine and get started!

Tim

1.
UNDERWEAR
Security vs. Freedom

Panties, bras, lingerie . . .
In defense of the corset

NOT LONG AGO, I was on a movie set with a charming young actress who hated wearing underwear. The director pulled the starlet aside several times to ask her to please put on some panties. Her character's skirts were so short that he was afraid something might end up on camera that shouldn't be in a PG-13 film. Not to mention that the constant flashing whenever she bent over was unnerving the crew.

Finally, she put on some underwear and everyone breathed a sigh of relief. Of course, she hated wearing a bra, too, and not long after she had a jumping scene in which her breasts bounced right out of her shirt.

Although this actress was clearly acting out (see, in my last book, Gunn's Golden Rule 2: "The world owes you . . . nothing"), this kind of antagonism toward underwear is typical today. Since the 1960s, there has been a general rebellion on the part of American women against constricting undergarments, consequences be damned.

There would be nothing wrong with this, if it in fact made women happier not to wear structured underwear. But I regularly meet people—usually women, but men, too—who are dissatisfied with the way their bodies look in clothes. They complain to me that their pants don't fit well or that they hate the lumpiness of their midsection under thin shirts. They say they wish they could be just a little smoother.

To which I say: you and everyone else throughout history! Didn't you see *Gone With the Wind*? Remember that scene where Scarlett O'Hara is desperately trying to reclaim her tiny, prebaby waist by means of a tight-laced corset?

Here's an 1899 boned corset—a rather extreme way to get rid of muffin top.

Long before the Civil War, women were engaging in similar behavior. In search of a smooth line, a trim waist, and curves in the right places (of course, the "right" places have changed from generation to generation), our ancestors created all kinds of contraptions for both men and women, including corsets made of whalebone and steel. Serious corseting continued well into the twentieth century. In 1946, Macy's sold a garment called the Wisp, a boned belt that could be worn under the wasp-waisted "New Look," as it was called, the aggressively hourglass style that came into vogue after World War II. Since the clothing revolution of the 1960s, we have imagined ourselves immune to this need for confinement. And yet, the desire to look a certain way still dominates our society. Fortunately, there are helpful garments out there for those who choose to wear them.

Shapewear—stretchy underwear that smoothes out lines and holds in bulges—is the answer to countless fashion-related complaints. These can be full bodysuits, underwear with a stomach panel, long shorts, or any undergarment with some body-specific engineering. Modern shapewear is far more comfortable and breathable than the corseting of the past. It's a great example of the evolution of textiles, and it lets people look better in clothes without lacing, boning, or metal stays.

"A girdle? Oh, no!" people invariably reply when I suggest they try a pair of Spanx, a Miraclesuit, Wacoal shorts, or whatever other brand of shapewear might answer the complaints they have about their body's look in clothes. "I would feel so *constrained*. I need to feel free."

This, to me, is a delusion. Wouldn't you feel *freer* (to flirt, to land that big deal, to wow everyone at a party) if you looked your best? The demand for minimally constrictive clothing is a very recent fluke in fashion thinking—only since the hippie movement has shaping underwear acquired such a bad reputation. Even during the rational dress movement of the nineteenth century, women never sought to completely eliminate what were then called stays. They just wanted women to be able to wear seven pounds of undergarments rather than the typical fourteen. Even women who took up wearing bloomers and tailor-made jackets sustained their curvy figures with corsets. They wore them even when exercising!

Ironically, Americans' disdain for corseting has paralleled an increase in our girth. We as a nation are in a vicious cycle of wearing looser and looser clothes because we are less and less comfortable in our bodies, and yet we are more and more insistent that we don't want to be "constrained." I believe our fear of tight underwear is a big part of why we are uncomfortable in our clothes. Tight underwear is your friend, America! (America does seem to be coming to this conclusion. Sara Blakely, the inventor of Spanx, is the youngest ever self-made female billionaire.)

Of course, I still respect people who prefer to let it all hang out. As in life, when it comes to your underwear, you have to make a choice between freedom and security. This is certainly the story of the corset, an object that shows up in various forms in many different cultures and has been a lightning rod for various notions of what women's bodies should look like.

The usual take on corsets today is that they symbolize the oppression of women. At the costume departments of museums, we gawk at the tiny waists and the intricate structuring of these garments. We imagine that in times when women were more restricted, as in Victorian England, corseting was tightest, and when women were more liberated, as in the 1920s, it was loosest.

Girdles, circa 1940.

DREW'S INIMITABLE
"A LA GRECQUE" CORSETS.

With IMPERISHABLE ELASTIC AND SUPPORTER combined. ANNUAL SALE OVER 90,000 PAIRS.
  The great advantage of this Corset is—a combination of Elastic Texture inserted at the Waist over the hip and stomach. This "Grande nouveauté" and exquisite design reduces the most portly figure to the standard of Beauty and Fashion. To avoid deception each pair is stamped DREW'S MAKE and Trade Mark. Price 16s. 6d.; in Black, 17s. 6d. To be obtained from all Drapers and Outfitters in the Kingdom. Postage 3d. extra. Wholesale only from DREW, SON and CO., Bath, England. Two Gold Medals. Two Diplomas of Merit.

This c. 1908 corset ad said the device "reduces the most portly figure to the standard of Beauty and Fashion."

This isn't totally accurate throughout history. Men's and women's clothing in the Middle Ages, for example, was basically unisex and shapeless, and yet women then were hardly empowered. Still, there's something to this idea of corseting reflecting women's role in society.

The most constricting underwear in American history was arguably the corset of the first decade of the twentieth century. The popular shape of bodies for the time was the S-curve, so named after the way corseted women appeared from the side: all bust and hips. This required devices like straight steel busks at the front and boning around the body. Garters hanging down from the bottom of the corset typically held the tops of stockings. Women also wore a chemise and drawers.[1]

Given the complex architecture of these shape-defining garments, imagine how refreshing it was when the important and colorful but largely forgotten French designer Paul Poiret created a corsetless, high-waisted dress in 1906. The message: women, who in America were hovering on the brink of winning the vote, needed to move around.

Underwear responds to cultural change and vice versa. When large breasts are in fashion, contraptions like the Wonderbra flourish. When skinny, Twiggy-like looks are popular, you see bandeau flatteners. The forties and fifties saw torpedo bras. Then the hippie movement "liberated" women from their mother's girdles. Was this really liberation? If you dress like a hippie in flowing dresses, of course you don't need a girdle, or even a bra. But what if you want to wear a silk shirt and a power suit into a boardroom?

It's my experience that, after the 1960s, women retained the idea that they needed to be free of corseting. When they started wearing non-hippie clothing, they felt uncomfortable without supportive underwear and yet they rejected underpinnings as oppressive. To me, it's ironic that so many people avoid shapewear now, because wearing tight shirts with skinny jeans is easily as constricting as a corset but does your silhouette none of the same favors.

This is not to say that there haven't been some diabolical inventions in shapewear's past. Claiming certain corsets were good for the back, manufacturers strapped women into garments that at times restricted their breathing. Fashion historian Colleen Gau examined the health claims made by corset manufacturers of the past. In 1995, she conducted a test of the so-called health corset,[2] which was worn at the end of the nineteenth century to give women that S-curve shape. She learned that it was pretty much impossible to exercise in one without passing out. That explains all the fainting Victorian women. They weren't weak; their corsets just ensured that they couldn't get enough oxygen into their lungs!

Again, we can't make too many assumptions. The cage crinoline that was introduced in 1856 may look to us like an iron maiden-esque torture device masquerading as an undergarment. In fact, the cage crinoline was liberating in its day. Before it came along, those huge skirts of the 1850s required six petticoats—not exactly conducive to vigorous activity or

Does Your Bra Fit?

» The shoulder straps should not dig into your flesh or hang loose.

» The cups should be neither overflowing nor gaping.

» A good bra will improve your posture as well as the drape of your clothes, and it will be comfortable enough that you'll forget it's even there.

» The back closure should be neither too loose nor too tight, and it should not pull up or sag down.

comfort. The cage crinoline made use of a rigid structure rather than layers of fabric, so it was lighter and comparatively freeing.[3]

The crinoline is probably never coming back, because modern life involves such hoop-skirt-unfriendly elements as compact cars, narrow sidewalks, and claustrophobic airplane seats. Then again, as fashion historian James Laver noted, women back in the nineteenth century wore crinolines even in crowded railway cars. "The laws of practicability," he wrote, "are of extremely limited application in any matter connected with women's dress."[4]

I'm not suggesting that we all go back to tight-lacing. Most women agree that the brassiere, in all its forms, is a vast improvement on the elaborate corseting their bodies were subjected to for so many years throughout the West. The term "brassiere" came about in America around 1904 via ad copy for the DeBevoise Company, which used this French word for a child's shirt to give the garment a French flair.

Universal cup sizing didn't start until the 1930s. Before that, beginning around 1910, stores had fitters on hand to assist women. At many department stores today, you can still find a fitter. Every woman should measure herself once every couple of years, and certainly after having a baby or gaining or losing a lot of weight. Having a well-fitting bra can instantly make you seem slimmer, and it can vastly improve your day-to-day comfort.

So, who invented the bra? This is rather like the question about where jeans originated. It's hard to say! Luman L. Chapman was issued U.S. patent 40,907 in 1863 for a shoulder-strapped bust supporter, but that was almost certainly not the first alternative to tight-laced corsets. Between that period and World War I, there were numerous other innovators, among them New York socialite Mary Phelps Jacob (also known as Caresse Crosby), who received a patent in 1913.

How, you may be wondering, does Otto Titsling (sometimes spelled Titzling), he of the silly song "Otto Titsling," sung by Bette Midler in *Beaches*, feature in the history of the bra? ("For Otto Titsling had found his quest: / To lift and mold the female breast.") Well, he is completely fictional, the hero of the amusing 1971 Wallace Reyburn satire *Bust-Up: The Uplifting Tale of Otto Titzling and the Development of the Bra*. In the story, Otto Titzling ("a two-tits-sling") has an assistant, Hans Delving ("hands delving") and a nemesis, Phillipe de Brassiere ("fill up the brassiere"). The moral: don't learn your fashion history from movie tunes.

While we're dispelling myths, I would like to address the matter of bra burning. Sometimes you hear feminists dismissively referred to as bra burners. Part of the legacy of the sixties is the mental image we have of women burning their bras in trash-can fires. Did you know this was a myth? It probably came about in the public imagination because at many Vietnam War protests, men were burning their draft cards, and in 1969 a protest against the Miss America pageant in Atlantic City involved a "freedom trash can," into which high

I dreamed I drove them wild in my *maidenform bra*

Maidenform bra ads of the 1960s showed women imagining themselves in all kinds of crazy places. (Another fantasy ad showed a woman actually *working* in an *office*.)

heels, bras, and other items perceived as oppressive were thrown. There was, however, no fire.[5]

Speaking of bras and freedom, the liberation implicit in a well-fitted bra has been somewhat ridiculously emphasized by manufacturers. A hilarious Maidenform campaign that lasted from 1949 to 1969 (twenty years!) showed models in various situations wearing nothing from the waist up but a bra. The slogans positioned the scenes as fantasies the woman was having. Two examples from 1952: "I dreamed I rode a streetcar in my Maidenform bra," and "I dreamed I opened the World Series in my Maidenform bra." A 1964 ad in *Life* magazine shows a woman sitting on the edge of a desk. The slogan: "I dreamed I went to work in my Maidenform bra."[6]

Clearly, an image of a woman dreaming of being in an office wearing just her underwear was a product of its time. A 1983 *Time* magazine article[7] discussed this ad campaign and reported that Maidenform dropped the fantasy theme of the ads in 1969, by which time women weren't dreaming of being in offices. They *were* in offices, and they weren't fantasizing about being shirtless.

New ads in the late 1970s showed models as doctors and lawyers. The new slogan: "The Maidenform woman. You never know where she'll turn up." Alas, they kept the bras in plain view, so you had pictures of nearly naked women in powerful situations, surrounded by fully clothed men, an image that didn't exactly scream social progress.

Of course, this question of whether underwear signals empowerment or subservience is eternal. Wearing a corset has long been a sign of wealth.[8] Between the late Middle Ages and the early Renaissance, the corset was a social marker, because it signaled that the woman had a maid on hand to tighten and loosen the garment.[9] In the 1800s, the corset was a sign of "middle-class self-discipline and of a restrictive sexual morality."[10] Women in the nineteenth

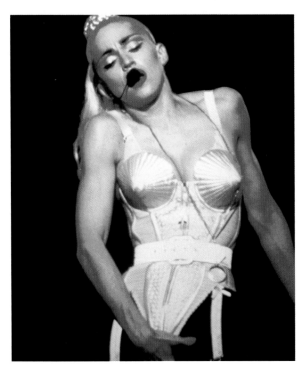

Madonna wore this famous corset by Jean Paul Gaultier on her 1990–91 Blond Ambition tour.

century were kept, in other words, too physically uncomfortable to entertain ideas about fooling around with men who weren't their husbands. Taking all those clothes off was just too much work, so they might as well stay faithful.

Some scholars, on the other hand, argue that the corset was a means of self-expression and that we can't blame objectification on such garments because the demise of the corset didn't exactly destroy our obsession with women's bodies.[11] The fashion historian Valerie Steele suggests that women wearing corsets today is actually a sign of empowerment. On her 1990 Blond Ambition tour, Madonna wore a gold corset by Jean Paul Gaultier when simulating masturbation to the song "Like a Virgin" and his famous cone bra over a pinstripe suit while singing "Express Yourself." She in no way seemed repressed by wearing those pieces.

Thanks in great part to Madonna, visible underwear became a major form of rebellion for young people in the 1980s and 1990s. The textbook *Fashion, Costume, and Culture* calls this trend "the emergence of open sexuality as an important element in clothing design."[12] In the nineties, young women often wore underwear as outerwear, or let their bra straps show. It was aggressively antifashion and not always the most flattering look. And yet it was liberating in its way and helped spawn an industry of underwear meant to be flaunted.

Witness the thong!

Perhaps you will remember how often thongs could be seen in the 1990s, emerging like whale tails from low-rise jeans. The boom in fitness and the rise of fabrics like spandex made people even more eager to show off their bodies. Designers like Calvin Klein brought out (at times disturbingly) thin models wearing next to no clothing. In 1980, the company produced the scandalous TV commercial in which a fifteen-year-old Brooke Shields asks, "You want to know what comes between me and my Calvins?" Answer: "Nothing." Her legs are spread and she's staring seductively at the camera from under a mane of hair.

Then there were the billboards of mostly naked young people such as Kate Moss and Marky Mark (Mark Wahlberg) lounging about erotically. But the Calvin Klein Jeans billboard near my Times Square office in 2009 was the most obscene to date. It showed four nearly naked, dazed-looking young people, one woman and three men, apparently mid-orgy. It's a jeans ad, but so often it's hard to tell the difference between Calvin Klein's jeans ads and underwear ads.

Now let's talk about panties. People tend to get carried away reading import into women's underpants. The writer Alison Lurie has a whole scheme of underwear colors and their significance. A woman who wears red underpants, for example, is said to "enjoy jealous scenes and prefer the sound of doors slamming and plates crashing to the music of Mozart." She continues to describe other colors, like "receptive blue," "dreamy violet," "cheerful yellow," and "jazzy orange."[13] Bet you didn't know when you grabbed a pair of panties out of your drawer in the dark this morning that you were signaling you were a dreamer or a plate thrower!

This level of overthinking goes back to the nineteenth century, when underpants for women were considered "unfeminine" and in violation of a biblical rule against women wearing men's clothing.[14] Isn't it amazing that underwear is a relatively recent development?

This anti-panty sentiment has cropped up at various times throughout fashion history. Groundbreaking American fashion designer and author

Before he was the serious actor Mark Wahlberg, Marky Mark modeled Calvin Klein underwear.

Elizabeth Hawes thought it was absurd that clothes needed to be protected from our bodies by underwear: "It is merely that most of us have been taught evacuating and having sexual intercourse are dirty and we therefore dream up the notion the parts of the body that perform these functions must be dirty even though well washed and healthy."[15]

Of course, by that point in history, people were actually bathing regularly, but just a hundred years earlier everyone was filthy. Until Beau Brummell, the Regency period arbiter of fashion and style (and the star of our suit chapter), daily bathing was far from common. The first deodorant wasn't patented until 1888.[16] For thousands of years, people were grubby and literally lousy with bugs. A 1900 medical paper found that in the huge skirts that were the fashion of the day there were "found large colonies of germs, including those of tuberculosis, typhoid, tetanus, influenza."[17]

To me, wearing underwear is part of practicing good hygiene, and that's part of why the proud underwearless recall to me the proud unwashed. One night when we were sitting together on Conan O'Brien's couch, David Duchovny declared to our host, the audience, and me: "I'm not wearing any underwear! I never wear underwear." I thought that was a little too much information, and I shifted away from him on the couch.

Women's drawers, as they were once known, didn't come into vogue until around 1900. After the influential hygienist Dr. Gustav Jaeger's wool long underwear became popular, the chemise and drawers were connected in one garment. Chemises and corsets went out of fashion after World War I and were replaced by bras and girdles (to which were attached clips for stockings). On cold days women might add a vest of wool, silk, or knitted cotton.

Beginning around 1920, women often wore pink rayon, knee-length knickers. In the late thirties and forties, wide-leg French knickers were popular. In the 1950s, their poufy dresses often required stiff petticoats. As women started wearing slacks more often, petticoats went out of fashion, but the camisole came back in.[18] Now we have access to pretty much all these different styles, and yet most women's underwear repertoires are limited to drugstore cotton panties.

Men's underwear has, by comparison, been relatively consistent over the centuries. Did the Greeks wear underwear? It's a question surely fielded by every junior-high classics teacher. The truth is: there's little evidence for undergarments.[19] Athletes were typically naked. Romans likely wore nothing under their togas, either. (So much for the perennial Latin-class joke *semper ubi sub ubi*: homophonically rendered by snickering twelve-year-old classics students as "always wear under wear.") In the second century BC, the Teutons defeated the Roman army. Under their tunics, the Teutons wore baggy trousers, or breeches, which the Romans saw as barbaric. The Teutons, for the most part, adopted the Roman way of dressing and got rid of their baggy underwear.[20]

In fact, baggy underclothes have symbolized barbarism for hundreds of years. In the eleventh century men wore braies, low-slung, ankle-length pants tied at the waist with a cord. Richer men's braies were tight; poorer men's were loose. Sometimes braies were tied with crisscrossing leg bands. Over the years, they grew shorter and shorter until they became something we would recognize as men's underwear.[21] The men's undershirt became outerwear as our modern T-shirt, but men's undershorts went in the opposite direction, starting out as shorts (outerwear) and becoming boxers (underwear).

Personally, I subscribe to the baggy-undershorts-as-barbaric philosophy and prefer jockey shorts. Boxer shorts ride up and can ruin the line of pants. Briefs don't have anywhere to go. Other people may not even notice when your underwear rides up, but you certainly do! If you find yourself tugging at your underwear throughout the day to keep it in place, throw them away. Keep in mind, too, that the problem may not be that your underwear is too small. It may be too big. Too-large underwear can create just as many hassles as underwear that's too tiny.

I find it incredible that what we consider essential underpants today were all but unknown to both men and women in England until the seventeenth century. "Charles II [who ruled 1660–1685] thought them immodest during a brief period when they were in vogue among the court, and even in 1800 they were greeted with cries of disgust."[22] "Gradually the outcry against wearing them died down, to be succeeded by an outcry against not wearing them."[23] David Duchovny would have fit right into the court of Charles II.

Speaking of men and underwear, I would encourage men to consider shapewear when they are wearing tuxedos or feel the need to pull out all the stops. I wear it if I need to look especially polished. I have three T-shirts that have elastic ribbing built into them. They reach to my hipbone. They're very slimming. They're hard to wrangle on, and I'm always sure I'm going to dislocate my shoulders taking them off, but they're worth it.

"I'm a *man*!" men often say when I suggest this. "I can't wear *shapewear*!"

I remind them that starting around 1810, the Apollo corset, a waist cincher stiffened with whalebone, was worn by men. It was often called a "Brummell bodice" or a "Cumberland corset" when worn by English men in the Regency period.[24] This was a group of men who brought masculinity back to menswear and defeated the fops and their powdered wigs and frills for fashion supremacy. They looked stronger and manlier in their corsets.

Now let's talk about sleepwear.

If you live alone, the matter of wearing nice sleeping clothes is between you and yourself. I would suggest that lounging around at home in silk pajamas may make you feel that life is slightly better than if you were lounging around in stained sweats. But if you live with a partner, he or she probably sees you rather often in your underwear and nightclothes. Wearing something attractive signifies that you care enough about your partner and yourself to keep up appearances even in private.

History is full of elegant home clothes. Ever wonder where that ratty bathrobe hanging on your bathroom door came from? Well, one of its lovely cousins is the elegantly named banyan. Starting in the seventeenth century, British men wore morning gowns, or banyans, before dressing for the day. These were usually made from some kind of printed silk or cotton with an exotic look. One high-collared, puff-sleeved morning gown formerly of the Brooklyn Museum collection dates from the 1820s. It looks like a patchwork quilt spawned with a trench coat,[25] and it puts our terry-cloth rags to shame.

The 1920s, '30s, and '40s also saw a flurry of "pajamas," although "dinner pajamas" and "beach pajamas" were far too elegant to wear to bed. Flipping through a *Vogue* from 1928, I found a pajama outfit consisting of a silver and green brocade jacket, chartreuse yellow lace-up pants and blouse, and green mules. The caption recommends this over-the-top ensemble for an afternoon tea or a casual dinner at home. One set of print dinner pajamas by Clare Potter even had matching shoes!

I wouldn't suggest you need to go *that* far with your sleepwear, but you can buy a lovely nightshirt or pair of pajamas for less than a full tank of gas. It seems a small price to pay to save your partner from looking at you in the same old threadbare T-shirts night after night.

And while you're already on the lingerie and sleepwear floor of your local department store, do go at least *look* at the shapewear. Plenty of women and men to whom I suggest shapewear feel insulted. They feel there must be some other way to achieve the silhouette they want other than foundation garments, but unless they are wearing couture clothing or have perfect posture, this is unlikely. I will say, though, that posture can go a long way toward making you look better in clothes—and wearing shapewear helps remind you to stand up straight.

Beyond feeling insulted, people complain that it is expensive. This is true. Good shapewear shorts or a shapewear undershirt can cost $30 to $60. That's not feasible for wearing every day. But for dressing up? It's well worth spending that on your underwear to make your fancy dress or suit look its best.

Some people also complain that shapewear flattens you out too much. I would say that this in my experience is only true of the cheapest kinds, those spandex tubes that you shimmy into. Shapewear with true engineering shouldn't distort your body. It should just neaten it.

So what kind is best for you? Finding the right undergarments can be daunting. Perhaps you'll benefit from something that goes around the waist. Perhaps you'll like the shorts. Talk to a salesperson about what you want to accentuate or deaccentuate about your body. See what they suggest. If you can't find anyone helpful, try on one of each style.

Let go of any thoughts you have that shapewear is for grandmothers. At the heart of people's objection to buying decent undergarments is that they think of them as for old people, and they don't want to admit they themselves have grown older. It's true that teenagers are typically good to go with the scantiest of underclothes. But the rest of us need a little help. American adults often want to stay in the same casual clothes that got them through college and believe these items help them look younger. Of course, the great irony is that you look much younger—sleeker, slimmer, in better shape—when you are more pulled together, and shapewear is a part of that.

Like any fashion change, it takes a bit of time to get used to wearing slimming garments—the results, however, are immediate. If it feels a little snug, just take a look at the S-curve corset of a hundred years ago and then try to tell me those stretchy Spanx are too confining. Together, let's work to turn vanity into a virtue!

WHAT SHAPEWEAR IS RIGHT FOR YOU?

» Do you want to avoid a panty line, conceal cellulite, or mitigate bulges around your hips? Try a pair of shorts.

» Do you also want a smoother stomach or to conquer muffin top? Try a slimming camisole or a pair of shorts with a high waist.

» Do you want to look smoother under a dress? Try a shaping slip of whatever length you need.

» Do you want to look smoother under pants? Try a full-body slimmer with built-in shorts that go to the bottom of the thigh.

» Are you a man who wants to conceal bulges in your chest or stomach? Try a compression V-neck, crew, or tank. It will also give you lumbar support and improve your posture!

2.

T-SHIRTS

From Underwear to Everywhere

Graphic tees, tank tops, V-necks . . .
Why a white T-shirt signals sexual availability

HOW QUICKLY the T-shirt has taken over our culture. Look around and you will see nearly everyone, people of every age and body type, wearing T-shirts. Typically a blend of cotton and polyester, some tees are tight; some are baggy. Some have crew necks, others scoop or V-necks. Some are solid, some striped, and some have pictures or messages on them. Some are fashionable and some are too sloppy even for farmwork.

Now that the T-shirt—named, of course, for its T shape—has attained world dominance, it's hard to remember that as recently as the 1940s, no one would dream of being seen in public wearing one. T-shirts were always—and later we will discuss the cases in which I believe they still should be—underwear.

Various sorts of T-shaped tops have been around for hundreds of years as underpinnings of everything from chain mail to silk suits. But they weren't clothes you'd wear outside. The early T-shirt existed to provide an extra layer of warmth and to absorb sweat. Until the twentieth century, the T-shirt's role was strictly to form a barrier between a man's body and the more valuable clothing he actually wanted the world to see.

In the late nineteenth century, a popular German hygienist named Dr. Gustav Jaeger encouraged men to wear undershirts made of wool as part of his "Sanitary Woolen System," which he claimed "affords to the body the greatest protection against Cold, Heat and Dampness, with the least obstruction to the body's exhalations."[1]

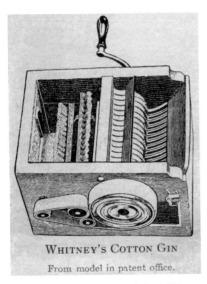

WHITNEY'S COTTON GIN

From model in patent office.

This 1793 patent model of Eli Whitney's cotton gin shows how the invention quickly separated seeds from cotton, vastly increasing the supply of cotton for British Industrial Revolution cotton mills.

Wool's days were numbered, though, thanks to America's boom in cotton. Eli Whitney's 1793 cotton gin increased the supply of cotton—as did slavery. Cotton was America's leading export by the 1850s, worth more than all of our country's other crops put together.[2]

Undershirts made of cotton were more comfortable, and those wool undergarments were already starting to vanish as central heating spread. Companies like Fruit of the Loom (founded in 1851) and Hanes (founded in 1901) sold lighter undershirts.

The stretchy cotton shirt we are so familiar with today is much more elastic than its ancestors, which were shapeless and baggy. We learn from fashion historian Dennita Sewell's essay on the garment[3] that "shirts changed very little in shape from their introduction in medieval times through the mid-nineteenth century. They were loose fitting, made of a woven fabric, and constructed with rectangular pieces that formed a T shape."

Most have short sleeves, but a popular variant is the sleeveless T-shirt, called a "tank top" since the 1960s. This is a reference to the tank swimsuit, so named for the 1920s term for a swimming pool: "swimming tank." Of course, it also has a nastier name. According to Elissa Leibowitz in *The Washington Post*, the term "wifebeater" has been around since the mid-1990s, familiarized by the TV show *Cops*: "Potbellied and ketchup stained, he is sitting on a couch swilling beers when police rap on his trailer door to make a domestic violence call. More likely than not he's wearing a ribbed, white tank top. A wife beater in a wifebeater." The term appears to have started as teen slang around 1993 or 1994. Now that you know the word's inauspicious origins, I suggest removing the term "wifebeater" from your vocabulary. Not only does it trivialize domestic abuse, it also became popular because of *Cops* . . . need I say more?

The invention of a sophisticated circular knitting machine during the Industrial Revolution made undershirts easier to mass-produce. As a result of the new technology, they also became somewhat more tightly fitted, but they weren't nearly as soft or breathable as today's T-shirts. The biggest advance in the undershirt ultimately came to America as so many items of clothing have—from France. During World War I, American soldiers discovered that the— *quell surpris*—French soldiers had lighter, more breathable underwear. When they came home from battle, they brought with them these new and improved undershirts.[4]

This *Life* magazine cover from July 13, 1942, shows an early graphic T-shirt.

Mass-produced white T-shirts quickly became de rigueur as men's underwear. The U.S. Navy made the white cotton tee its official undergarment in 1913. (The U.S. Army followed suit in 1942, then changed the shirt from white to khaki in 1944 so that it would provide camouflage in the South Pacific.[5] The name for the color khaki, by the way, comes from the Persian word *khak*, or dirt.)

And then one man threatened to take down the entire T-shirt business: Clark Gable.

In the 1934 film *It Happened One Night,* Gable's character is a newsman who travels with a runaway heiress (played by Claudette Colbert). In one scene when they are on the road together, they stop at a motel. While preparing for bed, he takes his shirt off and *he's not wearing an undershirt.*

Clark Gable, one of the biggest stars of the era, the epitome of sexiness, apparently didn't need an undershirt. While stripping in that scene, he even narrated his method of undressing to Claudette Colbert: "I have a method all my own. If you notice, the coat came first, then the tie, then the shirt. Now, uh, according to Hoyle, after that, the, uh, pants should be next. There's where I'm different. I go for the shoes next. First the right. Then the left. After that, it's, eh, every man for himself."

By appearing naked under his shirt, he signaled that he was too cool, too manly, too liberated for an undershirt. At that moment, American men took his lead, and T-shirts were suddenly part of the pre–central heating, fuddy-duddy, and overly health-conscious past.[6] This was convenient, too, because the Depression was raging, and no one was complaining about having one less article of clothing to buy.

Perhaps liberated men of the 1930s would have put an end to the T-shirt's popularity altogether . . . were it not for World War II. Million of Americans fought in the war, and they won it in T-shirts. This made the shirt "the emblem of manliness."[7] Returning soldiers kept wearing their standard-issue T-shirts in civilian life. Non-soldiers followed suit. A 1940s Sears, Roebuck and Co. catalog read, "You needn't be a soldier to have your own personal T-shirt."[8]

Clark Gable's going undershirtless in the 1934 movie *It Happened One Night* almost tanked the T-shirt industry.

Rebel teenagers scandalized respectable society in white T-shirts and jeans, as in 1949's *Bad Boy*.

No one wore a T-shirt like Marlon Brando in 1951's *A Streetcar Named Desire*.

If veterans gave the T-shirt a heroic cachet, two fifties films gave it an aura of sexiness and danger. In the 1953 movie *The Wild One*, Marlon Brando plays Johnny Strabler, the head of a biker gang and the ultimate bad boy. When asked what he's rebelling against, he responds, "Whaddaya got?" Marlon Brando's T-shirt was so tight that he reportedly had to be sewn into it.[9] He also wore a scandalously tight T-shirt in *A Streetcar Named Desire* (1951).

The T-shirt has long been a working-class garment. Men who did the manual labor of building this country often stripped down in the course of their work, revealing their functional white undershirts. There are many historic photographs of such T-shirt-clad workers through the decades, including tenant farmers, steelworkers,[10] and longshoremen.[11]

In the 1950s, young men from the suburbs wore the T-shirt to symbolize their allegiance with the workingman and the soldier rather than the men in suits and ties who filled their schools and churches. James Dean in 1955's *Rebel Without a Cause* continued this theme of the T-shirt as bad-boy uniform. Wearing jeans and white T-shirts signaled teenage disaffection—the T-shirt becoming the very symbol of rebellious youth culture, especially with a pack of cigarettes in the rolled-up sleeve. Beatniks like Jack Kerouac wore T-shirts to show their disdain for proper society, and so did greasers and bikers. Tommy Hilfiger in his book *All-American* recalls being sent home from school for wearing a T-shirt as late as 1969: "They took one look at me and said, 'You've got an undershirt on. Go home.'"[12]

So, what about slogan shirts? Since the twenties, there have been shirts with phrases on them. According to one fashion historian: "The beginning of today's merchandising industry took shape when children's garments were printed with Davy Crockett and Roy Rogers characters in the 1950s."[13] Mickey Mouse was another popular subject for early graphic T-shirts.[14]

The first campaign T-shirt appeared in 1948, for Republican Thomas Dewey: "Dew it with Dewey." (Of course, the shirts didn't work; Truman won.) Another politician, then-senator John F. Kennedy, was photographed wearing a T-shirt at home. Everything the handsome young politician and his stylish wife did became a fashion trend, so it was inevitable: T-shirts became the nation's favorite casual wear.

The first band T-shirt was a 1956 promotional Elvis Presley shirt showing him playing guitar in front of a green record.[15] Once mass screen printing became viable in 1959 with the invention of the stronger and more flexible plastisol ink, printed T-shirts were used to signify allegiance to celebrities, politicians, and brands. Band T-shirts really caught on in the 1960s. The Beatles sold shirts on their 1964 tour; the Monkees sold shirts on their 1967 tour.[16] Among the most successful band T-shirts of all time was the Rolling Stones' famous tongue shirt from 1971. The designer of that logo, John Pasche, recalls: "The design concept for the tongue was to represent the band's antiauthoritarian attitude, Mick's mouth, and the obvious sexual connotations."[17]

The Rolling Stones' lips shirt, shown here in a still from *Fast Times at Ridgemont High*, is one of the most popular band T-shirts of all time.

opposite: John F. Kennedy, shown here in the late 1940s, was an icon for a relaxed, all-American style.

The sixties also brought a wave of message shirts and tie-dyes to both men and women. The "I Love NY" T-shirt designed by Milton Glaser in 1976 was a huge hit. The happy-face T-shirt was born of an in-house marketing campaign in 1963 encouraging Worcester Mutual Insurance Company employees to deliver good customer service.[18] The shirt became massively popular nationwide in the seventies.

The T-shirt has often been a symbol of raw sex appeal and also of liberation for women. The unisex garment is an equalizer (outside of wet T-shirt contests). A T-shirt ad from the seventies reads: "The piece of clothing that emancipated America's top half."[19]

In the eighties, the rise of hip-hop propelled athletic wear to day attire. T-shirts with sports logos were suddenly everywhere. The TV show *Miami Vice* popularized the wearing of the T-shirt with suits, as well as the use of bright colors like pink for menswear. At the same time, Bruce Springsteen popularized dressing down in a T-shirt. His famous cover for the album *Born in the USA* (1984) showed him from the back wearing a white T-shirt and jeans, with a red bandana in his back pocket.

In the early 1990s, American teenagers, particularly black teenagers, started wearing Malcolm X T-shirts with this line from Ossie Davis's eulogy: "Our own black shining prince." According to Imani Perry, "At that time, the embrace of Malcolm X, particularly by young hip-hop fans, seemed

Joel Madden of the band Good Charlotte wears a Malcolm X T-shirt in 2008.

a deliberate counterpoint to the sanitized, mainstream, and universally celebrated image of Martin Luther King, Jr."[20]

A friend of mine from Texas recalls being sent home from school in the early 1990s for wearing one of these shirts. The school banned Malcolm X shirts, but students protested, saying the ban was racist. In response, the school banned all shirts with words on them.

The nineties grunge trend featured flannel shirts over often-ragged T-shirts. In this case, the T-shirt served its function as a tool of democratization. As Giorgio Armani writes in the introduction to Alice Harris's *The White T,* "I love the T-shirt as an antistatus symbol, putting rich and poor on the same level in a sheath of white cotton that cancels distinctions in class."[21]

The T-shirt has also increasingly become a way of broadcasting political issues, as if it were a walking billboard. The famous "Silence = Death" T-shirt emerged from a campaign started in 1987 by AIDS activists in New York City.

Che Guevara, as he appears in the iconic 1960 photograph by Alberto Korda, is one of the most popular T-shirt subjects. According to Michiko Kakutani's *New York Times* review of Michael Casey's *Che's Afterlife,* "the guerilla fighter became a logo as recognizable as the Nike swoosh or the McDonald's golden arches."[22] Fidel Castro used the image as a symbol for Cuba as early as 1967.

Che even showed up at the 1968 Paris student protests. From there, he became poster fodder for antiwar activists and the Black Power movement. Now even college students who know little about his life don Che T-shirts. "For many," Kakutani writes, "Che has become a generic symbol of the underdog, the idealist, the iconoclast, the man willing to die for a cause."[23] Che even showed up in a famous Matthew Diffee *New Yorker* cartoon—wearing a Bart Simpson T-shirt![24]

Today fashion designers often incorporate T-shirts into their work. Fittingly, a 2011 Dolce & Gabbana collection paid homage to the cultural history of fashion with T-shirts featuring images of James Dean and Marlon Brando (also Richard Gere, Muhammad Ali, and Steve McQueen).

The famous Diffee cartoon.

Of course, most people in America today wear T-shirts bought not from high-end designer showrooms but from chain stores, gift shops, sporting arenas, or concert venues. Bruno Collin writes in the foreword to *The T-Shirt Book,* "The T-shirt is something emotional. It embodies memories of a torrid trip to Ibiza or a time spent at a university."[25] A beloved tee is often a favorite item to sleep in, like a grown-up's security blanket.

The T-shirt is flexible, and that is its strength and its weakness. People don't often think hard about what size T-shirt they really need, because the garment is so forgiving and various sizes will seem to do just fine. T-shirts have become our national uniform, and it's often not until we take a trip to a different part of the world that we realize how underdressed the T-shirt can make us look.

Personally, I'm fascinated by how something like the T-shirt can go from being an undergarment that no one would ever think of wearing outside to being *the* staple in everyone's daily wardrobe. You see people wearing T-shirts out to dinner and to the office, even to the theater. The T-shirt's omnipresence is the triumph of American sportswear—and, in my opinion, its great tragedy.

I'm not going to go so far as to say T-shirts can never be stylish or appropriate in public, but certainly T-shirts should not be worn everywhere, in every circumstance. Unless dressed up by the rest of the outfit, a T-shirt is strictly casual wear. It makes no difference to me whether the T-shirt in question is expensive or cheap.

Once, I had a lunch meeting with a man at a high-end restaurant. He showed up wearing a T-shirt and jeans. He immediately went to the trouble of telling me that the shirt was Alexander McQueen and the jeans Dior. As if this mattered! He was in jeans and a T-shirt. A T-shirt is a T-shirt. Spending hundreds of dollars on it doesn't elevate it. He was underdressed, even if his casual outfit did cost more than my suit and tie.

I once had another fashion victim tell me, "This T-shirt cost twelve thousand dollars!"

What difference does that make? If that's the message you want to send about yourself and your fashion sense, you should wear the price tag, or that should be the message on your T-shirt: "Hi. This T-shirt costs more than a semester of college." Or: "Hi. I have money to burn. Please help me get rid of all this wealth." And my shirt, in turn, would say, "Great. Please write a $12,000 check to charity."

Not long ago I had an interesting question from the audience during a Liz Claiborne event: "What do you think about graphic tees?" This shows that people are still wondering about the appropriateness of these things, which I find heartening.

My reply: "I'll wear a graphic tee that says: 'AIDS Walk,' when I'm on the AIDS Walk. But generally graphic tees are for the young—and I'm not talking about the young at heart."

Still, graphic or colored T-shirts do seem to me a little less scandalous than white T-shirts. A classic white T-shirt looks like underwear to me. Looking at it in a positive light, that fuels the sexual aspect of the white tee. A white T-shirt sends an erotic message, and I think that must be part of the subtext to the Lady Gaga posters that went up all over New York in 2011 showing her in sunglasses, red lipstick, and a tight white tee.

Think also of the famous Calvin Klein ads of the 1990s, which showed young models seductively posed in very little besides white T-shirts. Looking at pictures like that, you feel like a voyeur. Unless you do want to be perceived in this seductive way, you should wear a T-shirt in a color other than white.

Or you should dress it up. At a mall event, we once took a woman out of the audience who had on a T-shirt and jeans. We had her up on the stage in all her casualness. Then we threw an attractive tailored jacket over her. The audience went nuts.

"See," we said, "it's so simple! You don't need a new wardrobe to look polished and sophisticated."

People often wear T-shirts that are either too big or too small. In the 1990s, XL white T-shirts became a uniform for hip-hop fans. For his performance of "The Real Slim Shady" at the 2000 Video Music Awards, Eminem entered Radio City Music Hall followed by dozens of young men with short blond hair, blue jeans, and white T-shirts, driving home the lyric: "And there's a million of us just like me."

In a revealing *Baltimore City Paper* article about the history of the extra-extra-oversized T-shirt, the T-shirt is described as "inner-city camouflage." A clothing chain executive is

Eminem performed at the 2000 MTV Video Music Awards with an army of lookalikes.

quoted as saying, "The culture of the customer is so everyone will look the same. If the cops are looking for a suspect, [he's invariably wearing a] long white T-shirt with long shorts. So they can't be identified. That was the real reason it all started."

The oversized white T-shirt is also about looking pristine. "It's able to satisfy contradictory cultural injunctions," the reporter suggests. "It's both cheap and extravagant, all-purpose and outrageous—and economical enough to afford the decadent gesture of wearing it once and throwing it away."

If the hip-hop look is all about the XXXL white shirt, the hipster look is all about too-small shirts. These tiny shirts can look great if you have the right build. Otherwise, they're not usually flattering.

For men who want to wear tight shirts but don't have the perfect body for them, there's no reason why you can't wear a tight white undershirt, or even shapewear, under a T-shirt. You can! Men don't want to own up to that level of self-analysis. They equate that with vanity

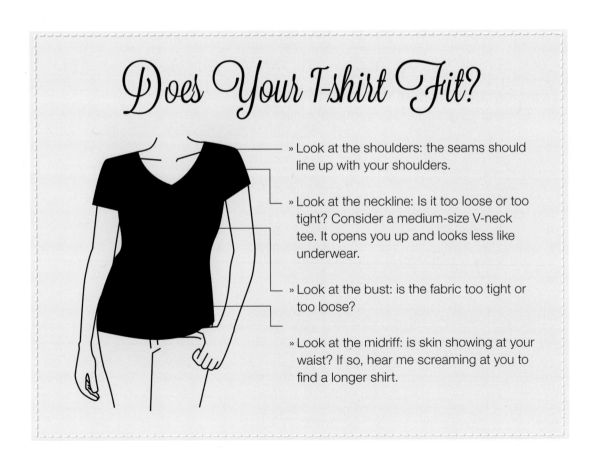

Does Your T-shirt Fit?

» Look at the shoulders: the seams should line up with your shoulders.

» Look at the neckline: Is it too loose or too tight? Consider a medium-size V-neck tee. It opens you up and looks less like underwear.

» Look at the bust: is the fabric too tight or too loose?

» Look at the midriff: is skin showing at your waist? If so, hear me screaming at you to find a longer shirt.

and vanity with femininity. It threatens their masculinity. That's ridiculous. There is nothing mutually exclusive about being manly and putting some thought into your appearance. Quite the contrary! Look at George Clooney and Brad Pitt. They may have a genetic advantage, but they also spend a lot of time and attention on their grooming and wardrobe.

But back to T-shirts. For those of us who aren't aspiring to look like a hipster or a hip-hop star, there's the question of how to tell when a T-shirt fits. The key is fitting the shoulder. The seams where the sleeves are attached should be exactly where your shoulder ends, not an inch toward your neck or toward your arms. That's my fit test.

Another tip: T-shirts with a V-neck or boat neck tend to be more flattering on both women and men. The traditional undershirt neckline is crew, so when you step away from that neckline, you're closer to looking dressed up. But avoid what I refer to as the V-crew neck—which is basically a high V-neck. To my eye, it's the least flattering of necklines.

That said, there is still the fundamental question of whether or not a T-shirt is appropriate in any given situation. T-shirts certainly have their place, but these days they are worn *every* place. Whenever you're putting on a T-shirt, it's best to keep in mind that it wasn't so long ago that they were only meant to be under clothes. Unless you can channel the sex appeal and rebellion implicit in a T-shirt into a pulled-together look, you may (for better or worse) be evoking the garment's not so distant past life—as underwear.

3.

JEANS

The Italian, French, German, English, Indian, All-American Garment

Low-rise, boot-cut, skinny . . .
Jeans, the great American wardrobe staple

FEW ITEMS of apparel are as ubiquitous as jeans. I assume that we all own a pair. (I have only had one person tell me, proudly, that she doesn't own a single pair of jeans, which I found startling because she wears other kinds of pants all the time!) For all their ubiquity, that pair of jeans in your closet is, historically speaking, a relative infant among the other items assembled there.

When I was a kid in the 1950s and early-to-mid '60s, no one—but *no one*—wore denim. Jeans were even on my elementary school's list of forbidden apparel and accessories. Other no-no's: collarless shirts (aka T-shirts), leather jackets, sneakers, and boots. What do you call someone who wears those items? A hood—a word that is no longer in use, meaning bad boy or girl. The denim-clad characters played by James Dean and Marlon Brando in the iconic '50s films *Rebel Without a Cause* and *The Wild One*, respectively, were what we called "hoods" in those days, and God forbid that you be labeled as one. (I'll add, parenthetically, that at my elementary school, one could still behave like a hood, even in oxford-cloth button-downs and gray flannel pants.)

But I recall owning a pair of jeans in those dark days. I can't imagine why. Did my parents think that jeans would toughen up their nerdy, reclusive, sports-shy son? Well, had I worn them more than once, toughen me up they would have—physically, if not spiritually. Jeans in those days were made of a much heavier denim and were unimaginably stiff; they could literally stand up on their own. I remember sitting on the edge of my bed and sliding into them. It was like walking with two leg braces; I couldn't bend my knees. Getting

Marlon Brando and other denim-clad hoods in 1953's *The Wild One*.

up or down a flight of stairs was a considerable workout. My legs were rubbed raw in the course of that single wearing. Surely, frequent wearing would have led to callused thighs. So, truth be told, I was fine with the school ban, although I did think it would have been nice if they'd also banned bullying.

My school's antijeans hysteria was not unique to my conservative Washington, DC, neighborhood. Communities everywhere devoutly believed that if your child were to wear jeans, a ticket to reform school was surely tucked away in the back pocket. In the 1950s, the Denim Council, a consortium of American textile mills, was formed to address the significant decline in sales due to this nationwide phenomenon. As we know, their fondest hopes were soon realized, as now jeans are the ultimate American wardrobe item.

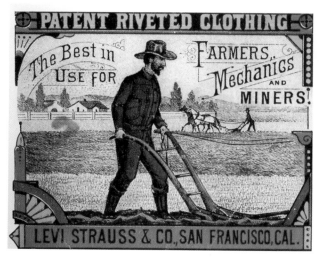

Levi Strauss was the first company to patent riveted jeans in America, as this early ad shows.

But let's back up. The history of denim may be the most fascinating of any category of clothing. I always maintain that fashion—clothing—happens in a context, a context that is societal, cultural, historic, economic, and even political. The turning point for jeans' popularity in America was the California Gold Rush of 1849. Thousands of people traveled west to seek their fortunes. Levi Strauss, a recent immigrant from Germany, was right behind them. In 1853, he opened a dry goods business in San Francisco to cater to this workforce. Strauss's American denim garments would hold up to the rigors of mining—mud, dirt, and very rough work. The seams in Strauss's clothing would be riveted for added strength. This riveting would become the iconic characteristic of the Levi Strauss brand. The brand name Levi's today is a stand-in for the word "jeans," much as Coke is shorthand for "cola."

Strauss invented the rugged-wearing pants that became known as jeans, but he didn't invent the textile. It is irrefutable that denim is centuries old and not American but Italian in origin, but the exact date of its appearance in unknown. We do know that in Genoa, Italy, in the sixteenth century, the textile—a sturdy twill made of cotton, linen, or wool—was called *jene fustyan* from *gènes,* the French word for Genoa, and *fustyan* for fustian, the name of the twill.

In the late 1620s, the Massachusetts Bay Company logged an invoice for "11 yards of wt. English jeans." In 1650, "19 pieces Jeines Fustian" were imported into Boston. However, by 1760, a full 110 years later, denim was the primary output of the United Company of

Philadelphia, the colonists' first mill.[1] And by the eighteenth century, *jene fustyan* was made entirely of cotton.[2]

In fall 2010 in New York, the art gallery Didier Aaron hosted an exhibition called *The Master of the Blue Jeans: A New Painter of Reality in Late Seventeenth Century Europe.* I expected to find a holy grail of sorts that would dispel the pervasive belief that blue jeans are primarily an American invention. Alas, it was rather a disappointment. It was a stretch to refer to the textiles in the paintings as blue jeans, although blue and fustian they were. It appeared that the show simply used the presence of a few blue working-class garments to aggrandize this anonymous artist under a catchy banner. Phooey.

While today's jeans are made of cotton, the twill that they are made of is stronger than fustian. That twill is called denim. Denim is traditionally yarn-dyed and woven with an indigo-blue face and a gray or unbleached fill.[3] The origin of the name "denim," though up for debate, harks back to the competitive relationship between Britain and France. It was long assumed that denim was an anglicized name for *serge de Nîmes,* a French textile dating back to the seventeenth century.

However, evidence has emerged that trumps this assumption. It appears that a heavy cotton twill was created in Britain in the eighteenth century and called "denim." The French *serge de Nîmes* was long thought to be a cotton twill, too, but we now know that it was wool. Accordingly, the new theory is that denim's origin is British and that the French name was given to the English product in order to give it prestige. The fabric from Genoa used to make sailors' pants was fustian, a sturdy blue fabric, but not what we would recognize as denim. In other words, the American wardrobe staple's likeliest origin is this: a German inventor used an English fabric with a French name to make an Italian pant.

At least that's my take! François Girbaud does not accept either the Genoa (jeans) or the *serge de Nîmes* (denim) origins and etymologies. He calls both "beautiful legends." Instead, he subscribes to the belief that the cloth was born in Amoskeag, New Hampshire, in 1831. Imagine trying to sell anything called "amoskeag"; you can see why manufacturers would prefer the jeans and denim stories, regardless of the truth. James Sullivan, in his wonderful book *Jeans: A Cultural History of an American Icon,* offers yet another theory. He cites the word "dungarees," another name for work pants and closely associated with denim and jeans, as originating from the village of Dungri in India. I'll leave it to the experts to battle it out, but I love how even asking a simple question about the origin of a pair of jeans can take us to every corner of the world.

When I was chair of the Department of Fashion Design at Parsons, I invited Lynn Downey, the historian for Levi Strauss & Co. in San Francisco, to present to my four hundred students a history of denim—from the company's perspective, of course. Lynn oversees a vast archive of clothing, photographs, recordings of oral histories, and letters from customers. The catalyst for my invitation was the then-recent discovery, in an abandoned mine, of the oldest extant pair of Levis. They date to 1879, seven years after Levi Strauss and Jacob Davis patented the first pair of jeans in 1872. Lynn brought to Parsons the 1879 jeans wrapped in acid-free archival cotton. They were the most shapeless pair of pants you ever saw. The wearer must have rolled them up and belted them, and the effect must have been that of a paper-bag waistband.

One thing I find interesting is that the only reason blue jeans are blue today is that the fabric was easy to dye indigo. Lynn has said[4] that there were other color choices available, including black, gold, and gray. In the year 1812, records show that Lord Byron ordered numerous pairs of "white jean trowsers" from his British tailor.[5] Blue has worked out, especially because it conceals dirt so well. But isn't it fun to imagine what would have happened if they'd gone with another color instead, and everyone around us was wearing, say, gold jeans?

Denim's transition into the world of fashion was not instantaneous. In America, denim spent close to a hundred years as a textile associated with laborers, particularly gold miners and cowboys. Denim figures prominently in the photographs of Walker Evans in *Let Us Now Praise Famous Men,* a document of Depression-era sharecroppers in Alabama for which Evans collaborated with Pulitzer Prize–winning writer James Agee. This would all create a stigma that would prove difficult to overcome.

It should be noted that the rise of denim in America is related not only to an identifiable need for sturdy work clothes but also to a

Miners wore Levi's into the California mines in the 1890s.

regional climate in the South that was ideally suited for growing the cotton plant. In addition to denim, cotton production according to James Sullivan, "included drill, a coarse fabric that would lend its name to one variety of prototypical jeans ('blue drillin's'), and duck or canvas,

which was perfect for tent cloth and sails.'"[6] Fustian, denim, and any twill textile of the like were relegated to the apparel of lower classes. According to a biography of Abraham Lincoln, the future president floated down the Sangamon River wearing "blue homespun jeans, jacket, vest, rawhide boots with pantaloons stuffed in, and a felt hat."[7]

Jeans' early popularity with workers is easy to understand. The upper classes dressed in silks and satins and fine wools, textiles that were soft and smooth to the touch and exuded luxury. Denim was heavy and rough; there was nothing luxurious about it. The actress Hope Williams was

Walker Evans's photographs in the 1941 book *Let Us Now Praise Famous Men* showed Alabama sharecroppers wearing denim.

shown wearing a pair of blue jeans in *Vogue* in 1928, but they were men's jeans, and she was on a dude ranch. In fact, dude ranches were extremely popular around that time, and women had to wear men's jeans there until the invention of Lady Levi's in 1934. They were given the batch number 701 to distinguish them from men's jeans, which were 501s. But, certainly, unless you were doing manual labor or getting up on a horse, you were unlikely to wear Lady Levi's out in public.

Up until World War II, American fashion was an unadulterated reflection of what was happening with clothing in Europe, especially in France. And denim was nowhere in the Parisian couture houses' refined textile vocabulary. But America was cut away from European fashion when the two hundred-plus couture houses in its epicenter of Paris closed due to World War II. It is at this moment that we begin to see the percolation and ascension of American fashion.

Among seminal American designer Claire McCardell's innovations was the intro-

None other than Nazi propagandist Leni Riefenstahl, shown here in 1939, was caught up in the American dude ranch craze that hastened the invention of Lady Levi's.

duction of denim into women's wardrobes. McCardell revered denim's roots. She liked its humble origins and working-class association. She used denim for sophisticated suits and coats, and even used Levi's signature double topstitching. This textile staple of the laboring masses struck a note of exoticism with the fashion crowd; they swooned over the designer's mixture of high fashion and low textile. In addition, McCardell stripped clothing of boning and infrastructure, thereby softening silhouettes and creating fashion that was comfortable and casual. This is why McCardell is attributed with the creation of American sportswear, a category of dressing that would distinguish this nation globally. And this is what earned her a *Time* magazine cover in 1955.

I have a theory about what I refer to as the "denim hiatus" in fashion, which I maintain lasted for close to twenty years, from the mid-1950s to the mid-1970s, when Calvin Klein brought denim back into the fashion arena for the first time since Claire McCardell. My theory is as follows: had Claire McCardell not died prematurely in 1958, and had the bad-boy movies of Brando and Dean not coincided with her untimely passing, then denim would not have experienced its eclipse as a garment for the middle and upper classes. It's merely a theory, mind you.

In any case, denim did disappear from the mainstream. Yes, denim was ever present among an antifashion crowd of laborers, motorcycle gangs, beatniks, and hippies, but those groups were severely marginalized when it came to the fashion world. (Later, fashion would be heavily influenced by all these groups, whose apparel would be dubbed "street fashion.") It wasn't really until the 1970s that women regularly wore jeans the way they do today.

In the category of designer jeans, history bestows upon Gloria Vanderbilt credit for being the first. She, ever so modestly, maintains that in a century-old American tradition of imitating European designs, she was merely inspired by the popular Italian brand Fiorucci, and wanted to create similar jeans at a more affordable price. And truth be told, it was Calvin Klein who put designer jeans in the face of the consumer. Certainly it was he who first featured jeans on a fashion runway. The year of his jeans launch was 1976, but it was ill-fated. Calvin and his business partner Barry Schwartz restrategized and relaunched jeans a year later to unconditional success. Interestingly, Calvin's new jean was derived from the classic Levi's 501: he deconstructed a pair, studied its parts and proportions, then lowered the rise and accentuated the rear end. *Et voilà!* A phenomenon was born!

Designer jeans have continued to be popular ever since, and their price tags have continued to rise. When Tom Ford was designing for Gucci, he created a pair of luxury jeans. They were artfully distressed, emblazoned with embellishments, and very luxurious, but they cost $3,100![8]

Jeans, like every other item of apparel in your wardrobe, experiences myriad iterations of silhouette and fit (baggy, pegged, boyfriend, oversized, skinny, high-waisted, low-rise) and textile treatment (dark, acid-washed, distressed, destroyed, pristine). The most controversial of these is the popular low-rise style. Some say Alex-

Silent film actress Viola Dana modeled denim overalls as early as 1917, but it would be many years before American women would wear jeans day-to-day.

Within the image (advertisement) the following text appears: "Levi's **jeaneration**" and labeled garment descriptions A, B, C, D, and size charts.

This 1970s Levi's ad from the U.K. shows the popularity of flare jeans.

ander McQueen should be credited for popularizing these in the 1990s, because he showed what he called "bumsters" on the runway in his 1995/6 "Highland Rape" collection. "[With bumsters,] I wanted to elongate the body, not just show the bum," McQueen said. "To me, that part of the body—not so much the buttocks, but the bottom of the spine—that's the most erotic part of anyone's body, man or woman."

Others would claim that the style was merely vulgar. Will it surprise you to know that I'm a fan of low-rise jeans? I am, and for a very particular reason. In 2007, I hosted a Liz Claiborne Denim Bus Tour across the nation, and I had a blast. Our purpose was to put before women everywhere a newly engineered series of jeans designs. And in my 4,500-mile experience, we found at least one pair of flattering jeans for every single woman. But it wasn't easy. The bus contained a communal space with mirrors and two private dressing rooms. We would begin our events outside the bus, usually at a tented location in the parking lot of a shopping mall, and present models of varying sizes—real-world sizes, mind you—in the various styles of denim. Then we worked one-on-one with women who stood in line, sometimes for hours, to have a style recommended for them and be fitted. When presented with a woman whose hips were appreciably wider than her waist (a frequent and not at all objectionable condition), I would always suggest a low-rise style. The response I received was universal: "No!"

"Why the objection?" I would ask.

"Just b-b-b-because . . . I can't!" the woman would invariably stammer.

But I had come around to the wisdom of the low-rise jean, and here's why: if you try to fit your slimmer waist, then the jeans won't fit your hips. If you try to fit your hips, then there will be too much fabric around your waist, the consequence being that you'll look sloppy. If we concentrate on fitting your hips only, which is what a low-rise jean is designed to do, then the jean will fit you perfectly.

I always added that I had no intention of letting anyone expose a muffin top or, worse, back cleavage; her top should cover the waistband of the jeans. Accordingly, she and I would be the only two people who would know that the jeans were low-rise. Everyone else would simply exclaim, "How fabulous you look in those jeans! Where did you get them?"

In my experience fitting women for jeans, the most flattering shape for the leg is usually one that falls straight from the widest part of the hip, with no flare and no taper. Owing to when I grew up, I associate bell-bottoms with hippies, so I generally advise against them unless you are, in fact, a hippie. Hipsters these days tend to wear skinny jeans exclusively. If you have the figure for a skinny jean, by all means do it! Regrettably, there are a lot of men and women walking around in skinny jeans that look like jeggings. And as far as I'm concerned, there is no place in this world for a jegging.

Straight-leg jeans tend to be the most slimming. Boot cut really seems to me like a euphemism for "wide leg," because a straight-leg jean can accommodate a boot just as well. And, of course, with a skinny jean you just put the boot on over the jeans.

When it comes to the wash of the jean, I've noticed that acid is back. I'm not a fan of that, or of destroyed or artificially distressed jeans. It seems like fashion victimhood to buy pre-ripped or frayed jeans. If you want that worn-in look, you can go to a vintage store and find jeans someone else has beaten up! Generally speaking, the darker the wash, the more versatile it will be in your wardrobe, because the darker it is, the more appropriate it is for nighttime. Of course, jeans are still not appropriate for the Oscars. I'm talking to you, John Travolta! Can you believe he wore jeans (paired with a tuxedo jacket) to the 2010 Oscars? I couldn't. He would have been better off in a white leisure suit.

If you have trouble finding a pair of jeans you love, you are far from alone. It is difficult to get the fit right. People really benefit from talking to a denim expert. This sounds self-serving, because Lucky Brand is part of the company that employs me, but in my experience the salespeople at Lucky Brand really understand fit and give good advice. And keep in mind: any jeans you buy today are bound to be more flexible, flattering, and comfortable than the ones from fifty years ago, just a blink of the eye in fashion history.

Which Jeans are Right for You?

» **Are you curvy?** Go for the lowest rise that will allow you to remain decent when bending over and pair it with a shirt that conceals the waistband.

» **Are you thin?** If you're high-waisted, you can try a high-rise to make your legs look extra-long. Otherwise, try a mid-rise.

» **Are you edgy?** Go for skinny jeans of any rise.

» **Are you more traditional?** Try mid-rise straight- or boot-leg jeans. I may be a fuddy-duddy, but I think once you're past forty-five or so, you should stick to a straight-leg pant that falls from the widest part of your hip.

» **Are you attending a Woodstock revival?** Your best bet: low-rise bell-bottoms. Go all out! Pair it with a tube top!

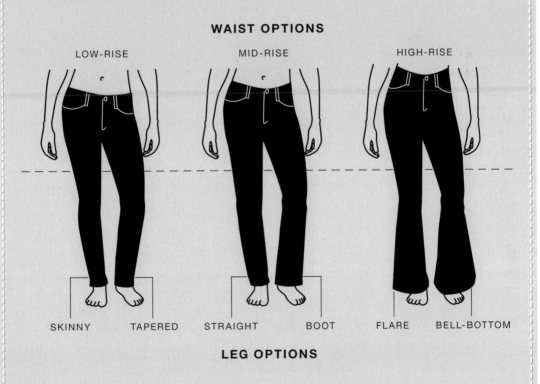

WAIST OPTIONS

LOW-RISE   MID-RISE   HIGH-RISE

SKINNY   TAPERED   STRAIGHT   BOOT   FLARE   BELL-BOTTOM

LEG OPTIONS

4.
DRESSES
From the Toga to the Wrap Dress

Cocktails, shifts, sheaths . . .
Are you a Cleopatra or a Helen?

ONE AFTERNOON, back when my grandmother was in her early twenties, she didn't show up for her weekly bridge club. So one of the ladies she usually played with called her house and asked if she were sick.

"Sick?" my grandfather said. "She's in the hospital. She just had a baby."

"*Baby?*" her friend said, shocked. "We didn't even know she was pregnant!"

This was the 1920s. You could get away with hiding a pregnancy in the dropped-waist dresses that were fashionable at the time. My very private grandmother was lucky to be pregnant then, and not a decade on either side of the twenties, when the popular look for dresses was far more fitted. With wasp-waisted dresses—so called because they yield an insectlike, hourglass shape—you couldn't conceal a big lunch, much less a pregnancy in its third trimester.

There has been a battle over the shape of women's clothing throughout Western history. In some eras, as in Europe after the French Revolution, there was a push for Grecian draping rather than tightly bound garments; this yielded the dreamy white cotton gowns of the 1790s. In other eras, as in 1720s England, petticoats created a stiff shell, making it hard at times to believe there was a woman under all that fabric.

The reigning waistline has moved up and down a woman's body over the years, from the empire-waist dresses of the Napoleonic era to the drop-waist dresses of the flapper days, to the natural-waist dresses worn by June Cleaver.

Actress and model Kay Laurell dresses in relaxed early 1920s fashion.

Women in the 1950s tended to wear variations of the New Look.

Today, there are many different silhouettes available to women—some narrow, others voluminous. And yet, even with so many options, finding a dress that fits well and is occasion appropriate can prove difficult, even for women with a great and natural sense of style. Finding the right dress—be it for work, for a date, or for a formal event—can be a source of great anxiety for women. I know few women who are fully satisfied with all the dresses in their closets.

It should come as no surprise that a flattering dress is the most rare and valuable of garments because it is the most difficult to fit. Unless you wear rompers or catsuits, the dress is likely the only garment in your closet that is one-piece dressing. That means it needs to fit in the greatest number of places: shoulders, chest, waist, and hips.

In my capacity as chief creative officer at Liz Claiborne Inc., I often brayed at the design-

At the turn of the twentieth century women wore large hats and long dresses. Heaven forefend you showed your ankles!

ers to stop making so many dresses and start making separates that, when put together, look like a dress. Many—I'd even venture most—women are a different size on top and on bottom. You can mix and match both styles and sizes if you have separates. And if you have a separate skirt, you can alter the waistline as your size changes, which you can't do as easily on a dress.

As we start this conversation about the history of the dress, I encourage you to lay out all the dresses you have (mentally, if not actually) across your bed, and study them. Do all your dresses look the same? Are they tight tubes or loose sheaths? What are they made of—wool, cotton, silk, spandex? What kind of waist looks best on you—high, low, natural? Which length is most flattering? What kind of neckline?

You are part of the history of fashion. The shapes you like best and the fabrics at your disposal are connected to the era and place in which you live. In this book, I've chosen to focus on real clothes worn by real women rather than on famous dresses. Enough with the importance of Givenchy's black cocktail dress for Audrey Hepburn in *Breakfast at Tiffany's* or the white halter dress that flies up around Marilyn Monroe in *The Seven Year Itch*. Yes, they are historically important, but how many women do you see walking around in white dresses with plunging necklines, or with near-hobble skirts hemmed with black feathers?

I appreciate the showmanship of avant-garde designers, the fantasies of Hollywood, and the aspirational nature of fashion magazines. But at the end of the day, for me, the priority is wearability. I want to study dresses that make real women look and feel beautiful. And I will argue that the dresses you see women wearing today on the street owe their shape, fabric, and fit not to a few stars' costumes but to thousands of years of history, beginning in the ancient world. As the centuries have passed, an evolutionary process has produced and discarded countless iterations of every garment (so long, bustles! Hello, A-lines!). Nothing that we wear is an accident.

There are many ways to categorize dresses—by era, by length, by dressiness—but they've all been done. I'd like to try something new. I'd like you to think about the dresses you actually own or covet and see them as two distinct types: the draped, which began for our purposes in ancient Greece, and the tailored, which I will trace to ancient Egypt. (Eerily-modern ancient Crete would be another place to start the conversation about tailoring, but Egypt is more vivid in the popular imagination, so let's go with that.)

Draped and tailored dresses probably hang side by side in your closet, but let's look at them as two distinct styles.

opposite: Audrey Hepburn in the famous black Givenchy cocktail dress from 1961's *Breakfast at Tiffany's*.

The Draped (Goddess, Flowy, Hippie, Wrap) Helen Dress

Do you like dresses that flow around your body in an easy, natural way? Dresses that are wrapped around you, possibly tied with a sash but otherwise loose and breezy? If so, you owe your taste to ancient Greece and Rome, where both men and women wore variations on what we know as the toga.[1] Large swaths of cloth were simply arrayed around the body. The rich wore wool and the poor wore felt.[2] The peplos of ancient Greece developed into the chiton, made of either two rectangles of cotton or linen, in the case of the Ionic chiton, or one, in the case of the Doric chiton.[3]

The draped goddess style of dress was worn by Rossana Podestà when she played the title role in *Helen of Troy* in 1956.

If this is your style, you should look for inspiration to Helen, known in her time (around 1200 BC) as the most beautiful woman in the world. For those of you whose Greek mythology is rusty: Aphrodite, the goddess of love, promised Helen to Paris, the prince of Troy. Unfortunately, Helen was already married to Menelaus, the king of Sparta, but that did not stop Paris from running off with her (or Helen from going with him). This event kicked off the Trojan War, which resulted in years of chaos and destruction.

For our purposes, we should note that when it was over (thanks to the Trojan horse), Menelaus captured Helen. He had planned to have her killed, but he couldn't bring himself to do it, such was her beauty. Here is a woman who inspired a war *and* left her husband, and he *still* finds her attractive. If that's not inspiring, I don't know what is![4]

Throughout Europe, variations on a draped style reigned more or less from the first through the thirteenth century. Any structure was typically achieved by means of sashes, belts, or jewelry. In ancient Greece and Rome, the fabric was often held together with pins at the shoulders. (In the Sophocles tragedy, Oedipus used pins from his mother's peplos to blind himself.)

Throughout the Dark Ages and medieval period, flowing tunics were the rule of the day. This draped style went out of fashion around 1340, and the next time we see the draped look in full effect is around 1800, thanks in part to the French Revolution. (No, I didn't ignore all those intervening centuries! They are covered in the second part of this chapter.)

Lilli Palmer and Christopher Plummer sported Greek chic in 1968's *Oedipus the King*.

Frances O'Connor wears an Empire-waist dress in 1999's *Mansfield Park*.

Rejecting the decadence of the upper class in all its guises, the rebels eschewed lace, ribbons, and velvet for simple white cotton gowns. Dresses of this time were made of flowy fabric tied below the breasts, which would come to be known as the empire waist.

A major influence on this style was Jean-Jacques Rousseau, who promoted "ideas of motherhood, education, sensibility, and humanity."[5] The new white neoclassical dresses symbolized this purity, love of nature, and simplicity.

Of course, as so often happens in fashion, the simple look didn't stay simple for long. The back of the white gowns grew in size. The natural shape gave way to the cinched waist. The nineteenth century saw a proliferation of petticoats, boned corseting, and other contraptions that conspired to make women look far less natural than Rousseau might have wished.

In the 1830s, puffy shoulders and skirts came into fashion. Broader shoulders had the effect of making the waist look smaller. In the 1840s and 1850s, broad shoulders went out but tiny waists stayed in, so you start to see more tight-lacing around that time.

After witnessing the physical harm done by this kind of extreme lacing, doctors and reformers began to protest. In the Victorian era, the dress reform movement, also known as the rational dress movement, dared to ask the question: Just how much should women corset their bodies? And while few at first dared suggest that the corset be jettisoned altogether, there was a revolt against tight-lacing.

In London in 1881, the Rational Dress Society proclaimed: "It protests against the wearing

Cartoonist and author Florence Kate Upton sports the huge sleeves so popular in the 1890s (one of several puffy-sleeved eras, another being the 1830s).

Rational dress fashions of the 1880s.

Designer Mariano Fortuny borrowed explicitly from ancient Greek fashion with his Delphos and Peplos (shown here) dresses of the early twentieth century.

of tightly-fitting corsets; of high-heeled shoes; of heavily-weighted skirts, as rendering healthy exercise almost impossible; and of all tie down cloaks or other garments impeding on the movements of the arms. It protests against crinolines or crinolettes of any kind as ugly and deforming . . ."

Once tight-lacing went out of fashion, there was talk of removing the corset altogether. Starting early in the twentieth century, designers started to create beautiful clothes that didn't require corsets, and they explicitly referenced Greece when they did so.

Directly inspired by Grecian draping, Mariano Fortuny created the Delphos gown in 1907 (as well as a two-piece version called the Peplos). It was elegant and in line with the mission of the rational dress movement.[6] These finely pleated silk tea gowns, often tied at the waist by thin silk cords, look so modern that it's hard to imagine they're more than a century old.

Fortuny wasn't the only designer explicitly referencing the classical era. In 1931, the brilliant Madame Grès opened a Paris studio called Maison Alix (later Maison Grès). She used silk jersey to make exquisitely draped dresses, including

Madame Grès was known for her expertly draped Goddess dresses.
These are from the 1950s but have a timeless quality.

the famous Goddess dress that would not have been out of place in the ancient world—nor on the red carpet today.

The former *Vogue* editor Diana Vreeland, my idol, called Madame Vionnet the most gifted designer in Western history. Madeleine Vionnet is largely forgotten (although certain designers have all but created shrines to her inside their studios), and that's a tragic loss. She created skillfully draped dresses that resembled togas.

The walls of her salon were covered with frescos depicting women wearing her dresses alongside Greek goddess.[7] She invented the bias cut—the technique of cutting fabric diagonally to the grain, which gives it greater stretch. If you ever have a chance to see a Vionnet in person—at the Museum of Metropolitan Art's wonderful Costume Institute or anywhere else—do it.

That reminds me: one day when I was at Parsons, I received a call from a Fifth Avenue socialite.

"I have a beautiful dress I'd like to donate to the school," she said.

"How generous," I said. "Do you know who the designer is?"

The influential designer Madeleine Vionnet (1876–1975) created neoclassical dresses.

"Vionnet."

"Vionnet?!" I shrieked as I ran out the door. "I'm getting in a cab right now!"

I arrived at the woman's apartment, panting.

The item in question turned out to be an A-line evening dress with heavy brocade that looked nothing like Vionnet's artfully draped work. I looked at the tag. It read: "Philippe Venet."

Alas. Venet, a quite different French designer, worked for Givenchy and Schiaparelli before opening his own couture shop in 1962. It closed in 1996. He has a place in fashion history, but he is no Vionnet.

According to James Laver in his 1937 masterpiece *Taste and Fashion,* wars have typically resulted in less confining clothes for women, as

Groundbreaking designer Paul Poiret fits a gown in 1924.

women were expected to work and could not easily do so surrounded by a dozen petticoats. Every time there is a loosening in the shape of dresses, womanhood, he says, breathes a sigh of collective relief: "'Now,' said the women of 1794, 'we can begin to enjoy ourselves.' 'Now,' said the girls of 1919, 'we can begin to enjoy ourselves.'"[8]

Paul Poiret, a great showman and egomaniac (his autobiography's title: *King of Fashion*), staged ridiculously expensive and elaborate fashion shows requiring, for example, a fleet of ships. But his work was revolutionary. Inspired by the Ballets Russes and taking his wife as his muse, he created glorious corsetless dresses—and even pants!—for women that let them move freely.

Given his expansion into home decor, he was probably the first designer to create a lifestyle brand. He's a kind of proto–Ralph Lauren. But Poiret's reign as king did not last

through World War II. He died in poverty on the streets of occupied Paris. I've often thought there should be a Hollywood film about his life. Paging Leonardo DiCaprio!

By contrast, a designer of the same era is the woman with arguably the biggest name in fashion history: Gabrielle "Coco" Chanel. The dropped-waist Chanel day dress, made of lightweight jersey, was a revelation. By wearing this dress, a woman sent the message that she was not a bird in a cage. She needed to move around freely, because she was part of the world.

If anyone ever doubts that a single designer can totally revolutionize the way we think about clothes, all you need to do is point them to Chanel. People are always calling designers revolutionary, but she really and truly did change the world. (Alas, her personal life is a little sticky. A biography published in 2011 suggests that she may have been a Nazi spy, code name "Westminster,"[9] but let's just stick to her contribution to fashion.)

Chanel's use of jersey, as in this 1927 day dress, revolutionized women's fashion.

opposite: Coco Chanel in 1936.

Before Chanel, women were rigged up in such outrageously uncomfortable getups that they could hardly breathe. The corsets, the fabrics, and the cuts—all seemed designed to make women feel as itchy and constrained as possible.

In 1916, Chanel took the knit fabric jersey—which before that moment had mainly been used for men's underwear—and used it to clothe women. The fabric let women's bodies be women's bodies, without anything being jacked up or pushed out. The fabric was comfortable, breathable, and—as it turned out—amazingly flattering to many women's bodies.

By the twenties, everyone was using jersey to make women's clothes, and so it is today that most women you see walking down the street are clad in a lightweight, stretchy fabric that a hundred years ago would only have been deemed appropriate for jockey shorts.

It's hard to imagine now what a revolution that was. Chanel took a great deal of heat for daring to show off women's bodies as they were, and she definitely fought back when people disagreed with her. She hated the ultracorseted look of Christian Dior: "Look at them," she said of women who wore such outfits, "Fools dressed by queens living out their fantasies. They dream of being women, so they make real women look like transvestites. . . . They can barely walk. I made clothes for the new woman. She could move and live naturally in my clothes."

According to the Metropolitan Museum's book *Chanel,* Marcel Proust, among others, didn't approve of women without their corsets. They looked too "ordinary," he said. But Chanel was insistent that this was what women wanted, and she was right.

"In inventing the jersey dress," she said, "I liberated the body, I eliminated the waistline." As part of this liberation, in 1926, she put the star of Jean Cocteau's play *Orpheus* in pants and a sweater. Within a decade, women throughout the West had sweaters in their closets.

Like Chanel, Jean Patou refused to heavily corset women's bodies. He shared with her what's called the *garçonne* look of the 1920s—some have called it dressing rich women as poor boys.

The message with the clothing revolution of the 1920s was that women deserved to be comfortable.

You see this same message conveyed years later with the draped dresses of Oleg Cassini, Donna Karan, and Issey Miyake. In the 1970s, Roy Halston dressed the "power ladies"

Halston's iconic
Ultrasuede shirtdress, 1973.

Jean Patou gown, 1931.

Trash bag or très chic? Tilda Swinton in Lanvin at the 2008 Oscars.

Diane von Furstenberg in one of her signature wrap dresses, with Andy Warhol, 1974.

of America in casual cashmere dresses, Ultrasuede shirtdresses, and floor-length jerseys. He used draping for the same reason the Greeks, the French Revolutionaries, Fortuny, and Chanel did: to make women look relaxed and self-assured.

In the confident toga spirit, Tilda Swinton wore a flowing black Lanvin washed silk satin dress to the 2008 Oscars. Some critics called it a trash bag. I thought it was great—for her. She was sending the message that she was a bohemian, not a Hollywood insider, and her daring made it that much sweeter when she took home the Best Supporting Actress award for her role in *Michael Clayton.*

One of my favorite dresses of all time is the Diane von Furstenberg patterned wrap dress, which in the 1970s created a whole new uniform for women in the working world. The wraparound dress style, which dates back thousands of years (think of the kimono!)—and was popularized in America in the late 1960s—is still popular today, with good reason. The wrap dress is a very flattering style on any body type. You just need to make sure you fit the shoulders, and the rest of the dress takes care of itself. It makes women look feminine, pulled together, and at ease in the world.

I encourage all women who are trying to update their work wardrobes to invest in a couple of flattering wrap dresses. It's easy, one-step dressing: it travels well, and it's easy to care for. With a wrap dress and heels—a complete outfit that can fit in the average purse—you're all set for a business meeting or dinner date.

Of course, the draped look is also easy to botch. Many of the dresses that you find at Walmart or your local department store, and from labels as diverse as Eileen Fisher and Jaclyn Smith, are in this Greek category. And they don't look great on everyone. But luckily, we live at a time when there are other silhouettes available. I feel bad for voluptuous women who lived through the 1920s, when those slinky styles were all the rage. Those cute flapper dresses can make a tiny woman look very saucy, but the same dress on a large woman can resemble a sausage casing.

Fifty years ago, shorter dresses were worn during the day and longer dresses were worn at night. Now women go to clubs wearing short dresses and, during the day, wear long dresses. Maxi dresses are back now, and I always say you need to dress these down. Maxi dresses, as a rule, should be worn with flats, not heels.

Many women I talk to tend to feel protected by the shapelessness and volume of these clothes and think that wearing dresses that are too big makes them look smaller. However, this strategy often backfires, making women look larger instead.

But this doesn't just happen at Walmart! I see a lot of what I call "Bad Greece" on the Oscars red carpet every year. A beautifully draped dress is a site to behold, but if the draping isn't artful, the dress can be a disaster. Rather than looking like a Greek goddess, a starlet can look as if she is wrapped up in bed sheets.

J.Lo's famous Donatella Versace dress at the 2000 Grammy Awards is a good example of Bad Greece. Known as the jungle dress, this sheer green silk bamboo wrap with jewels over the crotch broke the age-old rule that if you reveal a lot of your body on top, you don't reveal it on the bottom, too. I thought it was vulgar. Everyone else loved it, and it has been much imitated, to my consternation.

Three models in maxi dresses with empire waistlines, 1973.

The jungle dress is an example of draping that reveals a lot. More often, draping is used as a kind of shroud, to cover much of the body. Too often, a woman maintains that such a baggy dress is comfortable. Pajamas are comfortable! Comfort shouldn't be exclusively ruling your fashion choices.

The fact is: a draped dress that fits is going to be just as comfortable as one that's extra loose. In fact, it will be far more comfortable, because you'll know that you're carrying on a great tradition dating back to antiquity of women moving through the world with grace and elegance.

Of course, there's another road to take when dressing. I'll call it the tailored look. We'll begin in Egypt. . . .

The Tailored (Sewn, Structured, Fitted, Cinched, Corseted) Cleopatra Dress

Fabric wants to hang. Draping lets it be itself. If draping is nature, tailoring is nurture, forcing the fabric to take on a specific shape. Generally speaking, tailored clothes look more polished and sexual; draped clothes look more relaxed and sensual.

Cleopatra epitomizes this seductive, structured look. Princess Cleopatra VII became queen of Egypt in 51 BC, at the age of seventeen. Rome was poised to consume her empire, but she used her beauty and power to negotiate with Julius Caesar and Mark Antony. Her clothes were fitted rather than draped, and—amazingly to me, given how long ago she lived—tailored.

Jennifer Lopez in the revealing—I would say vulgar—Versace jungle dress.

While it seems like tailoring would be a much more advanced process than draping, both were present in the ancient world. The archaeological clothing timeline starts in 80,000 BC with beads. There is a record of flax fabric as early as 30,000 BC![10]

In ancient Egypt, beginning in 1600 BC,[11] both men and women usually wore a kind of tunic made of a rectangular piece of typically white linen, with holes cut for the arms and head, and sewn down the sides.[12] The longer and wider the tunic, the higher the status of the wearer.[13]

According to James Laver, "the characteristic costume consisted of a shirt with short, tight sleeves, worn either with or without a belt."[14] Sometimes there was also a tasseled

Are you a Helen or a Cleopatra?

If you prefer more draped looks, you are a Helen:

» You will probably look best in the silhouettes of ancient Greece, the French Revolution, and America in the 1920s and '60s.

» **Modern-day Helens:** Jennifer Lopez, Tilda Swinton, Jennifer Hudson

If you prefer more structured looks, you are a Cleopatra:

» You will probably look best in the silhouettes of ancient Egypt, the French royal court, and America in the 1930s, '40s, '50s, and '70s.

» **Modern-day Cleopatras:** Cate Blanchett, Helen Mirren, Reese Witherspoon

shoulder girdle, or cape. This tunic was typically paired with a loincloth, wig, and cloak. Essentially, in Egypt this formula did not change for more than a thousand years.

We tend to think of ancient cultures as sartorially primitive, but this look took work! There was sewing, fitting, accessorizing. Of course, as we know from the pyramids, those Egyptians were not a culture daunted by a task's difficulty level.

Simultaneously, the world of ancient Crete (3400–1000 BC) was producing clothes shockingly similar to more modern Western clothing. The breasts were sometimes exposed, but aside from that, some of their styles would have fit right in thousands of years later on the streets of Paris. There were even bodices. One fresco from c. 1400 BC Knossos shows a woman so elegant and polished that she looks like a French lady. Archaeologists nicknamed her La Parisienne.

Beginning roughly in the first century AD, it became a draper's world for hundreds of years. Clothes makers all

opposite: Elizabeth Taylor as Cleopatra in 1963.

over the West more or less took a timeout from tailored construction between ancient Egypt and the Middle Ages. Clothing throughout this long period of time was mostly draped and flowing. But when structure came back, it came back with a vengeance, and with only a few exceptions, it was more or less the rule until designers took women out of the corset in the 1920s.

In the Middle Ages, women wore a kirtle (kind of like a slip), a cotehardie (a garment that includes the bodice), a sideless surcoat (like a jacket), and a houppelande (aka a gown). But in the mid-1300s, all of a sudden, the silhouette changed. According to James Laver, under the reign of Philip of Valois in France, for men long tunics went out of fashion, in favor of shorter, tailored garments and tight hose.[15] And for women, starting around 1360, "we can see the beginnings of something we can recognize as fashion: a succession of rapidly changing modes," says James Laver.

Quickly, he says, three things that women would use for centuries to entice men came into play: décolletage, tight-lacing, and fancy hats.[16] The bodice of the gown became lower

This fifth-century Coptic tunic is made of linen and wool.

La Parisienne, the famously modern-looking fresco from Knossos, Crete, 1700–1400 BC.

English fashion in the fifteenth century: an ermine-lined gown with a side vent worn over a kirtle and with a belt. The long, tight sleeves could be turned back to form a cuff.

cut and tighter. A girdle confined the waist. Sleeves became huge. And people started to take note of every change in fashion. By the start of the fifteenth century, Laver says, every woman who could afford to was following fashion as best she could.

The Renaissance brought increased communication and influence between countries in Europe. Women wore rich fabrics like velvet, satin, and taffeta, embroidered with silver and gold thread, and decorated with furs. The main garment was the bodice and skirt sewn together, and over that was a gown that fit tightly in the waist and flowed to the ground.[17] The prevalence of rich fabrics like these continued through the reign of Henry VIII.

Spanish fashion continued to influence British fashion, even after the countries went to war under Elizabeth I. The most distinctive clothing feature of this era was the huge hoop skirt you start to see in the mid-1500s. In England in 1580, the queen took to wearing the

farthingale, which is rather like a hoop skirt that starts at your hips. These became all the rage. (With its farthingale, Spain was the trendsetter from the second half of the 1500s into the 1600s. Then France took over[18] and arguably continues to reign as the world's fashion leader.)

For a time, women (those who weren't doing manual labor) wore the Spanish farthingale, an underskirt that created volume by means of hoops of wire, wood, or whalebone.[19] The French

left: Lady Jane Grey was proclaimed queen of England on July 10, 1553, but beheaded nine days later.

below: Renaissance fashion of the sixteenth century.

farthingale, also known as a wheel farthingale, came next, but was mostly confined to the court. The skirt fabric fell straight down from the outer rim of a hoop around the woman's waist. The Italian farthingale's wheel was tilted at the back, giving the effect of a bustle.

Outside the court, the roll farthingale took off. This was popularly known as the bum roll. It was not flattering. Then, as now, if your clothing inspires nicknames that employ words like "bum" or "roll," you know you're in trouble. And it was just what it sounds like: a padded roll of cloth that went around the back of the dress and was joined in the front at the waist. You look at portraits of women in huge hoop dresses and it's hard to imagine how a potential suitor might go about getting acquainted with a woman in such a dress. You couldn't get within three feet!

While in most contexts these huge hoops are strictly period pieces, there are voluminous heirs to this kind of hoop skirt at the White House Correspondents' Dinner every year. Each time I've attended, I've felt as though I was on the set of *Gone With the Wind*. It's as though these women learned about fashion exclusively from Turner Classic Movies.

Suffice it to say: over this period of time, clothing sees a lot of structure and not a lot of Grecian draping. The seventeenth and eighteenth centuries were also all about tailoring, with plenty of stiff-boned bodices.[20]

Queen Elizabeth I wears a French farthingale.

The corsets were tight and the skirts were huge—the stuff that Academy Awards for Best Costume Design are made of—but what was the historical context for such huge gowns?

From 1590 to 1715, Europe was almost constantly at war. You might think fashion would stall given the social upheaval of the period, but the opposite happened. In this span of time, fashion changed constantly, influenced by art and philosophy.[21]

The eighteenth century brought a surge in industry and trading, like cotton from India and inventions such as the 1764 spinning jenny, a frame that sped up yarn production. In Europe the concept of "society" was emerging.[22] As Louis XIV grew older, he encouraged the court of Versailles to be less lavish and more formal. When he died in 1715, clothes became looser, as if in a great gesture of relaxing. The backs of dresses developed what's been called a "Watteau pleat," a box pleat running down the middle of the back that some people find quite elegant and others refer to as a "sack back."[23]

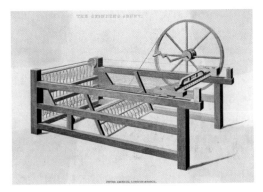

The 1764 spinning jenny sped up production.

This could almost be considered a return to the draping look, but we're going to keep the French ladies of the early eighteenth century in this tailored section, because of what happened to their skirts around this time. Hoops returned, and this time the goal was not to create circular volume but to maximize width. The pannier (French for "basket") could reach as much as fifteen feet sideways! Two women wearing panniers couldn't fit through a door together or sit on the same couch. Architecture had to change as a result. Doorways grew wider.

As we see so often, the more elaborate and lavish clothes get, the more they're headed for a fall. The vast panniers set the stage for the French Revolution–inspired detour from rigid tailoring into the simple white cotton dresses we discussed in the draping section.

But those circa-1800 white dresses and the return to simplicity they symbolized were short-lived. In the 1840s, the focus was on "the submissive slope of the dropped shoulders," according to Alison Lurie. The rule of the day: long corsets, heavy skirts, bulky shawls, and tight collars. Demure Queen Victoria, who took the throne in 1837, was this era's beauty

This 1780 pannier corset shows what was under those massive eighteenth-century skirts.

ideal. The fashionable Victorian woman found it difficult "to raise her arms very far, emphasizing her charming helplessness."[24]

Big skirts increasingly became a signifier of womanliness. "This was the age of the crinoline, and later of the bustle," writes Lurie, "and the increased importance of women in the domestic and social sphere was signaled by their sheer bulk. The oversize fashions also allowed them to display their father's or husband's wealth to the fullest extent."[25]

Variations on this massive skirt trend continued. The crinoline increased in popularity in 1860, thanks in part to Empress Eugénie, the woman James Laver claims was the last royal person to have a direct impact on fashion.[26] He said this, of course, years before Princess Diana and Kate Middleton!

This is around the period of time that couture was invented by Charles Frederick Worth. Worth was a British urchin, basically, who worked tirelessly to learn the tailor's trade. He turned construction into a high art—as you can see by his elaborate, plumage-covered peacock dress.[27]

Other fashion icons of the turn of the twentieth century were Maud Gonne (poet William Butler Yeats's muse) and Lillie Langtry (the British actress and companion to royalty). The

Queen Victoria, shown here in 1833, when she was still Princess Victoria, with her spaniel, Dash.

S-curved body was the ideal, and plenty of starching, lacing, and padding went into creating it. In discussing the crinoline, Laver suggests that these huge skirts symbolized the aloofness of women. The fact that men could only glimpse the occasional ankle made them obsessed with delicate ankles during this period.

By the 1920s, women were demanding greater freedom of movement, and so you see the rise in shorter, boxier, flapper-style dresses. But there was a backlash against the breezy look after the stock market crash of 1929, and the thirties and forties saw a good deal of tailoring, with longer hemlines and bias-cut dresses more flattering to curvier figures.

In more crass terms, the twenties were all about legs and the thirties and forties all about curves. What we find sexy in fashion changes from generation to generation. "The female body consists of a series of sterilized zones," writes James Laver, "which are those exposed by the fashion which is just going out, and an erogenous zone, which will be the point of interest for the fashion which is just coming in. This erogenous zone is always shifting, and it is the business of fashion to pursue it, without actually catching it up."

The post–World War II dresses of Christian Dior had serious *infrastructure*. He exemplified everything that was European about European fashion. Dior's "New Look," a term coined in 1947, had women looking sharp, in both senses of the word. Of course, the New

Lady Curzon, vicereine of India, wears the peacock dress created for her by Worth of Paris, 1903.

Lillie Langtry shows off her S-curve figure in 1885.

Barbara Stanwyck, future film star, shows off her legs in the 1920s, when she was a Ziegfeld girl.

Look wasn't completely *new*. The fashion shows of 1938 were full of corsets and other looks that were a backlash against the relative breeziness of the 1920s. World War II prevented those retro looks from coming back until the midforties. But come back they eventually did, and Dior's look ended the spare, utilitarian dressing of the war years, decadently requiring vast quantities of fabric for those full skirts.

"I wanted my dresses to be constructed," Dior said, "molded upon the curves of the feminine body, whose sweep they would stylize." Chanel said Dior "upholstered" women rather than dressed them.

Speaking of clothing as furnishing, let's talk about the Letty Lynton dress, a floor-length, ruffled, white organdy evening gown created by Adrian, head costume designer for MGM Studios. The dress was made for Joan Crawford's role in the 1932 film *Letty Lynton*, and it looks as though it could provide curtains for an entire household. But the dress was so

Christian Dior drapes fabric around a model in 1952.

popular that Adrian was pressured to do a ready-to-wear line. Something like five hundred thousand Letty Lynton dresses were sold at Macy's alone.[28]

Another popular but far more elite designer of the time, Mainbocher designed simple silk dresses that were incredibly expensive, costing more than $4,000 in 1945 money. After he created the pale blue wedding dress for Wallis Simpson, copies of the dress flew off the racks back in the United States. The two-time divorcée caused the scandal of the century by marrying the former King Edward VIII of England in 1936. The notorious couple had a huge influence on fashion—and inspired a movie by Madonna.

But the real influence on American fashion was France. Back then, everything the French did, we did. American designers went to Paris, looked at the collections, and turned out their own versions. Hattie Carnegie was among the champion copiers. Very little about her was authentic, including her name. She was born Henrietta Kanengeiser.[29]

Joan Crawford wears the hugely popular and totally ridiculous Letty Lynton dress, 1932.

Wallis Simpson in her wedding dress, 1937.

A poor Austrian immigrant to New York City, she worked as a messenger at Macy's. As part of her self-reinvention, she took the name of the richest person she could think of and became the first American custom designer with a ready-to-wear label. She copied European design shamelessly. At her shop during the Depression, Vionnet rip-offs sold for $50.

We've always been a nation of copiers, but during World War II, the Nazi occupation of Paris meant that American designers actually had to come up with their own designs. The result was the real birth of American fashion. Since then, American designers have had more of an impact on what we wear than we often realize. This country has produced some brilliant, original designers in the last sixty years. I'm not just talking about Oleg Cassini, the one quasi-American designer Jackie Kennedy wore (her tastes ran European).

The Metropolitan Museum of Art holds numerous dresses by Charles James, a god of structure and skill who got his start running a Chicago hat shop in the twenties. His famous silk four-leaf-clover dress of 1953 has a shiny satin bodice and a huge skirt that looks like leaves. The dress is exquisite, but in a 2011 interview, a couture veteran who once worked for Charles James revealed Austine Hearst's experience wearing the four-leaf-clover dress:

> When she wanted to go to the bathroom she couldn't. She had to take off the whole dress. It was so tight she couldn't bring it up. He was a genius, but forget it! His ideas were terrific, but then he couldn't think of the woman. You couldn't even move. He didn't think beyond: it looked great and that was it. He didn't care if the person could sit, go to the bathroom, or whatever. [30]

That's true of a great many designers even today!

But one American designer who did pay attention to women's needs is also one of my all-time favorites: the star of midcentury American fashion, Claire McCardell. She created stylish, functional clothes for real women. One of the most famous was her $6.95 Popover dress, which I consider the best-ever sweat-suit alternative. It was McCardell's answer to *Harper's Bazaar*'s challenge to create something fashionable that you could wear to clean the house and then to a cocktail party.

Claire McCardell took the boning and corseting out of clothes but retained the tailoring. It was really the best of both worlds. She paved the way for everything that's American about American fashion: effortless-looking chic that doesn't constrain the body but looks pulled together.

She also wrote a great fashion advice book, sadly out of print: *What Shall I Wear?* In this book, she talks about how women should dress to suit themselves, not the trends of the day.

Claire McCardell's 1942 Popover dress. Just pop it on, and you're ready to clean the house or go to a cocktail party!

Designer Charles James's voluminous, impeccably structured four-leaf-clover ball gown, 1953.

She is practical about fashion but also enthusiastic about taking chances. She dismisses trends. Just because red is in vogue, she says, doesn't mean *you* have to wear it. "Perhaps bright red will clash with everything about you," she says reasonably. She encourages women to ask one very important question when they're shopping: "Where would you wear it?"

The McCardell book clarifies what distinguishes American design. It's not Europe. It's not Asia. It has very specific dimensions. She also insisted that fashions only survive when they deserve to. Speaking of a collection of her dresses that were shown in a Beverly Hills gallery, she said: "The monastic dress was one of them, the flowing robelike design that the wearer shaped to her own waistline with a sash or belt. The dress appeared first in 1938. Yet, how can I say that? It appeared hundreds of years ago! Its design is a classic."

She's right; that simple dress has changed in a million different ways over the years. Its neckline plunged and rose. It acquired and lost shoulder pads. The pockets moved around. The amount of fullness changed. And yet it's remained essentially the same garment over hundreds of years and thousands of miles.

McCardell's parallel designer was Norman Norell. Whereas she did sportswear, he was known for evening wear. He was the first American designer to be accepted on the runways of Paris.

Another great American designer was Pauline Trigère, who was influenced by Vionnet and mastered bias cutting. When I was chair of the fashion department at Parsons, we received

hundreds of deaccessioned garments from the Metropolitan Museum of Art's Costume Institute. There was one Trigère I'll never forget. Not a single dart was visible, but it was perfectly tailored to its wearer's body. Well, we put it on a dress form and realized that the whole dress was shaped by darts *under the arms*. There were probably ten or twelve darts on each side, and that's what gave the dress its shape. It was astounding.

Geoffrey Beene, who died in 2004, was another great American designer. In the sixties he brought gray flannel and wool jersey to ballroom gowns, and he created his famous Sequined Football Evening Gown in 1967. He's known for saying things like, "Plastic is perfect in its own way. So is a diamond. Why shouldn't the two go together?"[31]

Why not indeed?

American fashion design has a wonderful history. Generally speaking, American designers have emphasized wearability and personal style. In her book, McCardell doesn't use the term "fashion victim" to describe people who let clothes wear them, but she does use "slaves to fashion," which is what you are when your look goes too far toward Bad Egypt.

For me, this overstructured look came to a head with the taffeta shantung dresses that dominated in the 1950s.[32] They look very out of fashion now. If you watch *Leave It to Bea-*

Norman Norell's 1953 mermaid dress.

ver, you see that June Cleaver looks ridiculous in those big dresses, walking around her house, supposedly cleaning. She's got this vast skirt and a little dust rag. *Really?* She doesn't look like she's been scrubbing a bathtub; she looks like she's lost her way from Cinderella's castle.

You could argue that her look came straight from Dior's New Look and wasn't all that uniquely American a style. Perhaps that's part of why I'm not as thrilled by it as I am by truly original American designs. As a rule, American design is extremely inventive. You get real characters here in America, like the brilliant fashion designer Elizabeth Hawes, who was a bestselling author (her hilarious books had titles like *Why Women Cry, or Wenches with Wrenches*), a union organizer, a fashion writer for *The New Yorker,* and a gifted couturier. Hawes Inc. clothed socialites of New York in the thirties.

Her elegant, creative gowns are now in the collection of the Metropolitan Museum of Art's Costume Institute, and they have charming names, like the Alimony dress, which can be paired with the Misadventure cape. Among the artists she collaborated with on designs were Alexander Calder and Isamu Noguchi. Alas, she died penniless in the Chelsea Hotel in 1971.

We have a glorious design tradition to be proud of here in this country, and it's a shame, in my view, that American designers of today know so little about American designers of the past. That's not to say that Europe doesn't have much to celebrate. Much over-the-top innovation in the sixties—my favorite fashion era to date—emerged from London and Paris. Exploding in international popularity were such eye-catching looks as André Courrèges's space-age collection and Mary Quant's minidresses.

Yves Saint Laurent collaborated with the artist Mondrian to create a dress in 1965 printed like one of the artist's canvases. This was carrying

Barbara Billingsley was the epitome of 1950s femininity as June Cleaver.

on the tradition of designer-and-artist collaborations that goes back at least to 1937, when the infinitely creative designer Elsa Schiaparelli worked with the surrealist Salvador Dalí on her famous lobster dress.

The sixties were also a time when see-through clothes came into vogue. Coco Chanel said, "Be a caterpillar by day and a butterfly at night."[33] Some women break out of their cocoon quite literally and put it all out there when dressing for nighttime.

This, too, evokes Egypt. Ancient Egyptian art shows dancers in see-through ankle-length linen dresses. The concept of the see-through dress has returned from time to time, perhaps most famously in Arnold Scaasi's pantsuit for Barbra Streisand's 1969 Oscar appearance. It caused quite a scandal.

"Though we had taken every aspect of the sequin outfit into consideration, we did not know that the flashbulbs used by the press would wipe out the flat surface of the black net," Scaasi wrote in his memoir, aptly titled *Women I Have Dressed (and Undressed!)*.[34] The next day's headlines read, "Streisand, Nude Under See-Through Outfit!"

Elizabeth Hawes encouraged women to pair her Alimony gown with her Misadventure cape, 1937.

Yves Saint Laurent's Mondrian dress, fall/winter 1965–66.

Elsa Schiaparelli's 1937 lobster dress.

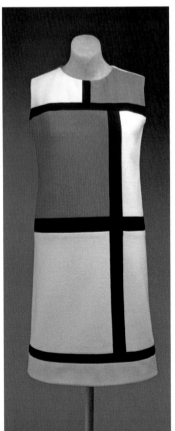

Some Scaasi critics pointed out that Yves Saint Laurent had done even more revealing see-through dresses in Paris. Scaasi acknowledged the influence, if just to imply that the French are more laid-back about revealing a woman's body: "Interestingly, in that epoch Yves Saint Laurent had done many *really* see-through clothes (without underpinnings) for his couture collections in Paris—naturally, the world press loved them, photographed them, and no one batted an eye!"

There have been plenty of other famous see-through outfits—among them Betsey Johnson's clear vinyl slip-on kit dress from 1966. It came with paste-on foil stars, fish, dots, and numbers for personalized underpinnings.[35]

In 1994 Elizabeth Hurley wore a revealing dress to the premiere of *Four Weddings and a Funeral*. There-

Barbra Streisand accepting her 1969 Oscar for *Funny Girl*.

after known as the safety-pin dress, the black Versace dress with gold pins lining her bare side, was voted the greatest red carpet dress of all time in a 2008 survey by the UK store Debenhams.[36] To me, that dress was a prime example of Bad Egypt.

There's been plenty of Good Egypt, too, of course. Interestingly, the flowy clothes many young people were wearing in the 1960s, like the flowing flower child dresses, were not considered fashion. The beacons of high fashion were designers like Paco Rabanne, who made tailored dresses that at times evoked knights' armor.

Everyday applications of this structured trend in 1960s fashion could be seen on the TV show *That Girl*, which ran from 1966 to 1971 and starred Marlo Thomas. When I recently met Marlo at an event, I was ecstatic.

Elizabeth Hurley in Versace's safety pin dress.

"In *That Girl,* you gave me my first education in the semiotics of clothes!" I told her. The mod dresses signified fun and confidence. With bright colors, bold patterns, and crisp lines, the tailored, flattering separates said "city girl."

Marlo gracefully acknowledged what a big impact the show had on fashion—and also how impossible it would have been for a real struggling actress to afford that kind of wardrobe, much less that apartment! She was delightful.

Some of the most fun dresses from the 1970s were those designed for Emma Peel of *The Avengers.* The designer was John Bates, known for backless dresses, striped tube dresses, pantsuits, dresses with matching tights, and op-art prints.[37] These clothes were often scandalously formfitting, but playful rather than lurid.

The 1980s are my least favorite fashion era to date. This was the era of Margaret Thatcher, *Dallas,* and the shoulder pad. The gaudy prints! The big hair! All of it is, for me, the antithesis of elegance. It was dominated by the most tailored of the tailored. Even talented designers lost their minds during this decade. Oscar de la Renta's high-society gowns are masses of ruffles and colors not found in nature.

Diana Rigg as Emma Peel in *The Avengers,* which ran from 1961 to 1969.

opposite: Marlo Thomas in *That Girl.*

Kathleen Beller, Pamela Sue Martin, Joan Collins, Linda Evans, and John Forsythe in *Dynasty*, which ran from 1981 to 1989.

Nolan Miller, designer of the clothes for the TV show *Dynasty,* created a ready-to-wear line, bringing those big-shouldered atrocities into every mall in America. Princess Diana's 1981 wedding dress, with its twenty-five-foot train and poufs everywhere, epitomized this period of excess and volume.

The 1990s, thankfully, were all about paring down, especially in music and clothing. One of the more famous dresses of the nineties was the white Calvin Klein tube dress worn by Alicia Silverstone as Cher in the movie *Clueless.* This is a classic example of a dress that's loaded with infrastructure, but looks simple, and doesn't have a lot of volume. You could probably make a dozen of these Calvin Klein dresses out of the reams of ivory fabric used to create Diana's wedding dress.

Many of the most popular designers since the nineties, among them Helmut Lang, have been enthusiastic embracers of the Egyptian school of dresses. It's funny how for all the work Vionnet, Chanel, and McCardell spent getting rid of the corset, modern designers like Jean Paul Gaultier and Thierry Mugler have been determined to bring it back.

It makes sense for stage costumes. Corsets, angles, and definition help make stars stand out even in huge arenas. Think of recent pop-star ensembles: Beyoncé's by Mugler, Madonna's by Gaultier, and Lady Gaga's by Alexander McQueen. But they can be tricky to pull off in real life.

So, what is the secret to wearing the Egyptian look well?

Proportion and fit. It's no surprise that many designers who excel at tailored dresses originally studied either architecture or sculpture. When done well, architectural dresses are true masterpieces.

So, how is this kind of dress done wrong? Bad Egypt is an awkward dress that wears *you*.

Armed with this history, look at the dresses in your closet. Hold each one up. Is it Egypt or is it Greece? More to the point: is it Good Egypt or Bad Egypt?

It's not easy to master any of this. I always say, if getting your fashion right were easy, everyone would look amazing all the time, and we know that's not the case. But know that when you get the tailored look or the draped look right, you're channeling Cleopatra or Helen of Troy, so you should carry yourself with all the pride and poise of a legendary beauty!

Alicia Silverstone and Justin Walker in 1995's *Clueless*. Earlier in the film she has this conversation with her father: "Cher, what are you wearing?" "A dress!" "Says who?" "Calvin Klein!"

5.
CAPRI PANTS AND SHORTS

The Plague on Our Nation

Bermudas, Daisy Dukes, hot pants . . .
From the battlefield to the beach party

THE BAGGY CARGO CAPRI is the single worst item of clothing in America today. There, I said it. Worse even than the dreaded jegging, the ubiquitous cargo capri is flattering on no one. I maintain that it dominates the country primarily because people hate shopping, and therefore they appreciate that with the cargo capri they only need to fit the waist and hips, letting the pant hem fall where it may. Alas, it's actually the hem length that makes the wearer look shorter, squatter, and sloppier than desired.

"I have big legs," cargo-capri wearers will say to me, "so I don't want to wear tight pants."

To this I say, if you are shy about your legs, the last thing you should do is wear shorter pants, baggier pants, or pants with pockets, much less all of these things at the same time. They will only make your legs look bigger and shorter. Think about sleeves. If you have thick arms, do you wear wizard sleeves? No! Tight capris can be flattering, especially on tall women, but baggy ones? I have yet to see it work.

At malls, I am tempted to set up the fashion equivalent of a guns-for-cash or needle-exchange booth and call through a bullhorn: "Throw your cargo capris into the flaming trash can, step behind the screen, and claim your wrap dress." I would find it very cathartic . . . albeit very hot beside the pyre given the ubiquity of the look.

I see women wearing capri pants nearly every day; they're not as bad as cargo capris, but they aren't the capri pants of Grace Kelly and Audrey Hepburn, either. Those 1960s capri pants were fitted. A designer named Sonja de Lennart is credited with introducing them in 1948, naming them after her favorite vacation spot: the Italian island of Capri. And in the fifties and sixties they became incredibly popular as people emulated their favorite starlets. They are far more stylish than the capri pants I see women wearing today, which are often shapeless and frumpy.

Laura Petrie, Mary Tyler Moore's character on *The Dick Van Dyke Show,* wore especially skinny capri pants on the show. In the sixties it was revolutionary. Up until then, most housewives on TV wore pearls and full-skirted dresses—even when they washed dishes. Laura seemed far more modern and comfortable in her trim capri pants—and they showed off her dancer's body. Emilio Pucci, the "prince of prints," helped popularize the style. He opened a boutique in 1950—where else?—on Capri.

Oh, cargo capris, how unflattering you are.

opposite: Grace Kelly, circa 1954.

HUMPHREY BOGART AUDREY HEPBURN WILLIAM HOLDEN

Sabrina

WALTER HAMPDEN · JOHN WILLIAMS · MARTHA HYER · JOAN VOHS

Produceret og iscenesat af BILLY WILDER

Manuskript: BILLY WILDER SAMUEL TAYLOR og ERNEST LEHMAN efter Samuel Taylors skuespil

EN PARAMOUNT FILM

A-S RASMUSSEN & NILSSON

So, with all of these great style icons paving the way for tailored capris, why did people start wearing their baggy, cargo-pocketed cousins? I blame our nation's increasing emphasis on being comfortable over being stylish. I believe these sartorial abominations are simply a hybrid of the capri and the pedal pusher—two styles never meant to breed, like miniskirts and ruffles.

Pedal pushers—so named for their obvious benefit to bikers, for whom long pants might get caught in the chain—are essentially long shorts. A woman on the cover of the August, 28, 1944, issue of *Life* magazine looks relaxed and happy in a collared shirt rolled up to the elbow and a pair of plaid knee-length shorts. The cover line: "Pedal Pushers." Thanks in part to the surf culture of Gidget and the beach party crowd, short pants became the height of cool for teenage girls. It was the dawn of teen culture. For teenagers, these casual pants—something their parents never would have worn—felt liberating and flirty. Carl Perkins even had a 1958 song called "Pink Pedal Pushers" ("The way she dressed / Was a-knockin' 'em

Mary Tyler Moore, circa 1965.

left: Pedal pushers of the 1960s.

opposite: Audrey Hepburn stars in 1954's *Sabrina*.

wild"). Another name for rolled-up beachy-looking pedal-pusher-length pants: clamdiggers. In Spanish, they're appropriately called *pantalón pirata*—pirate pants!

There are many variations on these, none of which I am particularly enthusiastic about. Researching online, I was met with a piece of fashion advice on a blog: "During summer, think of gaucho pants as the more sophisticated choice to capri pants."

Do not! They are wider, shorter, and end in the worst possible place, at the calf. And yet, I'd take a gaucho pant over a harem pant any day. Not that I'd want to choose. It's like picking between the bubonic plague and diphtheria. Harem pants, one of the more costumey looks of the 1980s, sport a dropped crotch, which to me suggests you are wearing a diaper. Do any of us think that's a good look?

Dukes of Hazzard (1979–85) star Catherine Bach created a craze for Daisy Dukes.

On the shorter side, short-shorts and hot pants are very on trend right now—denim ones are called Daisy Dukes, after the sex symbol on the TV show *The Dukes of Hazzard*—but you need to be a certain age and have a certain body type to pull them off.

In this country, until roughly the 1930s, children wore shorts far more often than adults. Boys typically wore shorts until the age of seven or eight, when they would switch to what were known as knickerbockers. It wasn't until the 1920s that you could even buy long pants for children in the United States, and it wasn't until the 1940s that it was common for children to wear them.[1]

In the UK many school uniforms still consist of short pants with long socks. According to Alison Lurie, boys go to school this way even in the winter, because bare knees symbolize toughness, evoking "the warlike costumes of the ancient Britons, the ancient and modern kilted Scots, empire-building explorers and heroic footballers. To cover them would be a sign of national weakness."[2] And yet, probably because I'm American, I think of bare knees as symbolic of the ninety-eight-pound weakling, or the sloppy shorts-and-flip-flops-even-in-winter college student—not exactly the picture of masculinity.

Shorts, of course, can be fetching on both men and women, as we've seen for hundreds of years. Men showed off their legs all over Europe for centuries, wearing tights with some kind of short pant. "Braies" is a term used from medieval times to the fifteenth century to describe shorts worn in the Saxon era as an outer garment but as undershorts in the mid-twelfth century when the Norman tunic covered them. Within a hundred years, the legs of these were tied at the knees by strings—a trend you often see now on the dreaded cargo capri.

Then from the Middle Ages to the seventeenth century, men wore tights and breeches. "Breeches" was the term for the upper part of the long hose that combined stockings and breeches together as tights from the end of the fourteenth through the early sixteenth century. After that point, the breech was typically a different color and fabric from the rest of the hose.

During the French Revolution, militants took the costume of workingmen and refused to wear aristocratic knee breeches, or culottes, and so were called the sansculottes. They wore pants instead, along with the red cap of liberty, and fought for freedom—sometimes violently. They were a formidable force, and infinitely more fashion forward than the aristocrats in their proto-capris.

You could argue that breeches look a bit like the "manpris," or male capri pants. Except that the male capri pants of today are often extra-cargo, with quite large pockets on their sides. When empty, these pockets look pointless. When full, they make the leg look bulky. Let's face it: it's a lose-lose garment.

Not surprisingly, the cargo pants' origins are military. Major William P. Yarborough developed the four-pocket cargo in 1942. The pants were intended to give soldiers more options for carrying supplies and to encourage "soldierly posture by discouraging the men from putting their hands in their pants pockets, thus keeping them from slouching."[3]

The crewmembers on *Project Runway* wear cargo shorts, but in their case it's utilitarian. They need the pockets to hold their walkie-talkies and keys and such. It's like a uniform. But why would you choose to do that if your job didn't require it? Unless you are going on a twenty-mile hike or working on a twenty-day shoot, a cargo style looks unnecessarily sloppy.

That's not to say shorts can't look great on men. They can even be dashing. Just think of British sportsman knickers, or their wider cousin, plus fours, so called because of the extra four inches of fabric used to make them. The Duke of Norfolk wore knickerbockers with a heavy wool jacket and matching cap in the 1880s when hunting.[4] And they continued as a British upper-class leisure garment through the 1920s. When the Prince of Wales, later King Edward VIII, took up golf, he wore tweed knickers with bright stock-

The French revolutionaries wore Phrygian caps with tricolor cockades, pantaloons (sansculottes), greatcoats, breeches, and short military jackets, 1793–94.

ings. And when on safari in Africa, he wore safari shorts along with his safari jacket and pith helmet. The shorts were reportedly designed by the prince himself, and the length was adjustable. Depending on the weather and height of the brush, they could be worn long or buttoned above the knee—the height of practicality.

But modern American manpris? I don't understand them. Unless you are doing something creative with your socks, like the Prince of Wales, or you are wearing a matching cap and jacket, like the Duke of Norfolk, the midcalf length typically just makes a man look sloppy—and shorter. Why not pick a short that actually looks like a short or a pant that looks like a pant? Commit!

Bermuda shorts are a fine option for people who want the comfort of the short without the extreme exposure of the hot pant. The British army wore these shortened pants when serving in warmer climates. In the 1950s, British subjects in Bermuda wore them as a trousers substitute, paired with a jacket, tie, and knee-high socks. Island law decreed that these shorts be modest: they were allowed to start no more than two inches above the knee.[5] When Edward VIII abdicated and became Duke of Windsor and was governor of the Bahamas, even he wore shorts.

The most flattering length for both men and women is usually within an inch or so on either side of the top of the kneecap. Most important, they should fit! Long-waisted women are pretty much the only people who can get away with high-waisted shorts. Sometimes people wear high-waisted shorts to try to mitigate girth, but this rarely works—in fact, the opposite is true. If you have a larger girth, you should mitigate it with lower-rise shorts (or pants) and a top long enough to cover the waistband.

I wear shorts sometimes. But I am cognizant of my age and my environment. I'm fifty-eight years old (with the age spots and varicose veins to prove it!) and live in Manhattan. I'm fond of saying that I have no ego, but I am vain. Accordingly, I know that my legs look like they belong to some species of fowl. I'll wear shorts outside my apartment *only* in my immediate neighborhood, *only* in the dog days of summer, and *only* for occasional errands. Would I wear them out to lunch? Perish the thought!

6.
SKIRTS
Mini, Midi, Maxi, and More

Pencils, hobbles, poufs . . . The shorter the skirt, the younger—not necessarily the sexier—the look

IT WAS NOON. I sat down at a café in New York, awaiting the arrival of my lunch date, a former fashion-marketing executive at Saks. I waited . . . and waited. At a quarter to one, I stood up to leave.

As I was nearing the front door, my lunch date entered the restaurant, walking an inch a minute. She was wearing six-inch stilettos and the tightest long skirt I'd ever seen. She was out of breath.

"I'm sorry it's taken me so long to get here," she huffed. "I can barely move in this skirt!"

"How are you going to sit down?" I asked, genuinely concerned.

She hiked up her skirt and collapsed into the chair.

We had a perfectly pleasant lunch, but at its end I was tempted to call a pedicab to get her back to her office.

The moral: the hobble skirt is not a practical garment, but if you insist on wearing one, give yourself
plenty of extra time between appointments.

Ironically, the hobble skirt was invented by Paul
Poiret, who is otherwise identified as one of the lib-
erators of women's bodies. In the early twentieth century, he was one of the first designers (Coco Chanel
is the more famous) to create fashionable dresses that
did not require a corset.

"Yes, I freed the bust," he wrote in his dazzlingly
narcissistic autobiography, *King of Fashion*, "but I
shackled the legs. . . . Women complained of being
no longer able to walk, nor get into a carriage. . . . Did
they not utter the same groans when they returned to
fullness? Have their complaints or grumblings ever
arrested the movement of fashion, or have they not
rather, on the contrary, helped it by advertising it?"[1]
And he's right: under protest or not, women did wear
the tight skirt.

Paul Poiret in 1913.

The tightness or looseness and the shortness or length of a skirt has long been symbolic
of a woman's—and a man's—place in society. Yes, a man's! For ages, it wasn't so much that
men wore pants and women wore skirts, but that people who had to work hard wore pants,
and people who were able to lounge around wore skirts. The less conducive to walking, the
more the skirt signaled the wearer's status as someone who didn't have to work. Through the
early twentieth century in America, boys and girls were both dressed in skirts until they were
about six years old.

Until the sixteenth century, men—priests, academics, judges, merchants, princes, and
many others—wore skirts, or robes. For men, the skirt was a "sign of leisure and a symbol of
dignity," writes Quentin Bell.[2] This is still true for men in high positions. After all, can you
imagine the Pope, or Professor Dumbledore, wearing *trousers*? Have you ever seen a depic-
tion of God wearing pants?

Of course, today skirts are generally worn by women, so let's talk about the evolution
of the skirt in women's wear. The skirt is basically a dress or robe that became a separate. I
like to call the skirt a topless dress. This begs the question: how did American sportswear
separates come about in the first place? According to *Time* magazine, we should give thanks
to Claire McCardell. As the story goes, "After lugging a trunk and five suitcases around

Europe, she decided to save space by making dresses in parts, switching the pieces around for variety—a bare top and covered-up top, for example, to be worn alternately with shorts, slacks or short or long skirts. That was one of the fashion world's first important experiments with separates, now a mainstay of American sportswear design."

Skirt length signifies many things, but generally speaking in this day and age, the shorter a woman's skirt, the younger she is (or is trying to appear). The fashionable woman of the 1920s was youthful, and so her skirt was short.

Mary Quant, 1967.

"In ages of prostitution fashion is dictated by the grand cocotte, and tends to favour the older woman," James Laver writes. "In ages of promiscuity fashion tends to favour the younger woman, the schoolgirl just escaped from her leading strings. The extremely juvenile fashions of the nineteen-twenties are a case in point."[3]

In other words, it's not that short skirts are automatically sexy and long skirts are automatically dowdy. It's just that right now we see short skirts as sexy because right now young women are seen as sexy. But when (as will inevitably happen) mature women are again seen as sexy, it's likely that the maxi and midi will make their triumphant return as sexy garments. Fashion reacts to culture and vice versa.

Most Eastern garb features long skirts. In the West we really stepped up and out lengthwise in the 1920s. Skirts haven't truly been back to the floor since then, with the exception of formal wear and maybe the occasional maxi craze, as in the 1970s.

The skirts of the 1920s are demure compared to the skirts of the 1960s. There has never been anything like the 1960s fashion revolution, and I don't think there will be again. The primary symbol of this revolution was the miniskirt.

Who invented the miniskirt? With two friends, fashion designer Mary Quant opened a clothing store in London in 1955 called Bazaar that would become a major part of Swinging London and the Chelsea Look. She thought clothing for the young needed to be youthful, so she introduced short skirts. She even wore one to Buckingham Palace in 1966 when she accepted the Order of the British Empire.[4]

Although miniskirts pervaded London quickly, Paris didn't respond to the baby boomer youth culture right away. But André Courrèges's autumn 1964 collection changed all that. He paired his miniskirt with calf-high boots—a futuristic look that was widely imitated.[5]

The miniskirt became a symbol of the sexual revolution. Many schools and churches banned the mini. The Italian Padre Pio, who was canonized in 2002, refused to hear confession from women in miniskirts. He posted a notice at the entrance of the Church of St. Mary of All Graces in San Giovanni Rotondo that read: "The church is God's house. It is forbidden for men to enter here with bare arms and wearing shorts. It is forbidden for women to enter wearing trousers, bare headed, with short, low-necked or sleeveless dresses." He died in 1968, just before long skirts made their return. By 1970 the hippies had rebelled against the mod look and introduced more flowing and romantic midi- and maxiskirts.

A 1970s U.K. catalogue offers plaid and solid miniskirts.

All of these skirt lengths cohabit on today's clothing racks. But this wide variety of choices can cause serious shopping anxiety. At the mall events I host as part of my role at Fifth & Pacific (formerly Liz Claiborne), women often stand up and ask, "Tim, can I still wear a miniskirt?"

"By virtue of the fact that you've asked the question," I say, "I see you have excellent self-knowledge." We talk about her age, body type, and what kind of message she wants to send. Often there is a realization that she has matured past the point where she wants to wear tiny skirts, and so we work to find something else she can wear to feel alluring but not like she's raided her daughter's closet.

Short skirts can look becoming, especially with tights, and especially if you have a non-scandalous top as a counterpoint. But there is a limit to how short you can go. Ideally, you should be able to sit down without the miniskirt riding all the way up. That's what Heidi Klum says. If anyone can yank a skirt, Heidi can, but even she has her breaking point. Sometimes she'll sit down for the judging on *Project Runway* and shriek, "Whoa!" because her skirt is suddenly leaving nothing to the imagination. "Cameras," she'll instruct our crew while pointing to her skirt, "don't go there."

Skirt Styles

Mini

Bubble

Pencil

A-Line

Peplum

Prairie

Hobble

Dirndl

LENGTH

MINI

MIDI

MAXI

And yet, she looks great in a mini. When you look like her, or you're sixteen, you can get away with a lot. When you are old enough to know to ask the question, that's a good indication that the look has become vulgar. Whenever someone asks, "How long can I wear these hot pants?" I say, "You can do it until you start asking yourself that question."

Of course, if you genuinely want to be perceived as the town tramp, that's another matter. Dolly Parton still wears trashy clothes in her sixties, but that's who she wanted to be and that's who she is, and bless her for it. She always says, "It costs a lot to look this cheap."

Wearing any kind of extreme look can be great as long as you own it. *Sex and the City* costumer Patricia Field has crazy, unnaturally dyed red hair and wears skin-tight clothes: that's who she is. Lady Gaga wore a lacy beekeeper hat and see-through pants to her sister's graduation. My first thought was: how inappropriate! But you know, that's who she is. And she didn't disappoint the crowd!

Plenty of women achieve an additional wow factor with skirt trimmings such as fringe. Native Americans of the Great Plains used fringe as a way to repel rainwater from clothes. In the 1920s, it was a way for flappers to add a little length to those scandalously short skirts. And in the sixties, it was a way for hippies to show their allegiance to the oppression of Native Americans and other minorities. Dennis Hopper's fringed jacket in *Easy Rider* (1969) helped the outsider image of fringe. But in the seventies, there was a backlash against fringe. Native American singer Buffy Sainte-Marie said such appropriation was insensitive.[6] Similar accusations were leveled at Ke$ha when she appeared wearing fringe on *Saturday Night Live* in 2010.

Sonja Henie sports a dirndl in 1938's *Happy Landing*.

But back to length. Minis can be very flattering—A-lines look great on many women, as do pencil skirts—generally more so than midis. Midis are back in fashion, but they often hit the leg at the widest part of the calf—an unflattering place. I remember seeing Barbara Walters say in a 1970 *Life* interview that the midi was the best length.[7] But the midi didn't really catch on like wildfire, and in spite of Barbara's best efforts, women continued to wear the miniskirt. In a New York *Daily News* survey conducted in 1970, 83 percent of women said they wore skirts above the knee.

Maxis are also on trend, but they can be dowdy. One long skirt style you see crop up from time to time is the dirndl, a long, traditional German skirt with a lot of pleats. In Episode 5 of *Project Runway* Season 9, Michael Kors compared Olivier's long gray skirt to a dirndl. It wasn't a compliment. According to Valerie Steele's *Encyclopedia of Clothing and Fashion*,[8] "Girls and women were told to proudly wear dirndls for Nazi Party–sponsored occasions and historic celebrations." It's frumpy, *and* it's associated with the Nazis. There is literally nothing to recommend it. Just say the word: "dirndl." Does that *sound* attractive?

Among the skirts that have come and gone (and which may yet come again) are the poodle skirt, hoop skirt, and prairie skirt. Also a trend that comes and goes: the bubble skirt, which bells out at the waist and then is gathered back in above or below the knee. The bubble dress was originally attributed to Cristóbal Balenciaga, for whom it was a signature in the decade between 1937 and 1947 (the year Christian Dior's New Look took over). A bubble dress with a fitted bodice became popularized in 1959, and returned in 1984.

Two designers on *Project Runway* with an affinity for the bubble skirt were Angela Keslar of Season 3 and Kimberly Goldson of Season 9. The trouble they faced in selling the judges on their bubbles was that the skirt isn't flattering on very many people on account of its volume. If you don't have the body for it, and if you don't pair it with a tight-fitting top, you can look like you're being devoured by a fabric balloon.

So, what's next for skirts? Will we ever again see them as everyday wear for men? Some male students of mine at Parsons would occasionally wear skirts. It usually worked for them, because it was part of a greater scheme of dressing in an avant-garde or countercultural way. But outside the traditional kilt, which you see even macho men donning in St. Patrick's Day parades, the male skirt hasn't in recent generations been a mainstream choice for non-bagpipers, and I don't know that it will become so in my lifetime.

Model at the fashion show Men in Skirts held at the Victoria and Albert Museum, 2002.

That's not for fashion designers' lack of trying! Various designers have tried to get men into skirts, including Jean Paul Gaultier and Vivienne Westwood. In the 1990s, there were even attempts to put what was then called the "New Lad" (the man catered to by "lad" magazines like *FHM* and *Maxim*) in a skirt. A *GQ* photo shoot from 2000, for example, had U.K. rugby star Kenny Logan wearing a dark Dries van Noten kilt with a gray T-shirt.[9] At the other end of the culture spectrum, some grunge musicians, including Kurt Cobain, wore dresses onstage, often paired with boots.

Given what we know about history and how common men's robes were for centuries, and how Scotsmen proudly wear the kilt, it's surprising that more American men haven't embraced the skirt.

I searched the Internet in an attempt to find out what, if any, skirts for men are currently available. I emphasize *skirts*; I ruled out kilts, sarongs, and caftans, because they have a timelessness that eschews fashion's ins and outs. My search produced over two million

results, almost all of which were fraudulent (as in, there's a skirt on the retailer's website, but it's not designed for a man). Then I had an "aha!" moment: Marc Jacobs! Marc wears skirts regularly. Furthermore, he looks altogether dashing and remarkably believable. Alas, more disappointment: there was not a single men's skirt in his ready-to-wear collection this year.

Apparently, even he recognizes that, at least for now, the man's skirt is not a profitable item for mass production in the Western world. So, ladies, enjoy the flexibility provided by this dressing staple, and remember to thank Claire McCardell for her vacation-inspired innovation in American separates. May you have such a world-altering revelation on your next trip!

opposite: Marc Jacobs wears a skirt at a spring/summer 2009 fashion show.

7.
BELTS
Friend to Soldiers and Vixens

Cinches, aprons, tool belts . . . Giving shape to the shapeless for thousands of years

ONE DAY at the offices of *More* magazine, where I'd been called to do a makeover on a lawyer, I bore witness to the power of the belt. The woman in question had a rather square body, and she had been wearing menswear-tailored suits, which only enhanced this impression. She looked, if I may say, rather like a tweed cube. We put a tasteful black jersey dress on her and added a wide cinch belt. Suddenly she was a pretty, professional woman with a waist!

Belts often play a role in fashion makeovers, because they do such wonderful things for bodies. They seem to be waning in popularity because of low-rise jeans, tunics, and other clothing items that hide the natural waist. Waistlines rise and fall, and the reigning style in any given era determines the popularity or unpopularity of belts.

For example, belts are rarely worn with empire-waist dresses, so when empire waists are in, belts are out.

The belt can work magic, and it was considered literally magical in ancient times. The belt may, in fact, have been the very first item of clothing, even before underwear! When unearthed by archaeologists, the "Ice Man," a body dating back to around 3,100 BC, had a lime fiber sheath wrapped around his waist.[1]

According to James Laver, our desire to wear clothing first emerged not because we felt shame (what's considered modest varies widely from culture to culture) or were cold (even in tropical climates clothes exist), but because clothes were seen as magical, offering protection against the "evil eye." And so, he argues, the earliest clothing was the amulet—worn on a belt![2]

One such amulet was the cowrie shell, which was supposed to protect against infertility. These shells have been found all over the world, even far away from the sea. They were apparently worn on belts around the waist, as well as on wrists, necks, and ankles. But the waist cord was the most important, says Laver,[3] and the more cowrie shells hung from this primitive belt, the higher the status and magical power of the wearer. In other words, even many thousands of years ago, you could tell who the richest person in town was by looking at what they wore. Cowrie-shell belts were the Louboutin heels of prehistory.

This practice of attaching ornaments to a belt has returned at various points. From the 1840s through the early twentieth century, women would sometimes wear a chatelaine, or a chain attached at the waist that had a hook on which could be hung sewing tools like scissors—rather like our modern tool belt.

Warriors hung their weapons from belts as far back as ancient Greece. Mythology has Orion carrying a sword on his belt, identifiable in the constellation bearing his name that is immortalized in the night sky.

From the thirteenth century to 1700, men wore a baldric, abelt diagonally across the chest or abdomen. This might hold their sword, dagger, bugle, horn, or pouch.[4] And at least as far back as the

Chatelaine, 1901.

1600s, wampum belts were a major part of Native American culture, used for trade and even to commemorate treaties and arrange marriages. Just as it's hard to imagine Robin Hood without this diagonal belt as well as one around his waist, on which he carried weapons and pouches of money for the poor, the World Wrestling Federation's championship wouldn't be the same without the belt prize.

Throughout history, the main function of the belt for both men and women has been to hold up clothes. In ancient Greece, women's floor-length robes were often belted. During the Greco-Roman

right: Copperplate engraving from Johann Bayer's *Uranometria* (1603) showing the constellation Orion.

below: Chiefs of the Six Nations at Brantford, Canada, with wampum belts, 1871.

R A Grider
1897.

period, women belted their tunic underneath their breasts and men belted theirs at the waist. From medieval times onward, the belt was called a "girdle," and women used it to give some proportion to flowing gowns.

Some women in the Middle Ages and then again in the nineteenth century reportedly wore a device called a chastity belt, designed to keep them pure. But contraptions like that don't fall into the fashion category. (We're not talking about latex masks, either!)

But back to belts and their alternatives. Among the more creative ways to keep pants up, suspenders have been around since 1787, though they were originally called "braces" and were made of leather. Cotton, silk, canvas, and velvet became popular brace materials. For some time in the nineteenth century they were even embroidered. The 1844 book *Hillingdon Hall* describes a colorful man as having a "pea-green cashmere coat lined with silk," past which could be glimpsed his "pink rowing shirt and amber-coloured braces."[5]

There *are* some pronounced advantages to suspenders, providing they fit properly. First, suspenders ensure that the pants remain securely in place, unlike a belt, which can shift up or down. Second, they allow air to circulate freely between the waistband of the pant and the shirt; this is especially advantageous in warm climates.

Errol Flynn in *The Adventures of Robin Hood*, 1938.

opposite: Iroquois wampum belts.

When suspenders were first invented, it was the era of the ubiquity of suits with vests. This meant that suspenders were never seen, because even if you were to remove your suit jacket, the suspenders were under the vest. As vests left the dressing vocabulary of a majority of men, suspenders, too, declined.

Today I associate suspenders with men only, though there are a few sartorially adventurous women who wear them, their goal, I deduce, to infuse their fashion with a wink of mas-

Ellen DeGeneres, wearing suspenders, with Portia de Rossi at the Daytime Emmy Awards, 2009.

culinity: think Diane Keaton, Ellen DeGeneres, Chloë Sevigny.

In the early 1990s, they were a way of dressing up jeans and a T-shirt. But the items with which the suspenders were often paired—high-waisted jeans, Converse sneakers, for example—served to undermine these otherwise good intentions.

Unless suspenders have a clothespin-like apparatus to attach to the waistband of your pants, your pants require buttons inside the waistband for their attachment, this being the preferred and higher-end suspender design. I have many suit pants that have those buttons, but I wear a belt instead. I only wear suspenders with my tuxedo. And that is only because a tuxedo is not designed to accommodate a belt, so suspenders are the only way to ensure that the pants stay up. And let me tell you that putting on suspenders is not for the lighthearted; that is, they require a level of concentration and fortitude that cannot be trivialized.

First, let's dissect a pair of suspenders: it has two long bands that attach to the front of the pant, roughly corresponding to each side of your pelvis; these bands go over your shoulders and cross your back to meet two-thirds of the way down your spine; at this juncture these two bands become one (band 3) and descend to the middle of your waistband in the back of your pants. Each of these three bands is fastened to the inner waistband of the pants with two buttons. One has to make certain that all of these particulars are in alignment.

It is extremely easy for one of them to end up backward, thereby messing up the entire contraption (yes, that's what suspenders are, a *contraption!*). This happens to me all the time: the front bands are correct, but the back band is fastened backward. But of course you don't know this until you put on the pants (suspenders *must* be fastened when the pants are off; there's no way that you can manage this otherwise, unless you have a valet, and who has a valet these days?). And then the pants have to come off and you have to contemplate what's wrong and how to correct it. It's like a Klein bottle or a Möbius strip. Aside from masochists, who wouldn't prefer a belt?

At various points in history, and in certain classes, the apron replaced the belt. Starting in the thirteenth century, aprons were worn by workers to protect their clothing. At various points in history women also wore the apron as a decorative item. Aprons were in fashion from the late sixteenth century through around 1640, again in the eighteenth century, and again in the late nineteenth century. The aprons of the 1870s, made of black silk and sometimes embroidered, were called fig leaves.

In the twentieth century belts became a major fashion accessory. One of my favorite modern belts is Elsa Schiaparelli's 1934 trompe l'oeil belt of black silk taffeta joined by plastic hands, which is in the Metropolitan Museum of Art's collection. Like so many of her designs, it's very witty and sure to inspire double takes.

Isabella de Bourbon models apron chic, painting by Jean-Marc Nattier, 1749.

Isn't it fun to think about the ubiquitous, unheralded belt's romantic relations? Too often, in spite of its being a core accessory in every woman's and man's wardrobe, the belt is taken for granted or misunderstood. So, let's talk about the best ways to make belts work for you.

I'll say it first: belts are so much easier for men! We have pants with belt loops that are fairly consistent in width, so our belt decisions are about colors and textiles rather than myriad widths and the added ingredients of patent leathers and metals that are presented to women.

However, ladies, I heap praise on your belt opportunities! Belts provide

HOW TO WEAR A BELT

Men should have four belts: one in black, one in brown for suits; one in black, one in brown for casual dressing. The brown should match the color of your brown shoes, be they light or dark. Personally, I prefer a darker brown to a tan. As for size, all your belts should accommodate the belt loops on your pants.

Women may want to invest in three belts: 1) A wide black belt in matte, patent, or stretch; 2) A mid-width belt that fits the standard loop on your jeans; 3) A thin wisp of a belt for solid-color tunics and dresses. Now some tips for when to wear which belt:

Wide belts work well with patterns.

Small belts work best with solids. Smaller belts get lost in a bold pattern.

If you're belting a tunic or a shirt, you have style options. It can cinch your waist or it can drape from your hip bones.

If you're wearing a belt with jeans, the governing width element is the belt loop size.

When it comes to color, metallics or patent leather can dress up a more casual item, and a plain leather belt can dress down a fancier piece.

you with an easy, effective means of transforming your items of apparel. You can use a belt to take a tunic from voluminous to fitted or a sheath from svelte to sexy. Belts can personalize anything you wear. It's not even remotely required that the belt correspond to your natural waist. It can be and should be used to help enhance your silhouette and give added proportion and fit to your head-to-toe look.

I suggest that we look at ourselves as being a sequence of thirds from our shoulders to our toes. When your apparel cuts you in half, a belt is a way of mitigating that effect. When this cutting-in-half happens with men, the culprit is usually an untucked shirt, which has become a ubiquitous look, regrettably. The only proportional solution is to tuck your shirt into your pants.

If you have a dress that has small belt loops that are not where the belt should be, cut them off. You should not feel constrained by those, because they don't always fall where the belt should. (In my experience, most belts that come with dresses aren't even the right belt for the dress!) The belt doesn't always have to sit at one's natural waist. The belt should be placed wherever it's most flattering on *you*.

All women should own a number of belts of different widths and different fabrics—leather, stretch, and patent leather. (A sturdy belt at a department store costs about $30.) It's a relatively inexpensive way to freshen up a wardrobe.

When it comes to color, women today don't even need to match their belt to their shoes and bag. In fact, matching can look matronly, studied, and too self-conscious. If you're wearing neutrals, you can use your belt, shoes, and handbag to make a color statement. Colors are a matter of taste, and with neutral garments you're fairly safe going with any color. Look at what's already in your wardrobe to remind yourself what colors you like best.

Elsa Schiaparelli's surrealist-inspired belt, fall 1934.

Men, on the other hand, must match. If a man is wearing a brown belt, he needs brown shoes—the same color brown. If you have tan shoes, you need a tan belt. If you have cordovan shoes, you need a cordovan belt. If a man's shoes and belt are mismatched, he'll look like he dressed in the dark. When men act as if color matching is hard, I say, "Cry me a river." Men should be grateful they don't have as many choices as women. Facing a rack of belts in every color, size, and fabric can be more fun, but it is also a whole lot more work.

Still, belts are our friends. They can make clothing go from dowdy to chic instantaneously. They can add a splash of color, keep pants in place, flatter an hourglass figure, or do all three at once. Experiment!

8.
DRESS SHIRTS
Prudery and Puffery

Collar stays, secretary blouses, French cuffs . . . Are you button-down casual or buttoned-up dressy?

ONE DAY when I was working in my office at Parsons, I heard angry voices echoing out of a workroom. I ran down the hall and found six professors screaming at one another. I broke up the fight and then learned what it was about: the dolman sleeve. The teachers were fighting over the definition, and no two were on the same page. I went back to my office to retrieve *The Fairchild Dictionary of Fashion*, a definitive resource for questions like this. I returned to the workroom and read from it: "'Dolman sleeve: Sleeve fitted at wrist but cut with deep armhole so that it somewhat resembles a cape from the back.'"

"*Fairchild*'s wrong!" one professor shouted. The bickering resumed.

I cut them off. "We can't have each of you teaching something different to your students," I insisted. "We're going with *Fairchild* on this one."

They continued to grumble, but they agreed to disagree in the interest of the students. After all, it wouldn't do to have a senior class full of students who had come up through the program with six different definitions of the dolman sleeve.

There are so many terms for shirts that it can make your head spin. By my count, Fairchild names 109 different kinds of sleeves (tulip, venetian, idiot, sultana, Magyar, leg-of-mutton, kimono, cape, barrel, lantern . . .), 194 necklines and collars (Peter Pan, camisole, bateau, butterfly, Capuchin . . .), and 19 cuffs (mousquetaire, pendant, gauntlet . . .). Now you see why professors of fashion can go a little batty!

And now you see why I'm not going into too much detail in this book. For the most part, the academics and experts speak their own language and understand only themselves when it comes to such things. This alienates people who do not have that extensive a background in the subject. In this book I am trying to strike a pose between the layman and the expert, so I'm going to do my best here to simplify the incredibly complex origins of the shirt.

This garment was collarless at first; a neckband was added in the fourteenth century and a standing collar in the fifteenth. Frills appeared in the seventeenth and eighteenth centuries. The nineteenth century brought removable collars and cuffs, but attached collars became popular in the 1920s. White shirts were the rule for hundreds of years, but in the mid-1800s, pink shirts (yes, pink!) were introduced, as well as prints with white collars. In the late nineteenth century, shirts acquired stripes. Men's business shirts were typically white until the 1960s, when color became popular, and now you see every combination of color and pattern.

One historical fashion question I've been asked repeatedly by people while working on this book is this: "Why do we button up men's shirts left over right and women's shirts right over left?"

Another tough one!

According to some, it's because of religion. Deuteronomy 22:5 reads, "The woman shall not wear that which pertaineth unto a man, neither shall a man put on a woman's garment: for all that do so are abomination unto the Lord thy God." This is one of the sins of which Joan of Arc, burned at the stake in 1431, was found guilty.

Some people say that it's because buttons, which you started to see on both men's and women's clothes in the West starting in the thirteenth century, were expensive, which meant any woman wearing them would have been dressed by a maid, and so the buttons were on the servant's right. Others say that the buttons on men's shirts changed when men started carrying concealed weapons and had to quickly unbutton their shirt and draw.

Then there's the cosmological angle: the Hasidic man's caftan buttons right over left to symbolize the victory of good over evil, because right is associated with the good and left with evil.[1] If we apply that to modern American clothing, only women are winning the fight for good!

I like the following theory best: when knights charged each other with lances, they charged with their left, shield side toward their foes. When shields were replaced with plate armor in the 1300s, the armor was mostly hit on the left side. Therefore, armor had to overlap on the right side so the lance would slide off rather than getting stuck in the joint. According to the Metropolitan Museum of Art's book on armor, that's why men's shirts and jackets are buttoned left over right even to this very day. It would make sense, then, that women, when they acquired buttons, would need a slightly different kind of shirt to keep from violating Deuteronomy. Every time I button up my shirt now, I feel myself channeling all those knights preparing for battle and feel much better armed for my morning meetings!

Knights in plate armor.

In the fourteenth century, men wore a gipon over their shirts. The gipon was tight and padded and either laced or buttoned down the front. This gave men a wasp waist and a huge chest. This would eventually evolve into a doublet, and for a while men wore shoulder pads that would put the ladies on *Dallas* to shame.

Now let's talk about collars. Nothing screams period costume quite like a ruff, those circular starched collars that were sometimes attached to the shirt or dress and sometimes freestanding. Whenever I see these images of women in their ruffs, all I can think is: Can you imagine stealing a kiss? The huge amount of fabric forms a barricade. It's like one of those Elizabethan collars—known more amusingly as "cones of shame"—dogs have to wear after

Queen Elizabeth I models the high ruff.

they've had surgery. But for hundreds of years ruffs have repeatedly appeared as symbols of status or sexuality.

From the 1560s through the 1640s, both men and women wore them as status symbols. Of course, people became concerned that you couldn't see enough of women's décolletage, and so the open ruff became popular among the upper classes. If you look at paintings of Queen Elizabeth c. 1580, you'll see that her attendants have closed ruffs and she has a high, open ruff that shows off her cleavage.[2]

Lest you believe that the thong panic of the 1990s was the first time people became incensed about clothing, believe it or not, the ruff drew heat for being decadent and obscene. In his 1583 rant, *The Anatomie of Abuses,* Puritan moralist Phillip Stubbes insisted that the devil invented the ruff. "If Eolus with his blasts, or Neptune with his storms, chance to hit upon the crazie barke of their brused ruffs," he wrote, "then they go flip-flap in the wind like rages that flie abroade, lying upon their shoulders like the dish-clout of a slut." Tell us how you really feel, Phillip.

The Puritans went in for the cascading short ruff. From 1615 to 1640, the relatively subdued falling ruff was popular. These cascaded down to the shoulders and are the look you may remember from your elementary school play about the Pilgrims. From 1625 to 1650, women wore a closed oval ruff, perhaps paired with a broad-brim beaver hat. In the 1650s, a new method of extracting starch from wheat was discovered, and so ruffs got bigger. The ruff returned in various forms from the 1740s through 1830 and from 1874 to 1900. You can see this ancestry today in lace collars.

Even in the absence of ruffs, necklines have gone up and down over the centuries, and at times styles have been downright scandalous. At the dawn of the Renaissance, Italian women wore low square necks offering a peek at their linen smocks, and men wore slashed doublets offering a glimpse at their linen undershirts, as you can see in the paintings of Leonardo and Raphael.

People often say that fashion coming from the streets was born in the twentieth century. That's not true. My favorite example comes from the 1500s. The sixteenth century saw a good deal of influence from German fashion. Perhaps the weirdest was the slashing

Pilgrims landing at Plymouth, Massachusetts, December 1620, wear the falling ruff.

fashion that started with German mercenaries and then caught on all over Europe.[3] According to James Laver, at the Battle of Grandson in 1476, the Swiss beat Charles the Bold, Duke of Burgundy. The Swiss soldiers used the silk they plundered to patch their ragged clothes. German mercenaries copied this look, cutting slits in their garments and pulling the lining through.

This rather weird look, called *landsknecht,* spread to the French court and throughout Europe in the early 1500s. In extreme cases, the doublet and breeches would both be slashed. Laver quotes one source on tights being slashed: "hose made in the German manner, the one [leg] yellow, the other black, slashed with sixteen cells of taffeta."[4] At first it was only for men's clothes, but women's skirts came in for slashing, too. This is such a proto-punk-rock look, and it was popular hundreds of years before Vivienne Westwood was even born!

In modern times wearing crisp, unripped shirts is a likelier sign of status. In chapter 5 of *The Great Gatsby,* Gatsby brags, "I've got a man in England who buys me clothes. He sends over a selection of things at the beginning of each season, spring and fall."

Fitzgerald then writes, "He took out a pile of shirts and began throwing them, one by one, before us, shirts of sheer linen and thick silk and fine flannel, which lost their folds as they fell and covered the table in many-colored disarray. While we admired he brought more and the soft rich heap mounted higher—shirts with stripes and scrolls and plaids in coral and apple-green and lavender and faint orange, and monograms of Indian blue. Suddenly, with a strained sound, Daisy bent her head into the shirts and began to cry stormily.

"'They're such beautiful shirts,' she sobbed, her voice muffled in the thick folds. 'It makes me sad because I've never seen such—such beautiful shirts before.'"

At least since the 1950s, looking cool and collected has been a recurring theme in shirt advertisements. The Man in the Hathaway Shirt sold men shirts under slogans like "How to keep cool when terrified." A 1958 ad shows him looking calm and charming in his crisp white shirt, eye patch, and thin tie despite being surrounded by dental equipment, the dentist lurking in shadow over his right shoulder.[5]

The seventies were experimental. The era brought some truly horrible fabrics and garishly wide collars, but we learned a lot about what not to do. Specifically, we learned that if you have 2, 4, or 6 percent synthetic fibers in a cotton, wool or silk, it gives you a flattering stretch and a better drape. If you use 100 percent synthetics, you wind up looking like a walking disco ball.

There have been various shirt crazes over the years. The 1981 film *Chariots of Fire* kindled an enthusiasm for preppy shirts, ties, and turn-of-the-century cricket sweaters.[6] But in general the man's shirt has been pretty consistent since the 1980s.

Now let's talk about cuffs. For a time, I tried wearing French cuffs, the kind that requires cuff links. But over time I started to think, *this is pure puffery*. What's wrong with a button? It's so much simpler. For the most part, I only wear one pair of cuff links. They were a gift. They are sterling silver and they say, "Make it work." Of course, if you're wearing a tuxedo, you want to wear French cuffs with cuff links that match the studs on the tuxedo. The studs on my tuxedo shirt are black enamel, so I have matching black enamel cuff links that I break out on formal occasions.

The button placement on the placket, the piece of fabric that runs down the middle of the shirtfront, is rarely the same across brands. For example, I don't like having the top two buttons unbuttoned, but on a J.Crew shirt if I button the second-to-top button, it's too high. You're either too buttoned-up or you feel too exposed. Can't you be in between Amish and a whore? Having more buttons might solve that problem.

If it's a dress shirt and you're wearing a tie, it doesn't matter, but if you're not, it can be awkward. I often wish shirts had more buttons. You'd have more options. But in

Hathaway Man shirt ad from the 1970s.

these challenging economic times, every button costs something to the manufacturer and the consumer. My great-aunt Virginia, who went by Si, was so petite she couldn't find anything that fit her, so she had all her clothes tailor-made. She looked fantastic, in part because she could control details like button placement on her shirts.

While we're on the subject of buttons, let's clear up one of the biggest misunderstandings when it comes to men's shirts. I hear people refer to "button-down" shirts all the time when they really mean dress shirts. Once, on a shoot for *Oprah,* the stylist kept telling me to wear a "button-down." I kept asking her if she was sure, because a button-down is a casual shirt. Finally I realized she just meant a dress shirt: by definition it has buttons, but it's not a button-down, which is a specific style.

A button-down shirt is one on which the tips of the collar have little buttons attaching it to the shirt. The button-down collar isn't meant to be dressy. For a teen, it's fine as formal wear. But for a grown man, it's casual and not meant to be worn with a tie. I will sometimes wear a button-down shirt with a knit tie for a more casual event, but I would never wear one with a suit.

A regular dress shirt has a collar without buttons on it. The collar does, however, need collar stays. They come with the shirt, generally. Because you don't have those little buttons as on a button-down, you need stays to keep the collar from turning up. Heat, humidity, or lack of starch will all force the collar up unless you have collar stays. It's like the undergarment for a shirt. And yet, you don't want to iron your shirt with the stays inside the collar, because they will leave their impression on it. So you take them out, iron the shirt, and put them back in. If they get lost (as they often do if you have the shirt laundered), you can replace them easily. Metal shirt stays, which you can buy in many stores and online for only a couple of dollars a pair, can replace lost plastic ones.

The tab collar is back in fashion now. To my eye, without the tie it looks nerdy. And I think you can only wear it with a single Windsor knot tie. It would be too thick otherwise. But I wouldn't wear it. It's too hipster for me.

Showing a little cleavage is often a good idea for women, especially if they're of a certain age. The Empress Alexandra, the last of the Romanovs, once said, "The arms are the last to go." My mother's comment upon hearing this was, "What is she talking about: a couch?"

It was one of my mother's better moments. A woman's arms generally show her age long before her décolletage. Helen Mirren's low-cut dresses at award shows have made her a sex symbol into her sixties. Besides, high-neck shirts like secretary blouses, which button way up and have a tie, seem matronly to me. They say "Marion the librarian."

Women's shirts usually have darts that help them fit better over the chest. Men's shirts only have these occasionally. I had one slim-fit Hugo Boss shirt with darts, but to be honest, it looked too much like a woman's shirt for my taste. Men's shirts do typically have a yoke, or horizontal seam across the back running several inches below the neckline, shoulder to shoulder, and sometimes with a couple of tiny pleats coming down from it. These give it some shape along the back.

Many office workers like shirts to have pockets, so they have a place to tuck a phone number or Post-it note. It's generally not considered as dressy a shirt when it has a pocket.

But if you're wearing a shirt without a suit and want a pocket for the occasional note, that's a personal choice.

Taking care of dress shirts is not easy. Now that collars and cuffs aren't detachable, you need to pay attention to them for signs of fraying and yellowing. The inevitable wear and tear can be delayed by being particular about the detergent you use and making sure it's compatible with the textile you're washing. Of course, no matter how well you take care of your clothes, age will eventually win out. There's not much you can do with a shirt once it yellows or frays, except to turn it into a dust rag.

You should, however, know how to sew on a button. I find few elements of clothing maintenance as irksome as getting a shirt back from the cleaner's and finding there's a button missing. To this end, I have a special spot in my top drawer for all those extra buttons that come with new shirts. Mine are next to my cuff links and spare collar stays. Will I have to make room someday for the return of the ruff? Only time will tell.

9.

TIES AND SCARVES

Color Me Beautiful, Hermès, and Other Cults

Neckties, bandanas, pashminas . . .
Men in the nineteenth century knew
dozens of ways to tie a tie; every
man today should know at least one.

IN *PROJECT RUNWAY*'S second episode of Season 2, "Clothes Off Your Back," the designers were told to make an outfit using only what they were wearing when the challenge was announced. Designer Kirsten Ehrig lost the challenge in part because she was unwilling to risk marring her Hermès scarf. The scarf, apparently, was worth more to her than being on *Project Runway*.

She wasn't the first woman to be obsessed with an Hermès scarf—sorry, *carré* (French for "square"), as they're called. Other companies, like Jacqmar, whose beautiful World War II–era scarves are collectors' items, have produced exquisite luxury carrés, but the cult around Hermès is extreme.

May I call to your attention the 1994 booklet entitled, *How to Wear Your Hermès Scarf*? It reads rather like the book *Green Eggs and Ham,* only instead of "Would you eat them on a train, or in the dark or on a plane?" you're faced with the choice of wearing them as a "headband or a belt; adhering to the simplicity of the corsair style or the tradition of the well-knotted tie; tied at the neck like a swimsuit top or playing in the breeze."[1]

The 2009 book *The Hermès Scarf: History & Mystique* is similarly rhapsodic: "How best to put into words that elegance, that delightful languor? How to express the soft and subtle

Caravaggio's 1610 painting of Salome, victorious after her dance of the seven veils.

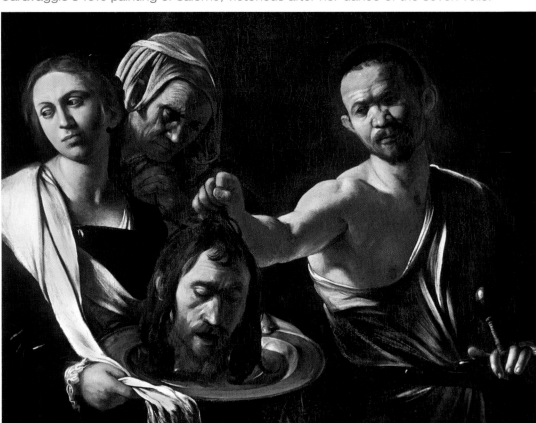

rustling sound we hear when it is taken in a hand, when it brushes against a cheek, when it is clutched by curious fingers or absently stroked by a light palm?"

The Hermès scarf does have a glamorous legacy. Hermès was known originally for luxury saddles and harnesses, but the company started producing silk scarves in 1937. For patterns, they took inspiration from the world of horseback riding they knew so well, but also from a wide variety of other realms: nature, museum collections, maps. The very first scarf was *Jeu des Omnibus et Dames Blanches*, inspired by an 1830s board game owned by Émile Hermès.[2] Many of the most popular designs today are aristocratic or horsey.

Some wealthy and compulsive people try to collect one of each of the hundreds of designs the company has produced since 1937,[3] and point to their celebrity pedigree as proof of their worth. In the late 1940s, the author Colette wore the Ex-Libris Hermès scarf as a bow tie.[4] An Hermès scarf showed up on Grace Kelly in 1956 as a sling for her broken arm. The Queen of England herself is a fan.[5] And so on.

The Hermès scarf obsession to me seems a bit like a cult. I wouldn't have said this even ten years ago. In fact, I remember chipping in for an Hermès scarf with a few other people so we could give it as a gift to our friend who loved them. It cost about $350 at the time, almost twenty years ago, but it made her very happy. At that time, I felt as if I was part of a small group who had discovered something special and unique. A venerable saddlemaker creating exquisite silk squares! What a find!

Since they've become ubiquitous, they've lost some of their allure for me. I'm turned off by the acquisitive frenzy surrounding them. Do you really want to be part of the cult? If you do, fine! But be mindful of it. You need to know what you're getting into. And you should know that they're not the only luxury scarves in town. Others include Bulgari, Oscar de la Renta, Gucci, Burberry, Tory Burch, and Coach. Not to mention, you don't need to buy a high-end scarf to look stylish. Every department store has scarves at a wide range of price points, in a vast array of textiles, many quite elegant.

People have been tying things around their necks since ancient times. The scarf has long been a symbol of erotic power. Salome's dance of the seven veils earned her John the Baptist's head on a platter. In ancient Greece and Rome, men used scarves as handkerchiefs. In the sixteenth century, they became love tokens given to women. In the seventeenth century, they held snuff. In the 1850s and 1860s, women wore large, often elaborately patterned shawls called paisleys over their wide crinoline skirts.[6]

Women wore long scarves in the early nineteenth century with their empire-waist muslin gowns. This was thanks to Napoleon's expedition to Egypt (1798–1801), which created an enthusiasm in France for all things Near Eastern. According to James Laver, Napoleon's ships brought back shawls of every material: "of cloth, of serge, of knitted silk, and even of rabbit's fur—and of all colors—red, blue, Egyptian earth colours—or embroidered with flowers and leaves." Among the first to wear these shawls? Josephine, of course.[7]

Since the dawn of Hollywood, starlets have worn scarves over their hair to hide out in public or to protect their hair in a breezy convertible. Isadora Duncan famously lost her life in 1927 when one of her signature flowing scarves became caught in the wheel spokes of her friend's Bugatti, breaking her neck.

And while we're on the subject of necks, women of a certain age have long used scarves to hide necks they "feel bad about," to quote the title of Nora Ephron's wonderful book. Scarves' utilitarian function extends, of course, beyond concealing aging necks. They are also used for warmth, or symbolic warmth, as in the 1990s craze for Nepal-inspired, and frequently pastel, cashmere pashminas. For a few years, it was as if suddenly every woman in America, even those in warm locations, had just returned from a chilly hike in the Himalayas.

Speaking of colors, in 1980, a woman named Carole Jackson hit the bestseller list with *Color Me Beautiful: Discover Your Natural Beauty Through Color*. Her concept: everyone's coloring is either warm or cool, and so everyone can be categorized as a Winter, Spring, Summer, or Fall. To find out which you are, you can study the book, or get your "colors done" by a Color Me Beautiful consultant. This was a huge fad in the eighties, and into the nineties.

Carole Jackson devotee Simon Doonan wrote in *The New York Observer* in 2001: "Finding our colors not only helped us find our true identity, it helped us buy sweaters."[8] A consultant he quotes says, "The 1970s were about beige. When jewel tones erupted in the '80s, women couldn't cope. They needed Carole. That's why *Color Me Beautiful* was such a hit."

When you had your colors done, you would receive swatches with your personalized colors that you could take with you when you went shopping. You were encouraged to dress in tones that complemented your coloring and to wear scarves in those hues.

This phenomenon may seem rather pseudoscientific, like astrology or the 1970s biorhythms craze, but from a fashion perspective, *Color Me Beautiful* was actually quite valuable. Not because of the color schemes it promoted, but because the book made people take stock of what looked good on them and what didn't. What people often forget now is that Jackson had elaborate work sheets in the back of the book. Women were encouraged to investigate their closets, to make sure they had matching shoes for all their dresses, jackets for work, and dresses for special occasions.

Yes, there was a lot of color misdiagnosis, which led to people walking around in crazy pastel shades when they would have looked better in red. And in truth, wearing a flattering color can only go so far

opposite: A cover model wears a cloche, a white drop-waist dress, and the kind of long scarf that proved fatal to Isadora Duncan.

★ 30ᵉ Année Nᵒ 511   Prix 2 fr. 00   Jeudi 17 Février 1927

le Sourire

Capotinage   Aquarelle de Suz. Meunier

toward making you look good. An appropriately hued trash bag is still a trash bag! Carole Jackson was also a little too quick to dismiss the universal power of the color black. But at least the book got people paying attention to their closets and thinking hard about what they looked best in and what they most wanted to wear.

Of course, one can also think *too* hard about what one wears, or what other people wear. In 2008, Rachael Ray appeared in a Dunkin' Donuts ad wearing a black-and-white scarf with some fringe on it. To some, this looked like a kaffiyeh, which some interpreted as an anti-Israel, pro-Palestine gesture. Dunkin' Donuts responded: "In a recent online ad, Rachael Ray is wearing a black-and-white silk scarf with a paisley design. It was selected by her stylist for the advertising shoot. Absolutely no symbolism was intended. However,

British WWI intelligence officer T. E. Lawrence, aka Lawrence of Arabia, c. 1920.

given the possibility of misperception, we are no longer using the commercial."

This whole uproar struck me, and most people who know their scarf history, as a little ridiculous. The kaffiyeh is a traditional Middle Eastern headdress that protects the face and head from sun and sand. Throughout the region, people of all religions have worn variations on this garment since biblical times. Lawrence of Arabia wore one.

Yes, it's true that Yasser Arafat arranged his kaffiyeh into the shape of Palestine and that it was used as a symbol of Palestinian nationalism during the 1936–39 Arab revolt in Palestine. But that's not how the Dunkin' Donuts shoot stylist shaped Rachael Ray's scarf.

For many years the kaffiyeh has been a go-to accessory for people of all nationalities and ethnicities faced with the challenge of sun and sand, including U.S. troops serving in Iraq. According to a 2005 article in the *Village Voice*, what it means is all in how you wear it: "Pro-Palestinian activists usually drape them loosely over their shoulders, as was recently seen at antiwar protests. World-music types bunch them to make a regular, long scarf, as girls did in the '80s. And the hippest kids fold the square in half to make a triangle and gather it around the neck, center point-down over their chests. This is similar to the way U.S. and British troops wear the scarves in Iraq and Afghanistan—to protect the face in sandstorms."[9] If anything, Rachael Ray's garment was patriotic, emulating the garb of our brave military men and women.

The kaffiyeh is far from the only scarf we've inherited from soldiers. Even the businessman's necktie has military roots. Starting in 1650, ties became a regular part of European men's wardrobes, thanks to the Thirty Years' War (Sweden and France vs. the Hapsburg Empire, 1618–48). The French soldiers were apparently taken with the loose neckerchiefs of the Croatian soldiers.[10] The word "cravat," which comes from the French *cravate* and predates the term "necktie," may actually come from the word *croate*.

Some scholars think a weather anomaly then helped the trend catch on. The years 1645 to 1705 (alternately cited as 1715) saw something called the Maunder Minimum, basically a low amount of solar activity. This was the middle of what's been called the Little Ice Age, during which Europe and North America experienced especially cold winters. Chilly Frenchmen must have figured those Croatian soldiers were on to something. Now, too, our major association with scarves is as protection from the cold, but there is so much more to the history of neckwear than just some wool to wrap around one's neck in winter.

The earliest examples of what we'd recognize as European neckties, worn by men from 1660 to the late eighteenth century, were typically made of lawn (a semitransparent linen), muslin, or silk. The strip of cloth was folded around the neck and tied in a knot or bow in the front. One style of white linen cravat was the steinkirk, named after a 1692 battle at which the soldiers only had time to twist their cravats loosely and tuck them through a buttonhole.

From the nineteenth century on, the cravat was starched and held up with a stiffener, and much attention was devoted to tying them. Beau Brummell, the hero of our suit chapter, is said to have been a tie-tying guru for England. Brummell famously devoted hours to "knotting, pleating, folding, and arranging them." And it was a skill that had prestige. People paid a lot of attention to neckties back then. *Neckclothitania or Tietania, being an Essay on Starchers, by One of the Cloth* (1818) was one of the publications from the era that detailed numerous ways to tie the cravat.[11]

Another, even more popular, was *L'Art de Mettre sa Cravate, par Le Baron Emile de L'Empese,* which was published in English as *The Art of Tying the Cravat by H. le Blanc* (1828). There were a great many fashion guides published in the early 1800s, so you can see that our generation was certainly not the first to fill its shelves with fashion self-help books. Considering how many dozens of ways men practiced tying ties back then, no man in America today has an excuse for not learning at least one method.

The name "necktie" emerged around 1830, but "cravat" hung around for a while, too. Women started wearing them in the 1830s as part of sport costumes like riding habits. Starting around 1840, the fabric covering the shirtfront was called a scarf, and the smaller piece of fabric around the neck was called a necktie.

Around this time, too, men began announcing their politics via their neckties. Those who wore black cravats were liberal; those who wore white were conservative. In the later 1800s, the rise in sporting clubs made "club ties" popular. Men wore ties with specific colors or stripes to identify themselves as members of a particular social scene.

This phenomenon endures now in the wearing of school ties, which started at Rugby School in the mid-nineteenth century, where jerseys were decorated with house badges, and then continued at Eton, which put its colors on caps, ties, scarves, and socks. Handmade silk Eton ties continue to be popular. Harry Potter fans participate in this trend, I've noticed, by wearing such items as a Gryffindor tie or a Ravenclaw scarf.

Victorian men wore clothes in such subdued hues that the necktie was an opportunity to act out with a little color. In March 1895, *Tailor and Cutter* called ties and scarves the "saving touch from the monotony of somberness. . . . Bows, scarves and ties seem to get more and more varied, and, in the majority of styles prettier and more artistic."[12]

That's true now, too. You'll see men at the office showing up in a traditional black suit and white shirt, but with a wacky tie featuring, for example, golf clubs, or Mickey Mouse, or candy canes for Christmas. For me, such novelty ties are too specific. Perhaps they're useful as conversation pieces, but that's only because they frequently need an explanation. I don't want to wear anything that needs an explanation. If you have to explain a joke, it's probably not that funny, and if you have to explain a garment, it's probably not that fashionable.

As the 1800s went on, jackets grew shorter and ties smaller. Most men were also working longer hours and didn't have as much time to spend on elaborate knots, and so the ready-made tie was born. There were four types of tie by the end of the nineteenth century. The first was the bow tie, which emerged from Regency fashion and took the shape of either a butterfly or a bat. The second, a scarf or neckerchief, was worn by working men and women. The ascot, a wide necktie looped over and held in place with a pin, was popular with the upper classes and was so called because of its suitability for wearing at Ascot Heath, the fashionable horse-racing spot in England. The ascot scarf was reintroduced in the late 1960s by Yves Saint Laurent, and became a status symbol in that era, too

Fourth, and most relevant for our purposes, was the long tie. When stiff collars relaxed and turned down, this kind of tie became even more popular. During the women's suffrage movement, women started to wear these ties, too, as a sign that they were the equals of men.

What really made the long tie victorious in the battle for tie supremacy was that in 1924 an American named Jesse Langsdorf patented a new tie-making process called Resilient Construction. He used three separate pieces of fabric, and bias cutting, to make a much more flexible and better-looking tie. Very little about the tie has changed since then, except the width, which has for the most part continued to be about three to three and a half inches, only occasionally deviating to two or five inches.

There have been tiny changes, of course. The Duke of Windsor made the Windsor knot popular. (I myself prefer a Windsor knot. Most people tie a half Windsor.) The 1930s and 1940s introduced synthetics. During World War II, Americans started wearing ties with stripes and plaids. This so-called Bold Look became more pronounced—and more garish—after the war. The mods wore skinny ties. In the 1960s, Michael Fish introduced the bright, wide kipper tie, aptly named because it did look like a kipper, or smoked herring, and its creator's name was, in fact, Fish.

How to tie a tie, 1906.

Today, more often then not, I see men wearing no tie at all, even in formal settings. You'd be amazed how often I meet men who don't own a single tie. Okay, maybe you wouldn't be amazed, but I am amazed! Perhaps if men knew that ties came from soldiers' uniforms, they'd be more likely to wear them?

Or perhaps they would enjoy the long tie more if they thought of it as a kind of bandana? For most men, the bandana conjures up images of Indiana Jones or the Wild West. Originally imported from India, the dark red or blue bandana with white or yellow spots was used in the eighteenth century as a neckcloth (literally tied around the neck), and later as a snuff handkerchief.

It was popular in the Old West and is now worn around the neck by farmers and modern-day cowboys as well as around the head by kitchen workers and other people who want to keep their hair out of their eyes. Gang members have worn them in their back left pocket to signify an allegiance—red for Bloods, blue for Crips. In all cases, the bandana is a sign of toughness.

Isn't that interesting, that one piece of fabric tied around the neck is a symbol of grit and another slightly more constructed piece of fabric tied around the neck is a symbol of professionalism? They are so similar! Tie-shy men, believe this: if you can wear a bandana, you can wear a tie.

So, what should you know when you go to pick one out? When you're shopping for a tie, you want to look for a lining that gives it some weight. Without that infrastructure, ties can be limp. I hate to say it, but when it comes to menswear, it's often true that the more expensive it is, the better it is. On the set of *Project Runway,* microphone wires are constantly being put into my ties. My Banana Republic ties will usually last a season, meaning a month of shooting, before needing to be retired. But the more expensive ties will show no wear and tear. Even after plenty of prodding, they're ready for another season.

"What about bow ties?" I am often asked.

Bow ties have been around a good long while, but for some reason they are often seen as a kind of bastard offspring of the proper tie. In the book *Jocks and Nerds,* two leading fashion historians declare, "The man who wears a bow tie may conform to every announced convention, but he will never be elected President and may never make it to corporate chief executive."[13]

That seems unduly harsh. Bow ties can be hard to pull off with a classic suit, and tend to look better with a sport coat and a pair of pants, but beyond that, it's just a matter of taste. When I worked in academia, I wore bow ties regularly. Then I worked for an unpleasant man who wore them all the time and that association ruined them for me. As a result, I gave most of my bow ties to my brother-in-law. Now the only time I wear one is with a tuxedo.

There is so much to learn about even the simplest items of clothing. I am learning every day. Case in point: the pocket square, that little piece of fabric that you can wear in the front pocket of a suit jacket. I have always admired men who can wear a pocket square, because I simply couldn't. In fact, the pocket square became a source of fascination for me—how it's folded (Brooks Brothers names four methods!), how it's placed in the breast pocket of the jacket, and how it coordinates with the wearer's shirt and necktie.

Over the course of the last five years, I have purchased about twenty pocket squares, mostly from Brooks Brothers. I had the sincere intention of wearing them, but I never could. The choreography of my attempts would be the same: select the correct pocket square for the colors that I intend to wear, place my suit jacket flat on my bed, insert the square in the breast pocket, stand back and observe, remove the square, refold it, replace it, observe, and try again.

opposite: Bow tie in a shirt ad from the 1970s.

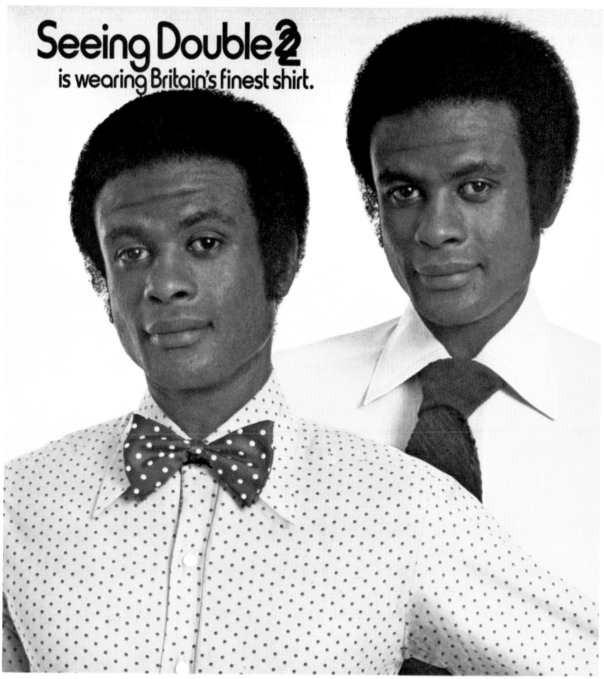

Seeing Double 2 is wearing Britain's finest shirt.

**Spots before your eyes?
It's That Shirt by Double Two.**

Yes, you're really seeing things – Dots before your eyes…

Contrasting stitching on the other shirt. Only That Shirt could be so fashionable – by Double Two.

Who else could make polka dots so eye-catching but so tasteful? Who else could make stitching so stylish?

the collar, cuffs and placket front.

You expect Double Two to put something extra into shirt design…extra styling, extra comfort in a slim-line fitting.

Now we're doing something extra with ties, too. Double Two shirts and ties are just made for each other!

That Shirt by Double Two – at around £5·00.

Double Two Ties and Bow Ties –

Double Two
SHIRTS
AND TIES

Double Two International,
Eagle House, 109/110 Jermyn Street,

Generally it would take three tries to get it right. Then I'd put on the jacket and look at myself in a full-length mirror. Without exception, I would sputter out loud, "You look like an ass." I'd extract the square and assure myself that I would never attempt this folly again.

Then, in the summer of 2010, I had a pocket square epiphany. Rita Ryack, the costume designer on *The Smurfs* movie, opened my eyes. Here's how it happened: I received a small but delightful part in *The Smurfs* as the executive assistant to a cosmetics mogul, played by the marvelous Sofia Vergara. Rita and I spoke on the phone about my wardrobe for the movie.

"You're Tim Gunn," she said. "I would never dream of telling you what to wear. Bring your own clothes and we'll make decisions together."

Fine. The first day on the set, Rita and I met in my trailer. I could see on her face that she was disappointed by what I had brought. She finally decided that my light gray suit with a pink shirt and foulard necktie would be best for the Central Park Boathouse scene. At the end of a very long day, she came to me as I was changing.

"I just saw the rushes," Rita said, "and your wardrobe isn't good enough."

"Isn't good enough?" I said. "It's as good as my wardrobe gets. My suits are all from Banana Republic, John Bartlett, and Zegna."

"I'm going shopping!" Rita declared. "And you're meeting me at a tailor tomorrow afternoon."

We met at the designated tailor, a fancy-schmancy establishment in the East Fifties off of Fifth Avenue. The very British Leonard Logsdail divides his time between New York and London. His walls are covered with autographed photos of movie stars. Being there was simultaneously exhilarating and intimidating. Furthermore, I felt like I was a fashion failure who had failed Rita's test and was doing penance.

Thankfully, I have very little ego, so I acquiesced to the terms and conditions under which I was there. Rita brought out the most sublime suits, shirts, and ties imaginable, at least by me. The labels were Isaia, Tom Ford, Ralph Lauren Black Label, Brioni, Charvet, and Gieves & Hawkes. I was in sartorial splendor. I tried on her choices while she judged and Leonard chalked and pinned. It was like something out of *Pretty Woman*.

Then she said: "I've heard you say in interviews that you won't wear a pocket square, but let's try it, okay?"

I was her dress-up doll, so why not? Rita's ability to coordinate pattern, print, and color are masterful; it's no wonder she has been nominated for a costume design Oscar. She educates and inspires. I learned so much from her in that incredibly special afternoon that my own sense of personal fashion changed forever.

But this epiphany came at a price: prior to this day, I didn't know what it was like to wear a $3,000 suit or a $450 shirt, or a $175 tie. It was—unfortunately—wonderful. This *Smurfs* epiphany made me take another look at my suits and ask, "*Is* this good enough?"

My ten-year-old Banana Republic suits suddenly seemed baggy and worn. I was enlightened but unhappy. Criticizing clothes I had been perfectly happy with a month before made me depressed. Rita's taste is too expensive to sustain, so now I am left aware of what the most exquisite clothes feel and look like but am without the means to fill my closets with them! I almost wish I'd been left in ignorant bliss. Alas. But when it comes to pocket squares, the epiphany was completely positive, and now I can share with you a trick she taught me.

Here's the key to getting the color and pattern of ties and pocket squares right: Look at your shirt and tie, assess the overall color story, and select a pocket square (this assumes that you have a number to select from) that corresponds to, but does not match, that color story. For instance, if it's a blue color story, go for lavenders or purples. If it's a pink color story, then try reds or corals. If the thought of these colors concerns you, then you can always use a neutral—gray is my go-to neutral for ties, especially if I'm wearing a gray, charcoal, or black suit.

Women can use this same trick when it comes to matching a scarf color to an outfit. Scarves are a great way to take an ordinary dress and make it look and feel special. I find that European women in particular are unbridled when it comes to wearing scarves. They tie them casually around their necks. They drape them over their shoulders. It's believable. American women don't often do that as well, but when they master it, they instantly stand out as stylish.

I often think that men tend to look contrived and peacocky when they add a scarf to everyday wear. I dubbed *Project Runway*'s Season 8 "Season Man Scarf," because the only men on the show not wearing scarves were Michael Kors and me. I wasn't tempted by the trend. But who knows? Maybe on the set of *Smurfs 5,* Rita will induct me into the cult of the man scarf. . . .

10.

VESTS

Take That, France!

Tweeds, silks, waistcoats . . .
Why vests are fashion's freedom fries

IN 2011, I appeared on a panel at Parsons, where I once was the chair of the fashion design school. At the end of the discussion there was a Q & A. An eager young woman raised her hand and asked me, quite sternly, "Is the globalization of the fashion industry creating a uniform?"

By the way she phrased the question, I could tell she had an agenda, so I asked her what it was. She suggested that American clothes were taking over the world and that something had to be done to protect native dress, lest Americans colonize the far reaches of the planet with their wicked jeans and T-shirts. I paraphrase. In any case, I did not play along.

"In other words," I said, "you don't want the Gap to open up in Southeast Asia? You want people in Mumbai to wear saris, not cargo shorts?"

She said that was more or less what she meant.

I said that such an attitude seemed to me like an attempt to keep people in the non-Western world from options. "Would any of us disagree that it's good to give people options?" I asked. Besides, I thought, this desire to preserve "authenticity" above all else is a failure to understand history. Cultures have been borrowing fashion from each other for thousands of years. There have always been cultures everyone wanted to emulate and those whose styles dominated other cultures far beyond their borders. What I should have said was: "You're looking for a fashion bully? Get mad at France!"

Well, that's just what the British did in the 1600s, and that's why we have vests today.

Vests have been falling out of fashion since the advent of indoor heating, but they are still worn by a few of us. I hope they will cycle back again, especially because they are one of the few garments promoted by the British, and I am tired of the French having the last word on all matters of fashion.

Britain and France have battled each other for fashion supremacy for many generations. There have been countless volleys, directly attacking the modes of the other. As early as the eleventh century, James Laver writes, monks "were complaining that the English had forgotten their usual simplicity, had trimmed their hair, shortened their tunics and generally adopted French modes."[1] British

A man of fashion in the court of Charles II, wearing the costume introduced in 1666 by the king and modeled after the Persian or Turkish coat.

tailoring is still widely considered the best in the world, whereas the French are the masters of dressmaking.

And the British-French fashion rivalry is still with us today. When Sarah Burton (who became creative director for the house of Alexander McQueen after his suicide in 2010) designed Kate Middleton's wedding dress, it had to be made in the U.K., even though the McQueen atelier was in Paris.

But back to the vest. In October 1666, the witty diarist and Member of Parliament Samuel Pepys reports in his diary that King Charles II, displeased by the decadence of popular French fashion, has introduced a waistcoat, or vest. Pepys's diaries are proof that history doesn't have to be boring. He openly discusses his extramarital affairs, his falling in and out of favor with the court, and gives a firsthand account of the Great Fire of London. He also discusses fashion in great detail.

Modeled after a clothing item from the Persian court of Shah Abbas (who ruled 1587–1629), this vest was intended to add some sobriety to the British costume in the wake of the Great Fire. It was also suggested as a rebuke to France and its decadence. Here in America, in 2003, there was the push to change the name for French fries to "freedom fries." Maybe instead we should have gone with the seventeenth-century British anti-France strategy and all taken to wearing vests.

Pepys describes the original British vest as "a long cassocke close to the body, of black cloth, and pinked with white silke under it, and a coat over it, and the legs ruffled with black riband like a pigeon's leg; and, upon the whole, I wish the King may keep it, for it is a very fine and handsome garment."

Still trying to get a visual idea of the first vest? It was "a knee-length coat with elbow sleeves, generally confined at the waist by a sash or buckled girdle, and always worn under a tunic or surcoat. This tunic and vest, mainly a court fashion in England, was the forerunner of the coat-and-waistcoat style and the origin of the man's suit."[2]

It was rather monklike, and in this sense King Charles II achieved his aim of sobering up menswear during his restoration of the monarchy after the Wars of the Three Kingdoms (England, Scotland, Ireland). Remember all that from high school World History?

But as we see again and again, fashion never tolerates sobriety for long. Quickly men's vests began to get more and more elaborate. They took on bright colors and embroidery in the seventeenth and eighteenth century.

In a very silly 1751 book called *Memoirs and Interesting Adventures of an Embroidered Waistcoat,* the author writes in the voice of a world-weary vest. The seen-it-all vest tallies the sexual conquests of its masters and recalls incidents it deems significant, like spills: "Our Templar was warm in caressing a favourite Wench, when the Moment of his Dalliance a large Bowl of Anagus was overset by the Struggle, and poured upon me its crimson Libations; he swore, he raged, and threatened a thousand Curses on Peter, for that he had suffered the most sensible Mortification in my Misfortune."[3] Once stained, the vest is discarded. Its next owner is an actor, who puts it on whenever he has to play the part of "a shabby Poet, or reduced Rake."[4] Ah, how the mighty embroidered waistcoat has fallen.

The French Revolution in 1789 put a stop to such ostentation as snazzy talking waistcoats, and the vest became more of what it is today: something modest to go under a jacket. The real godfather of today's vest is our beloved George "Beau" Brummell (1778–1840), the original dandy. As we learn in the suit chapter, for Brummell vanity wasn't connected to extravagance. His style was pared down and elegant. He did away with the style of men known as Fops, with their white makeup, powdered wigs, and ornate colors. Brummell (about whom there are several movies, including one starring Elizabeth Taylor as his love interest) wore dark suits, an elaborately tied white cravat, and a vest.

VEST STYLES

1. What size are you? If a vest is not hideously expensive, it probably comes in S, M, L, or XL. The proper fit of the vest is then determined by the tab tie in the back. The vest should not be baggy. You should be able to stick your hand into the front of the vest (to retrieve something from a shirt pocket, for example), but if you can fit your fist in, the vest is probably too big, or you haven't adjusted it enough.

2. Which collar do you prefer? Shawl collar, lapel collar, no collar (by far the most common)?

3. How many buttons do you like? The more expensive the vest, often the smaller the space between the buttons.

4. Do you want the vest to show above your jacket? The size of the V will determine how much shows. Many people don't want it to show, but to me, letting it peek out of the jacket is the whole point!

5. What material and pattern do you like best? It can be an item to play with. (If you go to someplace like Paul Smith, you can get vests in riotous paisleys!) Or it can be more neutral and subdued. It depends upon your taste.

Over the years there have been some variations. In the 1820s, the vest entered an interesting phase: as shapewear. The vest became tight, like a corset. Queen Victoria's husband, Prince Albert, helped popularize a tiny waist for men, and the way they achieved it was through a whalebone-reinforced, laced-up vest. See, men? Body consciousness isn't only for women! In the 1830s, vests provided much of the color in a man's outfit.

When Prince Albert's and Queen Victoria's son Edward—a man with an, um, less-cinched waist than trim Prince Albert—became king in 1901, the vest-as-corset conveniently went out of fashion. This was around the time it became fashionable to leave the bottom button of the vest unbuttoned—either because of the king's large stomach (his waist was forty-eight inches), or because it was deemed more convenient for horseback riding.

During World War I, rationing made it harder to justify the use of extra fabric. Indoor heating made that extra layer less necessary. The vest became identified with a tweedy, uptight dandyism—ironic because its original incarnation way back in the mid-1600s was a blow against foppery.

Aside from formal wear, we generally see the waistcoat most often now in the form of the outdoorsy down vest. According to the textbook *Fashion, Costume, and Culture,* the first manufactured down garment was made by Eddie Bauer in Seattle in 1936. Bauer developed the idea the hard way: from almost freezing to death on a winter fishing expedition. The down-insulated jacket he created in response was called the Skyliner. He went on to design flight jackets for the military during World War II.

The material wasn't new. Native Americans had used duck and goose down for centuries, even pre-1492, to make blankets and mattresses. But it hadn't been arranged around the body as a vest until 1936. And it was another thirty years before Americans apart from ice fishermen and fighter pilots took to regularly wearing them.

American Olympic skier Suzy Chaffee—known as Suzy Chapstick, because she did Chapstick commercials—wore bright down vests in the 1968 Olympics. The look caught on among outdoor sportsmen and then gradually throughout the population. And so, the down vest is yet another garment that comes to us from sports.

In the 1990s, puffy jackets and vests, like the one put out by Triple F.A.T. Goose, became all the rage, starting among young people in the inner city.[5] The down vest went from the street to the runway and continues to be popular, with good reason. They're especially great in the fall, when you're not quite ready for a coat, but you still want some extra warmth.

Dress vests today are typically made of wool or occasionally silk. Sometimes they come with a suit or a pair of pants. If the pants and vest are the same, you have a sense of seamless assembly. (I'm wearing such a set on the cover of my last book, *Gunn's Golden Rules.*) It's

Justin Bieber wears a vest on the red carpet at the Grammy Awards in 2010.

harder to match a vest when it's not part of a suit, and yet I prefer the vest as an independent accessory. I like when it stands apart in textile from other garments.

We've talked about men and vests, but of course women wear them, too. When people think of women in vests, they often think of Diane Keaton, who wore formal menswear as part of her signature bohemian look. But women have worn vests at least since 1794, when they became part of evening dress and stayed so into the nineteenth century.

On both men and women, a vest generally gives you a finish and a polish. Going back to Prince Albert, it's slimming, as long as you don't have too much girth. It finishes up a buttoned-down shirt nicely. It can dress up jeans and a T-shirt almost as well as a blazer. For occasions that fall between casual and formal, I like wearing a vest without a jacket, buttoned or open. Justin Bieber is among the stars who has walked the red carpet wearing a vest—recently a shawl-collared one by Alexander McQueen.

Now that I know the history, I also feel that every time I put on a vest, I'm doing a little something for the cause of putting the French in their place. Given the general success of the vest throughout history, I would say that the British won this battle, even if it is widely acknowledged that, in the matter of fashion dominance, they certainly lost the war.

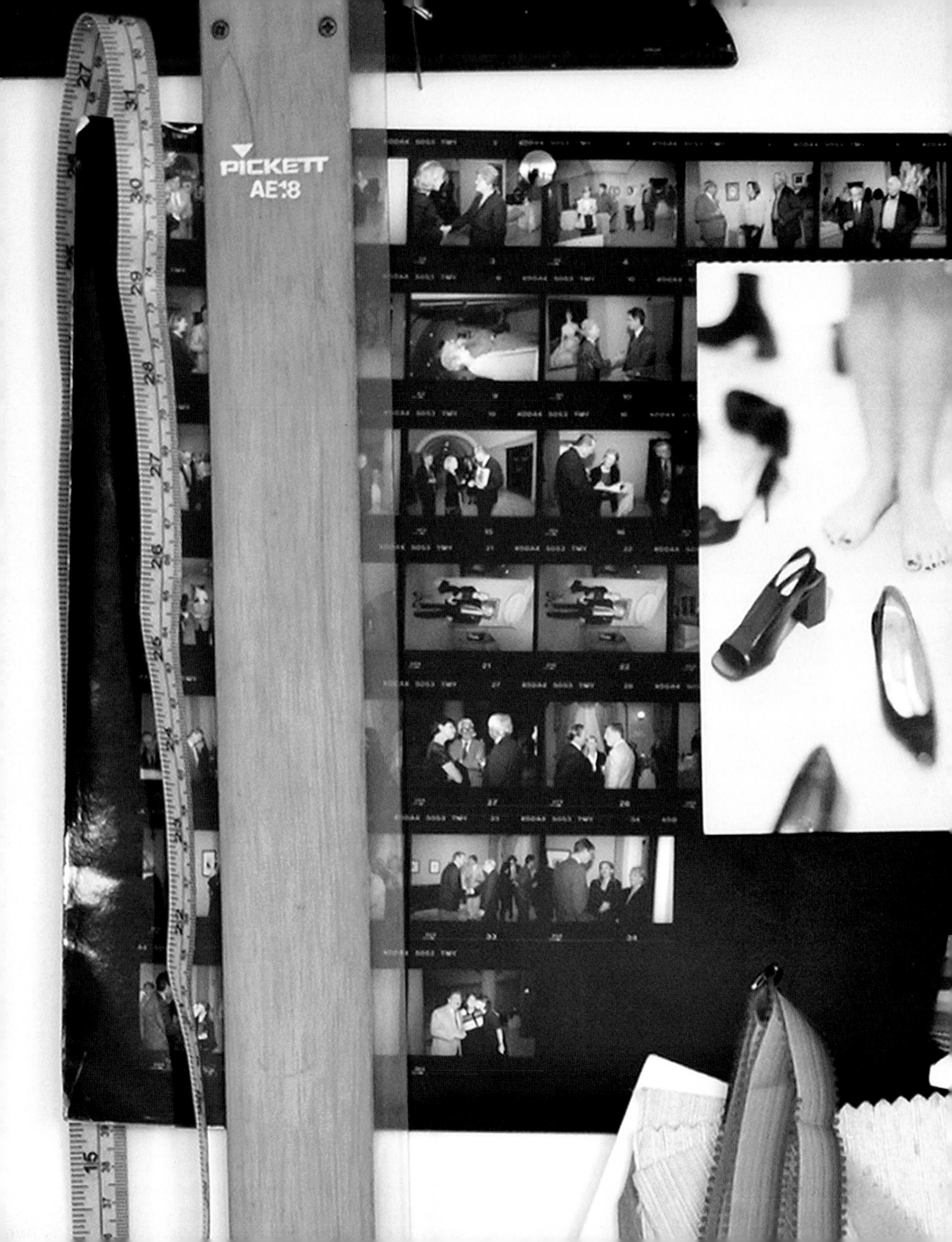
PICKETT

11.
SUITS
All Hail Beau Brummell!

Business wear, zoots, tuxedos . . .
Are you a single-notch or shawl-collar man?

ON ONE OF THE hottest days of the year, I was sent across the sweltering island of Manhattan to meet up with Heidi to shoot a promotional spot for a charity we work with. As I emerged from the subway, I realized that my light blue shirt had turned dark blue; I was soaked with sweat.

When I arrived, the producer took one look at me and said, "This won't do at all."

It took me a good long while to cool down and let my shirt change back to its natural color. Shortly thereafter, Heidi arrived, far cooler than I, thanks to her short shorts and tank top. It made me for a second regret that I couldn't wear the same.

To dress up as a man means wearing a suit. That means we men suffer in the summer, and dress-clad women suffer in the winter. Everything's a trade-off. Besides, in spite of their inconvenience on hot days, I love wearing suits. Properly tailored, a suit—from the French *suite,* meaning matching—looks better than anything else on a man's body. I loved the song Neil Patrick Harris sang on the hundredth episode of *How I Met Your Mother* called "Nothing Suits Me Like a Suit" (sample lyric: "Girls will go and girls will come / But there's only one absolute").

All things considered, the suit has a relatively short history: a mere four hundred years. In 1666, British king Charles II mandated that the standard of dress for the English court would be breeches (pants), a long coat, a waistcoat, and a cravat (the precursor to today's necktie). As we discussed in the vest chapter, Charles II was responding—as the English so often have throughout history—to a corresponding French trend, in this case one established by Louis XIV at the court of Versailles. Owing to the fact that the suit was associated with royal court dress, France abandoned it after the French Revolution, thereby leaving Britain as the sole caretaker of men's suit tailoring. It was there that the suit evolved to the carefully tailored and crafted look that remains to this day.

George "Beau" Brummell, watercolor by Richard Dighton, 1805.

However, what we consider to be the modern suit didn't appear until the nineteenth century in London. The modern suit owes everything—and I do mean every single thing—to George Bryan (Beau) Brummell (1778–1840). Most of us have heard the name, but few know—I certainly didn't until I started reading about him recently—what a transformative influence "the Beau" exerted upon clothing and Western society in general.

This isn't hyperbole. In the years 1799–1816, Brummell literally changed how English—and, later, European—men, and even women, dressed. Brummell's influence even affected how men presented themselves to the world; that is, one's carriage and bearing, one's subscription to wit, and "an air of languorous indifference." These became characteristics associated with a gentleman.

Brummell was considered a dandy, but in his time that term had a different meaning and resonance than it does today. Today we use the term to label a man who's an over-the-top fashion victim. Brummell was a minimalist. He said, "If John Bull [Everyman] turns around to look at you, you are not well dressed; but either too stiff, too tight, or too fashionable."[1] This also from Brummell's fascinating biography by Ian Kelly: "His [Brummell's] rules of dress have dominated male power dressing ever since. Without Brummell there would be no suit, for men or women, or tailoring in the Savile Row, Wall Street, or Chanel sense."

To put Brummell in context: he was educated at Eton and Oxford, served as best man at the wedding of the Prince Regent, the future King George IV, and had a childhood portrait painted by Sir Joshua Reynolds, the celebrated society artist.

It's difficult, if not impossible, to cite a specific moment or occasion that launched Brummell's fashion and style ascent; it seems to have just been part of his DNA. We do know that he observed the prevalent taste in menswear around him and criticized it for being too fussy. He sought a tailor who could bring tangible interpretation to his "vision" for dressing: streamlined, fitted pants, a starched linen shirt, and a trim waistcoat—minimal indeed.

This look became his uniform, and its eventual ubiquity would impact how the entire Western world dressed. According to the Berg encyclopedia, "garments worn by businessmen and women have remained almost static during the last 150 years. The black worsted wool suit has been the mainstay of business fashion essentially since the days of the English Regency period when it first replaced silk breeches and the cutaway coat."[2]

Since the Regency period, there have been very few variations on this look, but men do have a few options. Today, suits can be single or double-breasted, have one or two vents, and have one of a variety of lapel styles. Single-breasted suits may have one, two, or three buttons. Some suits come with a vest. More expensive suits may have working buttons on the sleeves. It can be very confusing, and increasingly so, as our culture becomes more and more casual, and both men and salespeople lose their understanding of all the various considerations that go into purchasing a suit.

Generally speaking, there are three categories of expense involved in suits: the most expensive, "bespoke," are completely original, one-of-a-kind garments on which every solitary stitch is done by hand. According to the book *Gentlemen,* bespoke means "cut by an individual, for an individual."[3] There are typically at least two or three fittings. The fittings and the suit cost $6,000 and up. In the 1960s, there were hundreds of bespoke tailors working on Savile Row. By the 1980s, there were fifty. Now there are probably half that.

Made-to-measure suits are also expensive, but they come from what's known as "slopers," basic forms that are already cut, but then customized for you. You could expect one fitting, and to pay $3,000 and up for the suit. Most of us go with the third option and buy our suits off the rack and then perhaps have them slightly tailored. Typically you will pay $600 to $700 for a good off-the-rack suit.

As a rule, if an invitation says "black tie," that means a tuxedo. Tuxedos can only be worn after five p.m. Technically, before five p.m. "formal" means a morning coat, which has tails. But who owns a morning coat? Even *I* don't own a morning coat, yet I own two tuxedos. If the invitation says formal and it's before five p.m., you're fine in a suit. There are more obscure dress requirements for certain occasions, but unless you're moving in rarefied circles, they are rare. "White tie," for example, means a dark suit with a tailcoat, a white tie, white shirt, and white vest, but events with such obscure dress requirements are quickly becoming a thing of the past.

But you could conceivably need a tuxedo—say, to buy or rent for your wedding. So what should you look for in a tuxedo? The first thing I look at is the lapel. There are various options: the peak lapel, the single-notch lapel, or the shawl collar lapel. I stay clear of the peak lapel, because its width can vary considerably, and so it can become dated quickly. The single-notch can vary a bit, but owing to its structure, it doesn't change much. My favorite for the tuxedo is the shawl collar, because it's the most timeless. For the most part, the only time shawl collars appeared on suits as opposed to tuxedos was in the 1980s, but the trend was short-lived and confined to hipsters.

If you're standing, I like a double-breasted suit, but if you need to sit down, that's a lot of buttons to contend with. I would never wear a double-breasted suit to a talk show, because you need to fiddle with it too much. It only looks good closed. My brother-in-law loves double-breasted suits, but every time I'm with him, I notice that he has to rebutton as soon as we stand up, and that interior button isn't that easy to access. You need two hands.

So, generally speaking, I prefer single-breasted suits. There can be one, two, or three buttons. I like two. The more buttons there are, the less of the shirt you see. It closes you up to have three buttons. You never button the bottom button on any suit, unless it's a one-button suit.

BRITISH HISTORY 101

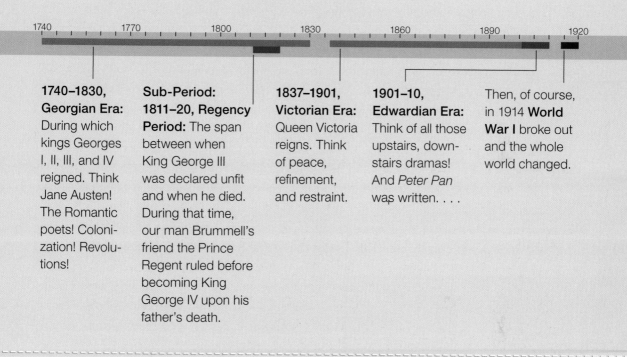

1740–1830, Georgian Era: During which kings Georges I, II, III, and IV reigned. Think Jane Austen! The Romantic poets! Colonization! Revolutions!

Sub-Period: 1811–20, Regency Period: The span between when King George III was declared unfit and when he died. During that time, our man Brummell's friend the Prince Regent ruled before becoming King George IV upon his father's death.

1837–1901, Victorian Era: Queen Victoria reigns. Think of peace, refinement, and restraint.

1901–10, Edwardian Era: Think of all those upstairs, downstairs dramas! And *Peter Pan* was written. . . .

Then, of course, in 1914 **World War I** broke out and the whole world changed.

The cost of a suit depends on the amount of craftsmanship, the kind of textile (such as wool, worsted wool, or seersucker), the quality of the textile, and the detailing. Is there topstitching in the lapel? Do the buttonholes in the sleeve work, or are they just for show?

The first thing to determine about a suit is the material. If a suit costs $50, it's probably made of nylon—which means it will look shiny and fall apart quickly. The lining of an expensive suit will typically be silk. A cheap one might be lined with polyester.

The best indicator of quality is a high thread count. So, how do you determine the thread count if it's not explicitly stated? Typically, if you see "Super 100's" on the label, that means it's a high thread count. Also, as a rule, quality menswear textiles come from Italy. Beyond that, it's hard to tell unless you have training. The general rule is to feel the fabric. Does it feel good? If it feels good, it probably is good. If you're not sure, go around a showroom and feel all the different fabrics. Touch the expensive ones and touch the cheap ones and note the differences.

When it comes to cut, generally speaking, the European suit will have two side vents (those slits in the bottom back of the jacket) that enable the wearer to easily put his hands in his pockets without causing the suit to pucker unflatteringly. The American suit will have one back vent. Jackets with no vents only look good if you're standing. The shape will become distorted if you sit down.

Britain has been the hands-down best place for suit tailoring for hundreds of years. Their only possible competitor is Italy, and the Italians have only been contenders since the Second World War. Italy has several centers of good tailoring, as opposed to one in Britain: Savile Row. Whereas the British suit is proper, the Italian suit is flashy, and pleats (which I discuss in the pant chapter and am not a fan of) are de rigueur in the Italian suit. Brioni suits are one example of the highest-end Italian suit; the company only makes five hundred custom suits a year.

But around the world, British tailoring is still considered the gold standard. Tailoring was Brummell's battle cry, and it continues to be at the core of English fashion. Even a cursory examination of the work of the often-outrageous late designer Alexander McQueen reveals the architectural structure and impeccable craft that is the hallmark of English tailoring.

While in London with the *ABC News* team for the wedding of His Royal Highness Prince William to Catherine Middleton, I paid a visit to Savile Row with the divine *Nightline* anchor Cynthia McFadden. At Hardy Amies and Gieves & Hawkes, for example, we were awestruck by the mastery of these tailoring artists. The evidence of their mastery is in the soft and supple quality of the suits, as opposed to the stiff hammered-and-nailed appearance of low-end American menswear. This is impossible for a novice to attain. British tailors are so precise they will often specialize in a specific item—pants, jackets, or vests!

The American suit is typically cut bigger, because Americans don't like feeling constrained. They should get used to it! One American trend that revealed this love of stylish comfort was the

Inside a Savile Row shop, 1970s.

craze for tweed sport jackets in the first half of the twentieth century. The American actor Douglas Fairbanks, Sr., appropriated the British Norfolk jacket,[4] and he helped spark a craze for the tweedy look among 1920s college men. When F. Scott Fitzgerald wore such a jacket in a 1925 *Vanity Fair* photograph, he fanned the flames of interest in this hybrid casual-dressy look. By the 1930s, movie stars wore sport jackets to signal their dual commitment to looking good and to leisure.[5]

The navy blazer's style is related to the tweed sport coat, but it is more evocative of yachting than fox hunts. There is an amusing but unlikely legend about the jacket originating on the nineteenth-century HMS *Blazer*, when the sailors had to be dressed up for a visit from Queen Victoria,[6] but the more likely case is that it owes its color and shape to prep school uniforms.

Every man in America should own at least one black suit. The Duke of Windsor wore midnight blue instead of black, because he insisted that in artificial light, midnight blue looked blacker than

Mary Pickford with Douglas Fairbanks, Sr., who wears a Norfolk jacket, 1920.

black. But he was a fussbudget. If you just have one black suit in your closet, you will be prepared for nearly every formal event that comes your way for the rest of your life. If you don't have one, buy one as soon as you can. Don't wait for someone to die. The last thing you should have to worry about in the wake of a family tragedy is finding something to wear to the funeral.

When it comes to suits in other colors, it's largely a matter of taste, but most men prefer suits in neutral colors, such as gray or navy. If they're inclined toward brighter colors, they will usually wear vibrant shirts and ties rather than a colorful suit. Lighter colors are typically seen during the day and during the summer, whereas darker colors come out at night and in winter.

Personally, I wouldn't consider a white suit. If you're Tom Wolfe, fine, but for the rest of us it's a tough look to pull off. Mark Twain wore one in all seasons, because he said it cheered him up. In 1906, he said, "I have found that when a man reaches the advanced age of seventy-one years, as I have, the continual sight of drab clothing is likely to have a depressing effect upon him. Light-colored clothing is more pleasing to the eye and enlivens the spirit." If you're that way, by all means go for a light suit, especially in summer.

Both colors and fabrics typically become lighter in summer. Summer-weight chino suits have a military origin. For decades, chino was a British army fabric, and then the American military adopted it, too. The fabric and dye are good at withstanding the harsh conditions of military life, especially in hot climates. The options are usually khaki, olive, or navy.

Seersucker, too, is a wonderful summer fabric. Seersucker is derived from the East Indian variation of the Persian *shir o shakkar,* which means "milk and sugar," a perfect name for a fabric with alternating smooth and grainy stripes. Seersucker is lightweight and never needs to be ironed. Alas, I don't often wear my seersucker suit, because much of my summer is spent taping *Project Runway,* and stripes give a distracting moiré (wavy line) effect on camera.

Of course, not everyone wants to follow the Beau Brummell dictum that to be truly fashionable you must not be noticed. So, how do you assert your own fashion sense while wearing a suit? In the book *Jocks and Nerds,* fashion historians Harold Koda and Richard Martin identify twelve male fashion identities of the twentieth century: Jock, Nerd, Worker, Rebel, Cowboy, Military Man, Sportsman, Hunter, Joe College, Businessman, Man about Town, and Dandy. They suggest that it's helpful for a man to find a distinct identity and then to dress accordingly.

Another way to think about your style is to look for icons to emulate. My style icon, for example, is Cary Grant.

"Who's she?" a student once asked me when I told him that. (Now when young people ask about my style icons, I just say George Clooney.)

I'm a classicist. But if you want to really stand out, there are some very inspiring historical examples of flashy menswear. In early-1940s America, some young black and Latino men took to wearing the ostentatious "zoot suit," based on the flashy suits

left: Tom Wolfe in his signature white suit, 1976.

opposite: Cary Grant, c. 1940s.

worn by Cab Calloway in the 1943 film *Stormy Weather*. The shoulders were padded and the pant legs tapered. At a time when Americans were being asked to conserve material and when people of color were marginalized, the zoot suit was a bold statement that the wearer would not conform and would not be ignored.

White teen hooligans in England did something like this starting around 1952, wearing long, draped, Edwardian-style jackets in black, maroon, or powder blue, tight drainpipe jeans tapered to the ankle, yellow socks, brass rings, and bootlace ties. Nicknamed Teddy Boys, they also often had crew cuts and carried switchblades. "Altogether," reports Nik Cohn, "the effect was one of heroic excess: garish, greasy and quite magnificent."[7]

A more conservative 1950s–60s style has made a comeback lately thanks to the TV show *Mad Men*. But what we see on *Mad Men* and in the collections it inspires is the twenty-first-century, far slimmer take on the early-1960s suit. The mainstream suit of the '50s and '60s was actually very roomy. To my eyes, the slimmer fit is far more flattering, and so I think it's a good adjustment to make when translating that particular vintage fashion to today.

In the 1960s, "mod" (short for "modernist") styles were based on the lines of Edwardian suits. The Beatles wore these suits, which were more colorful and casual, and they also started wearing Nehru suits when they returned from India. The Nehru became a suit substitute that was briefly accepted in the 1960s. Sammy Davis, Jr., and Sean Connery's James Bond wore them. Steven Seagal has been known to wear one. Johnny Carson even wore one for a while on *The Tonight Show*. (I thought he looked ridiculous in a Nehru, but maybe that's just me.)

I consider 1963 and 1964 the beginning of the fashion revolution, my favorite moment in fashion history. That was when

A zoot suit, 1943.

people started questioning the foundations of society, and clothing became genuinely shocking. That was when Parsons closed the lucrative interior design department because they thought it wasn't socially responsible to decorate rich people's apartments when the world was falling apart. Fashion, like everything else, became political, and very exciting to follow.

The 1970s brought bolder color and fabric choices for men. Tightness was in. George Frazier in *Esquire* dubbed this period in fashion history the Peacock Revolution,[8] because some men—in response, I believe, to the dirty and frayed hippies—dressed in wild colors and lush fabrics. Hippies and peacocks coexisted during that era, but the hippies must have outnumbered the peacocks one hundred to one. Most people were in between, but those were the poles. It was more affordable and easier to be a hippie, certainly.

A 1970s U.K. catalogue offers leisure suits.

The peacocks' brocade and velvet suits, which occasionally incorporated true plumage in the form of feathers, often verged on costume.

Leisure suits in full-on polyester were also popular during the '70s—the era that explored the threshold of synthetic fabrics. Now we almost never have 100 percent polyester, because we discovered that it looks and feels too artificial.

In the 1980s, men started wearing suits with T-shirts, thanks in large measure to Don Johnson on *Miami Vice* (1984–90). I was a young man then, and I thought it was great. You were still wearing a suit, but you could dress it down. I even liked the unstructured blazer, with its softer tailoring and fabrics. True, it became rather feminine. But it was a look. You could push the sleeves up. I found it fun, and it was a real statement.

Women of the 1980s tended to wear shoulder pads in everything, especially in "power suits." At first, this was a way for women in the business world to fit their bodies into menswear. Since the female body is so different, they had to create broad shoulders where there were none in order to wear men's clothes. For years women were walking around looking like

Don Johnson and Philip Michael Thomas in *Miami Vice* (1984–90).

linebackers from the waist up and sex kittens from the waist down, with their tight, short skirts, panty hose, and stiletto heels. It was the "business in the front, party in the back" mullet model, and a bit schizophrenic.

In a way, everyone who tries to make the suit flashy is attempting to get back to men's pre–Beau Brummell fashion audacity embodied by a group known as the incroyables (French for "unbelievables"). The incroyable costume is described by James Laver as "the last costume of fantasy to be worn by the male sex before it settled down for a century into its modified version of English country clothes."

The incroyables, Laver says, wore "violent colours, stripes everywhere, extending even to the stockings, the tails of the riding-coat incredibly elongated so that they almost touched the ground, the waistcoat so diminished that it scarcely covered the chest, the neck-cloth so exaggerated that it concealed the chin and made all men look as if they were suffering from goiter, the hair unpowdered and wildly disheveled, the hat neither the tricorne of the previous age nor the top-hat of the future, but a kind of crescent moon, of huge dimensions—such a headgear as might be made by folding a wide-brimmed hat in two and crushing it under the wheels of a passing car."[9]

Some ways of distinguishing yourself even when wearing a traditional suit are through subtlety and nuance: the number of buttons, the cut of the suit, and the type of lapel. You can also make more overt statements through bold shirts and ties. I am in favor of pattern mixing. I like to wear a striped shirt with a striped tie. I will even wear a striped suit with patterned shirts and ties, so there are three things going on at once.

The over-the-top look of the incroyables mocked the costumes of the aristocrats, 1795.

The colors should be in the same family, but not the same, and the pattern in the tie should be different from that of the shirt. My trick for figuring out if they're different enough: squint your eyes. If the shirt and the tie become one, it's wrong. You should be able to see a distinct difference in pattern even when your sight is blurred.

Of course, being ostentatious won't do for most offices, where to blend in is to show that you are part of the team. Traditionally, the three-piece suit is the uniform for businessmen the same way the military, athletes, doctors, and people in the service industries wear uniforms. I have a fondness for uniforms, because they democratize; that is, they negate fashion decision making. I also appreciate the clear semiotics of uniforms: they dispel ambivalence about who works in an establishment versus who is a visitor.

As we've evolved as a society, we've come to respect individuality and the personalization of one's appearance. Accordingly, the use of uniforms has diminished considerably. In some cases, the head-to-toe uniform has been replaced by a single item of apparel or an accessory that is to be incorporated into one's own personal wardrobe style, such as the staff apron at Walmart. And today, for better and for worse, there is a less rigorous uniform for white-collar workers.

Indeed, rules about what's appropriate in the office have changed greatly since women began ascending to positions of power. Traditional business clothes for woman originated from tailored menswear, and this is a trend that regrettably continues, even though women are a major presence in pretty much every sector of the working world.

I'm reminded of a visit I made to Capitol Hill while advocating for the Design Piracy Prohibition Act alongside Steven Kolb, executive director of the Council of Fashion Designers of America, and our liege and lobbyist, the fabulous Liz Robbins. A very timid teenage girl approached me and diffidently asked what I thought of her clothes.

It was obvious that she was wearing a uniform: charcoal gray pants, a white shirt with a tie, and a navy blazer. I deduced, correctly, that she was a Senate page. Putting my Socratic approach to work, I asked her what she thought of what she was wearing. She responded by asking me to follow her. I rounded the corner in one of the vast hallways only to be met by about two dozen identically dressed girls. I couldn't help myself; I exclaimed, "You young ladies are wearing men's clothes!" They laughed and nodded. They looked like they'd been dressed in their brothers' clothes, right down to their footwear, men's brown brogues.

Before we even engaged in a dialogue, I confessed that I was struck by the misogyny of it all. "Let me guess," I said, "when women were introduced into the ranks of Senate pages, the existing men's uniform wasn't altered to accommodate or acknowledge the difference in your physique, right?"

Correct. How infantilizing and trivializing those suits were, in the spirit of the *My Fair Lady* musical lament, "Why Can't a Woman Be More Like a Man?" This was 2010, after all! Doesn't it speak volumes for the cultural and social perception of women in the workforce, when you're told that even though you have a woman's body, you're only allowed to wear clothes made for men? The message sent by this policy is that if women are to be accepted into the exclusive ranks of men, then they have to look like men: buttoned up, stuffy, and no-nonsense. As if to show a little cleavage, to highlight a curvaceous figure, or to in any way appear feminine would discount, discredit, and disqualify them.

I strongly disagree with this idea. I feel that women should wear clothes that suit their bodies rather than forcing themselves into unflattering men's suits and that it is feminist to make a wide range of women's clothes acceptable business attire. But on the topic of women and business clothes, I have sometimes found myself in deep trouble.

Not long ago, I was promoting the 2011 film *The Smurfs* on the now defunct late-night show *Lopez Tonight* (George played Grouchy Smurf), but I know from experience that talk show interviews take on their own trajectory, so you never know. George brought up Hillary Rodham Clinton's style, or lack thereof, and asked me what I thought about it. (He also asked about the style of the cast of *Jersey Shore*, which it should not surprise you I find tragic.)

I said that when Secretary Clinton was the First Lady, I watched as her style evolved from unremark-

Secretary of State Hillary Clinton in China, 2009.

able to flattering and gorgeous. She really seemed to look like herself, or what I take her to be in her most sartorially shining moments: beautiful, confident, and elegant. When she became the senator from New York, I thought, "This is great! Now her style can truly ascend!" But it didn't. In fact, I perceived there to be a fashion retrenching. Back were the boxy pantsuits, the high necklines, the unflattering tailoring.

Why? Was it that as First Lady (emphasis on "Lady") she was supposed to play the role of wife, mother, and hostess and, accordingly, could emphasize her feminine side? And now the message was that if you want to play with the big guys then you better act like you're one of them and mimic their clothes, too?

Alas, my comments on *Lopez Tonight* triggered a hate fest. Blogs hammered away at my sexism and mean-spiritedness. I felt unduly maligned. I hadn't attacked Secretary Clinton's character. (In fact, I'd praised her to the skies.) I'd just commented on her apparel, for goodness sake. My argument was that women wearing only slightly readjusted menswear for business purposes is very dated. Now that women have been in the working world for a good while, there are so many options for women to look both attractive and professional.

Now, please don't misunderstand me and think that men have to dress like men or women like women or else they're breaking some kind of fashion rule. I certainly don't believe that all men have to dress masculinely and all women have to dress femininely, especially given the fact that what is deemed appropriate for men or women changes so much over time.

Take, for example, the color pink. Pink is considered the ultimate girly-girl color, as though by religious decree. But the blue-for-boys, pink-for-girls color code wasn't standard until after World War II. In 1916, *Infants' and Children's Wear Review* insisted upon pink for boys and blue for girls. In 1939, *Parents* magazine claimed that pink was a good color for boys because it was a pale version of red, which was the color of Mars, the war god. Blue was good for girls because it was the color of Venus, and of the Virgin Mary.[10] So, pink for girls is a relatively recent trend, and utterly random. Good luck turning back the pink-on-pink Disney princess train now, though!

There is a long history of women wearing menswear to gorgeous effect. Androgynous looks can be exquisite. Just think of Marlene Dietrich and Greta Garbo! In 1931, *Women's Wear Daily* reported: "Most of the smart women who are returning to Paris from the Riviera . . . are boasting that their clothes come from men's tailors."[11] Even way back in the 1670s, you had women in France and Germany wearing riding habits made by tailors rather than dressmakers.[12]

Students of mine at Parsons often played with gender expectations in exciting ways with their garments. People in the transgendered community, too, often use fashion to assert their inner identities rather than their biological ones. Look at the New York City wit Fran Leibowitz, who pulls off menswear—including French cuffs with cuff links—with aplomb.

If Mrs. Clinton were doing any of this, I would be all for it. But her pantsuits suggest to me that she is making herself deliberately frumpy. It makes me sad, because I know how radiant and attractive she can look. Of course, when she does show cleavage, she is criticized by hateful blogs, so I understand why she'd rather play it safe and bury herself in jackets.

In any case, she is far from alone in her dated menswear looks. Many women in the business world still believe that they need to dress like men to be taken seriously. The most common thing I hear from women who wear male-tailored clothes to the workplace is that it's because they don't want to risk being unprofessional. However, it *is* possible to be both feminine and professional. There have been many innovations in women's business wear over the years. Look at House Minority Leader Nancy Pelosi. She's powerful and authoritative, and dressing like a woman doesn't diminish her authority in any way.

Liz Claiborne (whose company I began working for in 2007) was one of the designers who offered an antidote to that boxy menswear look for women in the business world. With her eponymous line of women's apparel in 1975, she created clothing that was neither macho nor frilly. It was such a respite from the ultrafeminine dresses that prevailed at the time. Furthermore, her apparel transitioned from workplace to dinner out on the town, thereby giving women a multifunctional wardrobe.

The Chanel suit is another good example of a tailored look that was also relaxed. It was a defining aspect of her post–World War II collections. Ironically, it was reviled in Paris. And yet, it was all the rage in America. American fashion magazine editors went crazy for them. I am a big fan of the Chanel suit. For me, it's as much about the textile as it is about the silhouette. I find the suit to be enormously flattering on most women. It's a huge status symbol even to this day, and it's fairly timeless. Even twenty-five-year-old women look great in them.

In the 1980s, Donna Karan provided another seminal moment in business clothes for women: she addressed the profound difference between men's and women's shapes. By using fabrics with stretch (jersey), her designs draped anatomically, conforming to a woman's shape, thereby accentuating curves—shoulders, bust, and hips.

How to wear business clothes when you're curvy is a question I hear a lot from women in the workplace. One woman wrote to my *Marie Claire* advice column asking about how to wear a blazer over a very large bust. I told her to ditch the blazer and wear something knitted with some stretch, belting it to give it shape.

But for those without the large-bust issue, wearing a blazer is often the best way to dress up in the professional world. People who have a casual work environment should always keep a blazer on the back of their chair. If the boss calls you in, you can throw it on; it's such an easy way to show respect!

My view is that there are so many different kinds of workplaces today. You need to be appropriate to your environment and be true to who you are. You need to know how you want to present yourself to the world. And until you know the specifics, it's more respectful to err on the side of dressy. This is why you need to dress up for job interviews.

In any case, whenever we put on a suit today, we should thank Beau Brummell, without whom we might still be powdering wigs and pulling on tights. Of course, some of us are bringing back the tights, in the form of jeggings! Which brings us to our chapter on pants, or the lack thereof. . . .

12.
PANTS
The Truth About Dress Reform

Khakis, trousers, cargoes . . .
No, leggings are not pants—jeggings either!

WALKING DOWN Forty-second Street in the summer of 2011, I couldn't help but notice the window display at the Gap directly across from the Condé Nast Building (which houses the offices of *Vogue*, among other magazines). Female mannequins in the window were dressed in what could only be described as tights, paired with shirts and jackets. The slogan stenciled on the window: "Leggings—the denim alternative."

As you probably know, I have a great respect for the law, but I was tempted to break that particular window or to spray-paint a correction. In no way are leggings—in other words, *tights*—a "denim alternative." Tights are a bare legs alternative or a panty-hose alternative. They are not an alternative to actual pants.

Thankfully, a clever blogger created a flowchart entitled, "Am I Wearing Pants? A Self-Check Guide for Girls to Help Prevent GLHP (Girls Leaving the House Pantsless) Syndrome." Among the important questions this flowchart[1] suggested you ask about your "pants" before leaving the house: "Do they have pockets?" "Can you wear them to yoga?" "Are you sporting a camel toe?" Follow-up questions included: "Be honest—is it stretchy jegging denim?" Sample conclusions: "Gaaah, you're wearing tights!" or "Huzzah! You're probably wearing pants." I was happy to see I'm apparently not the only one who's shocked by the tights-as-pants trend.

Striped leggings, 1987.

When it comes to menswear, leggings and jeggings are less of a plague than in women's wear, but that just makes it even more startling when men do wear them. Once when I was on Conan O'Brien's late-night show, we had a long discussion about this phenomenon. Amazingly, Conan showed up on his show the next night wearing—you guessed it—jeggings! He got a big laugh, and thankfully that was to my knowledge the last time he wore them.

It's a shame that actual, non-stretchy, non-denim pants seem so unpopular these days, given their glorious history for both men and women. I say men and women, because our notion of pants as being for men and skirts for women is quite ahistorical. It's not even close to true that the first pants for women were the bloomers of the nineteenth century.

If you can believe it: over the course of human history, women have probably worn pants more than men! In much of the East,

Bloomers, 1851.

men wore robes and women trousers. The Greeks basically had unisex robes. When the Persians defeated the Babylonians in the sixth century BC, they turned them on to unisex pants.[2]

According to Quentin Bell, the Russian Empress Elizaveta Petrovna (who reigned 1741–62) was proud of her pretty legs and frustrated that skirts always hid them. She solved this problem by holding "metamorphose" parties, at which women wore pants and men wore hoop skirts. This apparently suited her figure well but made everyone around her miserable, because they didn't look quite as good "metamorphosed." "It may have started as a joke," writes Bell, "but it became a prodigious bore."[3]

Given this long history, it's now surprising to me that women wearing pants caused such a scandal in the nineteenth century. New York resident and reformer Amelia Jenks Bloomer is typically credited with the garment, but she's poorly understood. She was first and foremost a temperance activist. In 1851, she published an article in a feminist magazine she edited called *The Lily* in which she suggested women wear a kind of "Turkish Costume" of loose pants gathered at the ankle and covered with a short skirt.

She and a friend adopted the outfit after their friend Mrs. Miller was inspired by the work clothes worn in the Oneida community in 1848. "Millers" apparently wasn't as funny a name as "bloomers," and so Horace Greeley's *Tribune* used the latter as the name with which to ridicule this garment. Mrs. Bloomer wore them while lecturing against alcohol, and was teased so much for the pants that she finally gave them up.[4] When a similar style returned years later, they were better accepted and retained her name, but she didn't live to see herself (and her friend Mrs. Miller) fully vindicated.

In the early 1900s, fashionable women sometimes wore harem pants, thanks in part to Paul Poiret's Ballets Russes–influenced evening wear. After World War I, wealthy Americans liked to wear French evening fashions for their cocktail hours. (Did you know Americans invented ritualized cocktailing? Score one for us!) French designers such as Chanel and Vionnet created palazzo pants, silk tops, and wrap jackets for just this purpose. In fall 1966, Norman Norell introduced sequin pajamas perfect for the cocktail hour. Next time you're heading out after work for happy hour, imagine yourself wearing some of those!

In the 1940s, the ahead-of-her-time fashion designer Elizabeth Hawes pushed pants for women. And she walked the walk. During World War II, she closed her custom dress house to work in a factory and to write a column for the left-wing daily *PM*. One article was called "Girls in Slacks Have the Most Fun at Coney Island."[5]

Women's pants of the 1940s and '50s typically sat in the middle of the waist—no low-rise back then! Cigarette pants were the most popular women's pants of the 1950s. They had a wide waistband, which usually had a thin belt across it, and a flat front.

Palazzo pants have survived better than the cigarette pant. They can still work today. I think of them as dressy rather than casual. You want to pair a wider pant with a slimmer top. It's hard to navigate one's daily world of errands in a palazzo pant, but they can be fun when put to their original use: drinking.

Among the earliest pants for men were worn in the Persian Empire in 550–329 BC.[6] The first truly elegant pants were probably the ones French men wore in the first part of the seventeenth century. The slim, high-waisted pants elongated their silhouettes.

We know that in the 1850s, and then again in the 1940s, women in pants made people nervous. But did you know pants have been fraught for men as well as for women? Specifically, at least since the 1700s, there has been concern that taking off men's pants not be too easy. The button-closed front was used until the long waistcoat that covered it became shorter around 1760, at which point the front button fly was replaced by "falls," a panel buttoned around the sides. Falls were replaced by a button-fly front on evening pants

opposite: Actress Dolores Gray wears high-waisted pants at home, 1950s.

DOWN TO THE SEA IN SHIPS: SUMMER HOLIDAY FASHIONS.

THE cruising holiday is so popular this year that aboard ship fashions have played an important part in the season's collections. The vogue for red, white, and blue, for instance, has a distinctly nautical air, that is seen to the best advantage on the deck of a liner. For Mediterranean waters, the Matita model sketched above on the left has a cool little jacket of white linen. The second outfit, from Harvey Nichols, is ideal for the Norwegian fjords or our own coast-line. The well-cut trousers are of white flannel, and can be obtained for 25s. 9d., and the tricolour tuck-in jersey is 39s. 6d. The woolly cardigan is one of many new designs. On the right is an attractive jersey-fabric suit which is useful ashore and afloat. It is completed by a chic double-breasted waistcoat in fancy piqué. The three-piece outfit can be obtained for 6½ guineas at Debenham and Freebody's.

PAT CHARLES.

since around 1840. The zipper was especially nerve-wracking as a pants closure, because it was so easy to undo. That's at least part of why it took so long to catch on.

The zipper was invented for shoes in the 1890s by a traveling salesman from the American Midwest named Whitcomb Judson. Various entrepreneurs and inventors worked on similar products, but as late as the 1920s, they were still only used for rubber overshoes, money belts, and tobacco pouches. It was around this time that the B. F. Goodrich Rubber Company came up with the name "Zipper." But it was still another decade or so before the zipper found its way into clothing.

Elsa Schiaparelli used zippers in her 1935 collection, as closures and as decoration. Edward Molyneaux used them for his slim-fitting 1937 coats. High-end men's tailors starting using them as a closure for flies by the end of the 1930s and then they turned up in ready-to-wear pants. By the 1950s, they were the main pant fastener. In her 1973 book *Fear of Flying*, Erica Jong coined a term for a "zipless" sexual encounter. She explains it in this way: "When you came together, zippers fell away like rose petals, underwear blew off in one breath like dandelion fluff."

And *that* danger of front zippers falling away easily is why, if women in the 1940s and 1950s wore pants at all, they often wore side-zip ones. The front zip was considered too provocative.[7] In some parts of Europe into the twentieth century, there were even laws against women wearing men's pants: "Women wanting to wear men's trousers therefore had to sew up the flies and put in a side zip."[8] Today a majority of pants have a zip closure.

Generally speaking, the best fit for a dress pant is one that falls straight from the widest part of your hip, with no flare nor taper. That's the safety zone.

When it comes to waistlines, there are basically three: high, low, and in between. If your hips are larger than your waist, a low-rise pant is usually a good idea. But of course no one should be baring a midriff.

Let's talk about pleats. I maintain: never. I recently went to Brooks Brothers to buy a new tuxedo. On the rack they had a beautiful one in a great midweight wool. I loved everything about it, until I tried it on and realized the pants had pleats. I asked for a plain-front pant. They said the only pant it came with had pleats. They only had plain-front pants as tuxedo separates, and they were made of a far less luxurious textile.

"Why do you only have the pleat option?" I asked.

"That's what our customers want," the salesman said.

"But they shouldn't be wearing pleats!" I insisted.

"You should tell them that!"

In the end, I bought tuxedo separates in the less elegant fabric. I just couldn't do the pleats. For me, wearing pleats would be like walking around in Crocs.

Pleats make the waist area roomier, and so people think that's what they should wear if they're on the large side. They're wrong! Pleated pants are not meant to accommodate the belly, because the waistband is still fixed. In fact, pleats will make you look larger, because there will be extra fabric there. Yes, some men with wider hips like pleats because they make it easier to get into their pockets. I think it's better not to carry much in your pockets in the first place, but I can respect that as a personal choice.

Now on to cuffs, a fairly recent development. Folded-up pant cuffs are attributed to King Edward VII. In the second half of the nineteenth century, he turned up his trouser legs to protect them from dirt, and it became considered fashionable. You never have cuffs on formal wear or military uniforms, but otherwise it's a matter of personal taste. I'm not a fan of cuffs on pants for women or men, because in my opinion it visually shortens the pant and looks less modern and more casual. Any man who's at all self-conscious about being short should never wear cuffs. They make your leg look shorter. My brother-in-law cuffs everything. I used to, but I've started to see it as old-fashioned. It also draws attention to that part of the suit, so it puts more pressure on you to make sure your shoes are shined! But I understand that some people like a little added weight at the bottom of their pant leg because they feel it helps the pant hang well.

As a rule, these days pants have a stuffier and more formal vibe than jeans. This seismic shift occurred in 1969, and when the pant-jean chasm erupted, I was on the wrong side of history. The prep school I was attending at the time organized a formal outing to the Woodstock Music and Art Fair. Six of us, dressed in Weejuns, gray flannel pants, and blue sport coats with the school's crest, climbed into a van. I had more of a cultural interest in the

> ## SHOPPING FOR PANTS
>
> When shopping for pants, I advise women to bring along two pairs of shoes—a heel and a flat—so they can see which height of shoe the pant looks best with. Pants typically have a specific height and style of shoe that they suit. One pant will not service both a flat and a stiletto. You see people wearing heel pants with flats and the pants are way too long, or you see them wearing flat pants with heels and the pants are way too short. It's better to work this out when you're shopping rather than on the morning of a job interview!

event than a musical one. After all, I was still studying the classical piano, and that certainly wouldn't be found in the mud of Max Yasgur's farm.

We arrived in the midafternoon. Traffic was terrible. Walking around the grounds, I kept thinking about how odd it all was. Here were acres and acres of people. I don't like crowds, so I always kept the van in my sight. And I tried to get over how filthy it all was. My shoes were ruined instantly.

My roommate had really wanted to go. He had a pronounced Park Avenue accent. At one point during our walk around the farm, he went up to a bunch of hippies splayed out on the ground—high on pot, acid, alcohol, and everything else imaginable—and he said, in his upper-crust accent, "That's *uh vehry* nice dog you *hahve* there."

It wasn't a dog. It was a child. I grabbed Jim's arm and said, "Let's go."

And that was the end of our two-hour visit to the Woodstock Festival. On the way back to Connecticut, in our splattered flannel pants, we looked at each other dejectedly.

"That wasn't so great, was it?" one of my classmates said. No one knew exactly how to answer him.

Upon reflection, I'm glad to have been there. It was a historical moment that had little to do with me, but it was important all the same. I didn't know at the time that it was going to be the defining moment of our generation. I did know my schoolmates and I would have been less dramatically out of place if we'd been wearing bell-bottomed jeans instead of preppy trousers.

13.
HOSIERY

From the Mayflower to the Bedroom Floor

Socks, stockings, panty hose . . .
Tights should look like tights.

AS PART of my official duties at Liz Claiborne Inc. (now renamed Fifth & Pacific), I travel around the country to host fashion events. We take questions at the end of the runway show, and there's hardly a time when a woman doesn't ask me about stockings. It's likely she was raised to believe that you were supposed to wear panty hose in more formal settings. Generally, the question is some variation on this: "Are bare legs vulgar with a skirt or dress?"

I always say no. Bare legs are usually the more fashionable option. As pants have become more popular for women, panty hose have continued to fall out of favor, and as a rule, I say good riddance.

But tights can be great. My advice is just to always wear a stocking that looks like a stocking. Women sometimes tell me they feel naked without tights, and would feel exposed without their tan panty hose. But generally when I see women with this look, they seem old-fashioned, and uncomfortable. Black tights are far more flattering. They make one's legs look younger and thinner.

THE TIGHTS WITH NOTHING TO HIDE.

No toe or heel seams. No nasty thick fabric around the thigh. Just beautiful sheer throughout 15 denier tights in the most fashionable shades, with that silky finish you expect to pay a fortune for. Only 85p RRP.

Mirage by Aristoc

A 1980s U.K. panty hose ad.

I don't use "nude" for the color tan, because a huge percentage of the women in this country are not white. "Nude" is not an appropriate word for a pair of tights that only resembles a white woman's nude legs. I'm told that Kate Middleton has provoked something of a renaissance for the tan stocking, but I am still against it. If you do want to wear tights, wear black or a color that enhances your outfit. The 1966 movie *Blow-Up* is full of daring dress-and-tights color combinations, if you're looking for inspiration.

Panty hose didn't even appear until 1959, when a Glen Raven Cotton Mills designer came up with a combination of tights and underwear that included spandex and so kept its shape. First they were just worn by dancers. Then, thanks in part to the popularity of the miniskirt, panty hose caught on, with assorted variations. For example, did you know that the reason we have sandal-foot tights (tights without a toe seam) is because of the craze for clear vinyl footwear in 1966?[1]

Before that time, tights were generally made of cotton or silk, although Dr. Jaeger's health campaign (about which more can be found in our underwear chapter) made wool tights popular for a time. The tilting of the crinoline in the 1800s could reveal a good amount of women's legs, so leg coverings, typically cotton stockings, were introduced. They were at first just two tubes of fabric joined to a waistband, worn without underpants. Once women's underpants (then called drawers) came into fashion, the garter belt came into vogue to hold up women's stockings. They held the corset down while holding the stockings up.[2] When shorter skirts came into fashion in the 1920s, there was a switch to prettier silk stockings, held up by garters.[3]

Men no longer needed to worry about tights, as they had for hundreds of years. In the eleventh century, men's stockings came to just below the knee and had a patterned top—like golf socks. They grew longer from there, and in the twelfth century reached to mid-thigh. Knitting didn't really sweep England until Elizabeth I's reign (1558–1603). Until then, tights were tailored to fit the leg and made from linen or wool. Sometimes they were footless and sometimes they had a stirrup at the instep. Sometimes they even had thin leather soles,

Models from *Blow-Up*, 1966.

rather like mukluks, the soft boot worn by aboriginal people in the Arctic. Sometimes they were decorated with bright colors or stripes. [4]

In other words, men in the 1100s would feel right at home staring at the hosiery wall of an American Apparel store today. Men started wearing pants instead of breeches at the beginning of the nineteenth century but came back to colorful and sometimes argyle hosiery in the 1920s in order to liven up their breeches when hunting or playing golf. Typically made of wool, silk, or cotton, socks developed ribbed cuffs in the 1840s so they wouldn't fall down as easily.

One of the biggest trends in American sock history was the bobby-soxer phenomenon of the 1940s. There's a fun 1947 Cary Grant film called *The Bachelor and the Bobby-Soxer*

Bobby-soxers, 1953. Note that the bobby, or ankle, socks are proto-punkly paired here with dog collars.

in which a teenage girl (played by Shirley Temple) falls for an older playboy. Female fans of crooners like Frank Sinatra were nicknamed "bobby-soxers" because they wore "half hose," or short "bobby" socks (the term appears to have the same etymology as the bobby pin and the bob haircut). The short socks often appeared as part of girls' school uniforms and were a way of feminizing masculine shoes like the saddle shoes bobby-soxers usually wore with their poodle skirts. In the 1950s, "sock hops" were all the rage. They were called that because shoes had to be removed at the entrance to the dance in order to protect

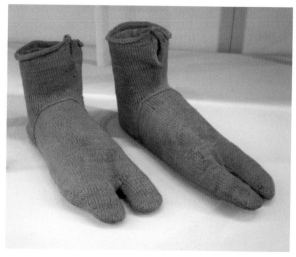

Sandal socks from Egypt, knit with a single needle, AD 300-499.

the gym floor varnish. Men have been behind most of the rock-and-roll fashion trends of the last sixty years, but the bobby-soxer look unquestionably belongs to young women.

Socks go back way further than that, though. The oldest surviving examples of hand knitting (which isn't the same as two-needle knitting) are Syrian socks dating to AD 200. Knitting was probably perfected in the Arabian countries between AD 500 and 1200, and came to Europe via the Crusades (1095–1291). The Victoria and Albert Museum's oldest knitted (with a single needle) items are a pair of socks from around AD 300 to 499 from Egypt. They have a separated toe and are meant to be worn with sandals.

Do not try this at home! Seriously, unless you are a fifth-century pharaoh, socks with sandals is a terrible look. On both men and women, it comes off as aging and inappropriate. If you're wearing socks, wear a shoe! Don't wear a sandal. I think of Europeans as being very fashion conscious, but their proclivity for wool socks with sandals is one egregious exception.

When it comes to fabric, socks have experienced a learning curve. At the Bata Shoe Museum in Toronto there is a sock crafted by the Anasazi Native American tribe of Arizona that dates to AD 1200. It was made from human hair, the sole reinforced with yucca! Can you imagine how itchy those must have been?

I will talk a lot about the difference between knitting and weaving in the sweater chapter, but I have to stress how amazing I find it that knitting as we know it today didn't really exist until a few hundred years ago. Weaving came first, along with a kind of single-needle knitting called *nålbinding*. Knitting with two needles didn't come into vogue until around the time Columbus discovered America. But by the time America was settled, it was something

Tom Cruise in *Risky Business*.

women did constantly. Crossing the Atlantic on the *Mayflower* in 1620 took sixty-six days. How did those Pilgrim women pass the time? Knitting socks!

Mechanizing the knitting process was one of the major events in clothing history. English clergyman William Lee was "annoyed with his fiancée's preoccupation with knitting during the courtship but grateful for her financial support (from knitting) during marriage."[5] So in 1589, he built what he called a stocking machine to accomplish the same goal while ensuring his wife could continue to pay enough attention to him. Alas for Lee, Queen Elizabeth rejected the patent application. She acknowledged its cleverness but was afraid it would put too many people out of work.

The queen was smart to acknowledge the subversive power of knitting. When the colonists finally revolted against England, hand knits became symbolic of the colonists' independence. Martha Washington herself knitted with the officers' wives in the army camps, a show of support for the troops. For generations, knitting socks for soldiers would continue to be a favorite way for women back home to honor the troops.

This was true during both World Wars I and II. One Red Cross manual from 1917 cautions American women about the dangers of bad knitting: "Remember a man may not have the chance to change his socks for many days, and a lump or knot brings a blister. If the blister breaks, blood poisoning may set in and result in the loss of a foot or even a life. We cannot afford to lose our men through negligence or ignorance."[6]

But no pressure, ladies!

William Lee's stocking machine became more complex in 1857, when a drive mechanism was attached. Now stockings could be knitted flat and then sewn up the back in a seam. Generally, hosiery in the 1800s was made of cotton, silk, or fine wool. In 1856, new synthetic dyes made it possible to produce brightly colored tights.[7] Also popular were stripes or embroidered "clocks"—little decorations on the side of the stocking or on the back of the heel.

Women wore heavy black stockings when swimming or exercising. Early in the 1900s, women wore silk stockings for formal occasions and cotton ones during the day. Rayon was introduced in 1914, but these stockings sagged. The Du Pont Company introduced nylon at the 1939 World's Fair, and that was a far bigger success than rayon, because it didn't shrink or sag. In 1924, shorter skirts caught on, and so tights mattered more; just as in the 1960s, short skirts would create an explosion in the stocking industry.

Many styles of tights and socks are now available to us in a wide variety of fabrics. My general rule of thumb for women is that tights and shoes should usually match, because it makes your legs look longer. So, if you're wearing black shoes, you should wear black tights. But if you're wearing socks, the sock should match your pant or skirt so that you don't end up with a "boot" effect, with the shoe and sock merging so that you lose the distinction between shoe and sock.

And for men? White socks are the standard for athletic wear, or if your parents are out of town and you are sliding around on hardwood floors. (The 1983 Tom Cruise film *Risky Business* is probably the most famous moment in the history of the white sock.) But white socks should never be worn with suits, unless the suit and shoes are white, too, in which case you are probably Tom Wolfe or Mark Twain and aren't asking me for fashion advice, anyway. I see so many businessmen make this white-sock mistake, and their athletic socks counteract the polish of their business clothes.

I understand that it can be confusing. The MetaFilter message board question "What color socks should I wear with brown shoes and blue jeans?"[8] generated dozens of pieces of conflicting advice. A couple of posters suggested white. Others said: gray, black, tan, dark brown, orange, green, argyle, or navy. No wonder men tend to throw their hands up when faced with this kind of fashion conundrum!

WHAT COLOR SOCKS SHOULD YOU WEAR?

» With athletic shorts or pants and sneakers: *white athletic*

» With white pants: *white formal (the thinner kind)*

» With blue jeans: *navy or gray*

» With black jeans: *black*

» With black pants: *black*

» With brown pants: *dark brown, no matter what color the pant is, unless you are adventurous and can pull off pink!*

» With gray pants: *black or gray*

» With a skirt: *match the color of the shoes or skirt. The head-to-toe look should be of a piece, so usually matching shoes is safest.*

» Red, green, or other colored pants: *socks as a rule should match or complement the pants. Gray is often a safe bet if you're stumped.*

» With golf pants or a loud print: *Are you really going out in those? I hope you're playing golf! If so, a neutral that matches one of the colors in the pant.*

So, what's the rule of thumb? Some say you should always match your socks to your shoes. Others say you should always match your socks to your pants. The correct answer is pants. And so in the case of jeans and brown shoes, I would go with navy socks.

One note on sock-and-pant etiquette: if you're wearing socks with dress pants, you should reveal no leg skin. It's like a bare midriff: you don't want to see it. It's different if you're wearing shoes without socks, which is fine in casual settings. Going sockless is totally acceptable if, for example, you're going to a picnic in. In that case, show all the leg skin you like. But if you have socks on, make sure they're long enough to hide your shins even when your legs are crossed.

Owning socks and tights of various colors and patterns is a way of expanding your wardrobe's potential. Men who want to get creative should look to their hose-and-breech wearing ancestors, or to the Duke of Windsor and his sportsman cronies. Women should look to the silk-stockinged flappers of the 1920s, the ankle-socked bobby-soxers of the 1950s, or the mod ladies of the 1960s. Throughout history, people have had fun with their hosiery, and you can, too!

14.
SHOES
The World at Your Feet

Heels, boots, slippers . . . The more
impractical the shoe, the richer the look

SAVAGE BEAUTY, the astoundingly popular 2011 Alexander McQueen retrospective at the Metropolitan Museum of Art, featured a number of examples of extreme McQueen footwear, including his spring/summer 2010 Jellyfish Armadillo boot, the famous many-inch hooves Lady Gaga made so popular in her "Bad Romance" video. But the shoes I was most struck by in the show were his chopines.[1] They are a direct reference to the original high-fashion high heels.

Venetian chopines of the fifteenth century appear all but impossible to wear. Open-toed, backless, and quite high, these dramatic clogs had no heel, per se. The foot's weight was thrown entirely forward onto an open-toed platform. They were worn by court ladies and by prostitutes. Much like today's stripper shoes, they are sexually

Chopines, c. 1600.

Turkish pattens shown in a 1742–43 pastel drawing by Jean-Étienne Liotard.

charged because they force the wearer into a seductively off-kilter posture, and because they reveal a good deal of the foot.

Modesty got the better of the shoe industry in the seventeenth century, when high heels with closed toes and backs replaced the chopines. That means the backless heels we so often see now are actually an older design than what we think of as a traditional pump! It wasn't until the late 1930s that sling-backs and open-toed heels gave us another glimpse at the toes and heels.

Heel height has fluctuated ever since, as have platforms. One goal of a high shoe is to elevate the wearer out of the muck. Before there was pavement (asphalt didn't even appear until 1824, in Paris), streets were very muddy. People often wore one kind of shoe indoors, like a satin slipper, and another outside, perhaps with some kind of overshoe. One type of overshoe was called pattens, which were made of leather, wood, or iron, and lifted the wearer up a couple of inches or more from the sidewalk to protect the sole of the shoe from grime. Men and women wore these from the fourteenth- to the mid-nineteenth century, when street conditions started to become slightly less disgusting.

At the end of the eighteenth century, heels were three or four inches high. They then became flat until around 1850, when the heel was low and chunky. This low thick heel was popular until the 1890s, at which point heels became high again for a decade or so, then became low at the turn of the century until the 1920s, when higher heels came into vogue for evening wear. By the late 1950s, fashion dictated a four-inch-plus spike heel for evening.[2] Thanks to *Sex and the City*'s heroines, a fetish for high-priced high heels entered the mainstream.

Speaking of high-end shoe designers, in 2011 it was fascinating to see the design company of Christian Louboutin try to stop the company Yves Saint Laurent from producing high heels with red soles, claiming that Louboutin was the originator of the red sole. Louboutin lost, and I was glad. He was not the first person to paint a sole, and I am wary of patenting a color, like Tiffany blue. Why should we grant that entire history to Louboutin and say there are no predecessors and should be no successors?

Christian Louboutin shoe with the designer's famous red sole, 2006.

left: Kristin Davis, Kim Cattrall, Sarah Jessica Parker, and Cynthia Nixon at the *Sex and the City* sixth-season premiere party, 2003.

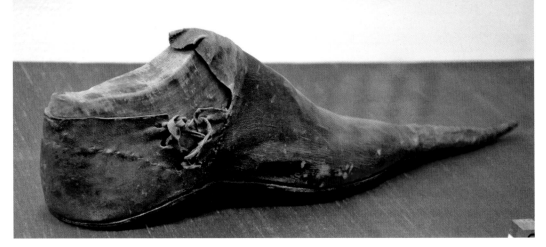

Poulaine, Spain, fifteenth century.

Detail of a fifteenth-century illuminated manuscript of *Renaud de Montauban* showing the piked shoe style.

Length of the vamp has also varied greatly over time, with the most extreme versions being the long, pointy, piked shoes (also called poulaines or crackowes) of the fourteenth and fifteenth centuries. An edict was passed in the 1300s banning all but the wealthiest citizens from wearing long poulaines. The clergy opposed these shoes for anyone, regardless of their station, perhaps because it was hard to kneel in prayer while wearing such pointy shoes. Also, perhaps, because they were overtly phallic, especially when men wore flesh-colored ones with attached bells. The plague of 1347 was even blamed on the obscenity of the poulaine—nature's retribution against inappropriate footwear as defined by the Church. Nevertheless, these poulaines were very popular from 1370 through 1410 and again later in the fifteenth century for both men and women.

A round toe replaced the pointed toe at the turn of the sixteenth century. By 1515, toes were square, and sometimes the shoe was slashed.[3] Square toes were in fashion again from 1825 through the 1870s. Even in the twentieth century, various toe styles came in and out of fashion. Round toes were popular with women of the 1920s and 1930s; square toes were popular with mods of the 1960s and then again in the 1990s. Poulaine-like pointed toes were in fashion in the 1990s. Now rounded toes are back again.

But even as height, toe style, and vamp length have fluctuated over time, the rule of thumb, then as now in the era of Lady Gaga, is that the fancier the person, the more ridiculous the shoe. "Perhaps the most effectual guarantee of social standing is obtained by means of unpractical footwear," writes Quentin Bell,[4] who also notes that the heel started as a male shoe, and "seems to have a military origin and indeed to serve a practical need in that the heel is of obvious use in holding a stirrup."[5] Isn't it fun to think about the women of *Sex and the City* owing their Manolos to ancient cavalry soldiers?

Certainly there are exceptions, but as a rule, the clunkier the shoe, the lower the social status. Think about a clog versus a sabot, a gigantic wooden shoe, which is like walking around in a giant baked potato. The clog at least has some shape to it. The bigger, chunkier, and clunkier the shoe, the lowlier its origins. If you think about the opera shoe, it's very dainty. It was about demonstrating that you're of such a high class that you don't need to walk far.

But an exception to this status game, and a sign of widespread fashion democratization, is the flip-flop, once worn only on beaches but now appearing on the feet of rich and poor in nearly every social situation. My position on flip-flops is that they have very little appropriateness outside of a beach, a swimming pool, or in tropical climates. When I spent four months in equatorial Kuala Lumpur, Malaysia, I never wore them, ever, but since then I have overcome my aversion, and now own a pair. On hot summer days on the Upper West Side of New York City, I will wear them to pick up the morning paper and get a cup of coffee at Dunkin' Donuts.

And now that I know the origin of the humble flip-flop, I object even less to wearing them, at least casually. The flip-flop has a multimillennial legacy. I'll cite Diana Vreeland's recollections of her first encounter with this humble example of footwear in her memoir, *D.V.*

She was in Pompeii, touring the ruins. As we know, the volcanic eruption that devastated the city in AD 79 captured all manner of activities in situ; that is, the volcanic ash exploded with such voracity than whatever was happening at the moment was frozen in place forever. Vreeland came upon a preserved diorama of a woman having *relations* with a slave. Vreeland deduced this by the slave bracelet that the young man was wearing, along with his footwear. His shoes were not the elaborate sandals of the aristocracy or warriors, but something she deemed sublime it its simplicity. In Vreeland's words, "It had just *one* thong which went between the big toe and the one next to it. . . ."

The ubiquitous flip-flop.

Vreeland had this sandal reproduced (after scandalizing her prudish shoemaker with *far* too much detail about the Pompeian sexual scenario that inspired it), and she wore it in Capri, in New York, and wherever she fancied. She regarded it as a "low" accessory to mix with her "high" apparel. *Et voilà*—the precursor of today's flip-flop. As with all things Vreeland, she was ahead of her time.

That sandal existed even before Pompeii, however. We have tangible evidence of the proto-flip-flop's existence in Egyptian stone carvings. Then, for the Greeks, the sandal was a class delineation; that is, the upper and middle classes wore them and the poor went barefoot. It is noteworthy that the Greeks didn't wear shoes inside, as is the case with many societies and cultures today—Scandinavia and Japan among them.

I don't wear shoes in my apartment, either. I walk around in socks or slippers. I don't want to bring New York City street and sidewalk residue into my apartment, nor do I want to potentially disturb my neighbors below me. (I'm on the top floor, so I'm lucky, because my former apartment was below a team of thundering, stiletto-wearing cattle, or so it seemed.)

Compared with the Egyptian sandal, the Greek sandal bore more lacing—as, generally speaking, Grecian apparel showed more leg. These lacings were partly practical and partly decorative. In addition, the Greeks introduced cork soles to their sandals. Cork came from the bark of the cork tree, which grew in abundance along the Mediterranean coast. Given that it was lightweight and water resistant, it was even more durable than leather.

The Greek sandal morphed into a laced boot for horsemen and included shin guards for warriors. According to James Laver, Greek prostitutes wore gilded sandals, possibly at times with a "follow me" symbol written in nails on the sole, shrewdly creating advertising footprints with every step.[6] By contrast: in Rome, no one went barefoot. The poor wore thick socklike shoes of felt. For the upper echelon, Rome introduced more elaborate sandals.[7]

Still today you can see women walking around wearing these sorts of gladiator sandals. A couple of years ago, I was with Nina Garcia on *Good Morning America*. Robin Roberts (whom I adore) asked us about fashion trends for that particular season. In my typical way, I declined to respond, saying that I didn't want anyone to run to a store just because I endorsed a trend. Besides, a trend is good only if it works for you, your wardrobe, and your lifestyle. Robin looked disarmed—and disappointed—and turned to Nina, who had no such anxiety.

"The gladiator sandal!" she declared.

"The gladiator sandal?" I echoed with a question mark. "How many women possess the time to deal with a gladiator sandal?"

It wasn't very polite of me to challenge Nina, but I couldn't help myself. I mean: the gladiator sandal?!

An even older style, though, than the gladiator sandal, is the caveman's footwear. Can't you just picture him: wearing a one-shoulder tunic of leather and animal skins wrapped with straps around the feet and lower legs? There is a cave painting from Spain dating as early as 15,000 BC showing a man in skin boots and a woman in fur ones. The bulky caveman boot certainly has a modern heir: Uggs. I feel they are aptly named and don't belong in this millennium, but I realize I'm in the minority on that.

Proto-Uggs in *When the Dinosaurs Ruled the Earth*, 1970.

Espadrilles date to the 1920s.

Keep in mind that all footwear until the middle of the nineteenth century was different from our modern shoes in one respect: they were made up of two straight shoes rather than one left and one right shoe. Shoes without distinction between the left and right are called "straights," and would you believe that until 1900—*1900!*—many shoes were just that, such that you didn't need to distinguish one shoe from the other?

Since the turn of the twentieth century, many styles of footwear have come in and out of fashion. The espadrille is among them. It originated in 1920s Spain and was for men only. Later, women joined the ranks of wearers. Espadrilles have a particular context; that is, as disposable summer footwear. They're made of canvas with twisted rope soles, come in myriad colors, prints, and patterns, and they're a great look.

Another classic is the ankle boot, which first appeared for women around 1804. They were especially popular in the middle of the nineteenth century and then again in the middle of the twentieth century, when they were called Chelsea boots, after the mod hub in London.

Large boots have been popular with workers and soldiers as long as there have been heavy things that can fall on feet, but they have also entered the fashion arena at various points. Even before tan Timberlands took over American city streets, Wellingtons, named after Arthur Wellesley, the first Duke of Wellington (1769–1852), entered into British civilian dress because of the Napoleonic Wars. English women of the 1840s even wore dress Wellingtons to the opera. They looked like slippers peeking out from under the skirt but had a practical upper part that made it a boot—although the upper fabric often resembled hose.

Even before that, Beau Brummell promoted Hessian boots. Earlier still, the seventeenth century brought the cavalier boot, which replaced the slouchy sixteenth-century boot, which in turn replaced the thigh-high brown leather boots of the fifteenth century. When the English burned French warrior Joan of Arc at the stake in 1431, one of the charges against her was that she was wearing men's boots rather than women's boots.

The 1960s were the golden age for women's boots. André Courrèges introduced white leather boots around the same time as the miniskirt, and they proved the perfect match for the era's futuristic look. Nancy Sinatra's 1966 hit "These Boots Are Made for Walkin' " helped establish the go-go boot as a symbol of female power. (Hippies preferred the humbler lace-up granny boot.) Dr. Martens were introduced as orthopedic shoes in the 1940s, but entered into fashion via punk in the 1970s and grunge in the 1990s.

Traditional pump-style heels have returned again and again to the fashion arena, and it's no surprise why. Most women benefit from looking longer, and heels accomplish this better than anything. They also have a long pedigree as a mode of flirtation. It's hard to imagine any other item of clothing serving the same purpose of the glass slipper in Cinderella. The mystery of the Brothers Grimm fairy tale the Twelve Dancing Princesses is how the king's daughters manage to wear out their dancing shoes each night, even though no one sees them leave their bedroom. The patent-leather, round-toed, ankle-strapped Mary Jane started out in 1927 as a children's shoe but became popular with coquettish adults in a heeled version.

Women have their own tolerance level for heels. Some women love a four-inch heel. Some don't like anything higher than a two- or three-inch heel.

"I just can't do heels," some women tell me. "Am I disadvantaged?"

To which I respond: "I know plenty of fashion editors who only wear flats." Any height can be flattering. I would never force a woman to wear a shoe she couldn't walk in.

If you're petite, you can certainly accept your height and wear flats or low heels. Even the old rule about wearing flats when you date shorter men is out of date. Shorter men don't want to be patronized, and often they are attracted to taller women *because* of their height, not in spite of it.

Now, let's talk about color. I hear from so many women who have trouble matching shoes to dresses. My advice: in so many cases, metallic hues can be your savior—in shoes, belts, and

Long before grunge, Dr. Martens were known for their air-cushion sole, as this 1960s ad shows.

opposite: Frank Sinatra hugs his go-go-booted daughter Nancy on a TV special, 1966.

handbags. Women sometimes balk when I say that. My response: if you're wearing jewelry, it's probably silver, gold, or platinum. Why not do the same with your accessories?

Once you have the style and color chosen, you need the right size shoe. I know many women, especially in Europe, who purposefully wear shoes that are too small. They think it's more flattering even though they're in constant pain. No one should be in pain! You should buy shoes that fit, keeping in mind that leather will stretch and plastic won't.

You should also not buy shoes that are too big, because you'll fall down. I have a friend who was constantly toppling over in heels. It turned out that she was actually a size nine but had been wearing a 9½. Once she started wearing the right size, she could run around in heels all day without incident.

STILETTO ALTERNATIVES

Women often ask me if fashion requires the wearing of heels. It certainly does not! It's a matter of taste and style. Flats are perfectly acceptable. But if you want to look longer and leaner without wearing a high heel, one way to achieve the same effect is to wear a lower-heeled shoe that has a platform. You'll add the same number of inches but more stability. And you won't have to worry about your heel getting stuck in a sidewalk crack!

Now, an important public service announcement for both men and women: shoes require maintenance. In the life of a shoe, shoe menders may need to occasionally replace the tip of the heel or the sole. I find most people don't acknowledge that it's the one item you wear that receives the largest amount of wear and tear. It needs upkeep. For this reason, too, you need to circulate shoes. Wearing the same shoe every day isn't good for your shoe or for your feet.

Living in New York City puts a huge amount of wear and tear on one's shoes. We are not a car culture; we're hoofers. I walk everywhere and that includes, of course, getting to the subway. And the subway isn't a static experience. It requires that one go down stairs, up stairs, hike along a platform to the exit, and then walk to one's destination. I should get a pedometer and record how many miles I walk in any given week—a lot! And all of this walking takes its toll on footwear.

For this reason, in the 1980s, it was common to see women like Melanie Griffith's character in *Working Girl* wearing sneakers with their panty hose, then changing into sky-high pumps once they arrived at work, but now women tend to wear more practical shoes all day, or to carry little flats that fit into a purse in case they need to take off their heels and run for a train.

I understand that people would rather just throw out shoes when they get old, but I encourage you to develop a relationship with a cobbler instead. It's better for the environment and will save you money. My mother had a college roommate who owned a pair of alligator pumps, real alligator. They were very expensive and my mother coveted them. She returned to their room one evening and found the pumps in the waste can. Why? The soles were wearing out. My mother was aghast. Maintenance! If you had a Rolls-Royce and its oil was running low, would you abandon it and buy a new one?

People on job interviews underestimate the importance of a shined shoe. The wrong shoe or poorly maintained shoes can ruin one's look and impression. I have a vivid recollection from a meeting of the Board of Governors at Parsons. A candidate for dean was being presented. He was a handsome, well-spoken fellow in an impeccable black suit, white shirt, and black tie. All was going well, until the cocktail reception following the meeting. For the course of the meeting, we had been seated. We stood for the reception and there they were, the candidate's ancient shoes: scruffy, unpolished, black dress shoes that looked as though they had walked ten thousand miles over rugged terrain. It was startling. And it was such a discordant note considering the rest of his outfit. I saw one of the board members take the president of the university aside, gesture to the candidate's shoes, and say, "Never!"

When I was doing press for my last book, *Gunn's Golden Rules,* I appeared on *Good Morning America.* When I appear as a guest on talk shows, hosts will often ask me what I think of their clothes. Well, I was shocked when *GMA*'s George Stephanopoulos eviscerated his own footwear. He gestured to his loafers and said apologetically that he hadn't shined his shoes. Indeed, they seemed as though they hadn't been shined in quite a while, and they were falling apart at the seams. I wouldn't have called attention to it if I were him—especially because his comment persuaded the cameramen to take a lingering close-up of the decrepit footwear!

Polishing one's shoes is so easy that I don't quite understand why people put it off. Polish that dries is a phenomenon of the twentieth century. In Victorian times, polish never dried, and all this wet polish had an impact on furniture, resulting in the attachment of fringe to the bottom of upholstery—chairs, settees, and divans. When excessively soiled by the pol-

ish, the fringe could be replaced. Polish today is quick and easy and there's no excuse for an excessively scuffed dress shoe.

That said, may I tilt at that shoe-maintenance windmill called shoe trees? Does anyone actually know of someone who has and uses them? I don't. And it's one of the very few lies that I tell. When buying a new pair of shoes, the sales associate almost always asks me whether I also want shoe trees. "Thank you," I respond, "but I have plenty." I find that it's easier to lie than it is to engage in a conversation about what their benefit may be (I get it!). They're expensive (roughly $30 for cedar ones) and their use requires *time*. I'd rather spend my allotted shoe-maintenance time on polishing.

I must confess that I'm a bit of a shoe junkie; I have a lot. When it comes to dress shoes, I have a special affinity for monk straps (reminiscent of—you guessed it—monk's shoes), the two sides of which are fastened together with a distinctive buckle.

I am not as big a fan of lace-ups, because I'm usually in a rush. I choose shoes that are easy to get on and off at the threshold of my front door. Lace-ups are not among them. So I tend to stick with monk straps, slip-ons, and pull-on boots. The one go-to lace-up that I do own are the black patent leather oxfords that match my tuxedo. They're classic, timeless, and always reliable. I'll add that I used to own a pair of those effete patent pumps with a large grosgrain bow on the vamp. Frankly, they *killed* my feet, because the vamp was so low cut. After an evening on the red carpet, I'd feel as though I needed workman's comp.

Whatever kind of shoes you like, and however well you take care of them, you should know that footwear has traditionally been associated with honor. In biblical times, the sandal was a symbol of fair trade. Ruth 4:7 reads: "Now this was the manner in former time in Israel concerning redeeming and concerning changing, for to confirm all things; a man plucked off his shoe, and gave it to his neighbour: and this was a testimony in Israel."

And shoes don't only signify integrity; they also symbolize luck. It's for this reason that shoes have been tied onto the backs of wedding cars and hidden in the chimneys of buildings to act as a talisman for its inhabitants. In this sense, shoes are your very own good luck charm, and they follow you wherever you go.

opposite: It's traditional to tie shoes to the car of the just married, as here in 1936.

15.
ATHLETIC WEAR
Attack of the Playclothes

Sweat suits, swimwear, hoodies . . .
Get thee behind me, yoga pants!

ALL OVER AMERICA, you see women in yoga pants and men in sweatpants, even when they are not on their way to or from a yoga class or softball field. When I fly, I see so many sweat suits—even pajamas—on my fellow travelers that it's as though the airplane were the sleeper car of a train bound for summer camp or a gym in the sky, not a public space for business people and vacationers.

To me, this is an example of the "monkey house at the zoo" phenomenon I'm always talking about: when you walk into the monkey house, you're struck by the horrible stench, but after a while you stop noticing that it stinks. But this is not progress! You may have lost your sense of smell, but the place doesn't smell any better than it did when you walked in. Replace the smell of monkey excrement with the sight of people wearing yoga pants at a nice restaurant and you have my analogy.

I blame Casual Fridays. This fashion holiday has only been around for twenty years, but what a toll it has taken on workplace fashion! The first Casual Friday, called Casual Day, happened in 1991. It was a nationwide fund-raising event cosponsored by Levi Strauss & Co. and United Cerebral Palsy. The concept was that employees could "buy" the chance to dress informally by making a donation to the UCPA.

Casual Day was such a popular event that many businesses continued the tradition, establishing a day of the week when its workers could dress down. According to a follow-up study by Levi's, by 1996, 90 percent of American office workers were allowed to dress casually on Fridays.[1] To which I say: well played, Levi's! Who knows by how much they have increased their company's profits by sneaking jeans into the boardroom.

The Casual Friday trend in workplaces has avalanched into Casual Everyday for many Americans. I am forever meeting people—*employed adults*—who have nothing but T-shirts, jeans, and cargo shorts in their closets.

"Don't you need at least one suit or nice dress for weddings or funerals?" I always ask.

They insist there's no need. Either they don't go to any special events, or the ones they do go to are casual. This usually strikes me as delusional on the part of the individuals in question, but maybe they're right. Perhaps America has become such a land of casual comfort that we are careening toward a sweatpants-at-the-opera future.

For now, though, seeing casually dressed people in formal settings is still shocking—to me, at least. And I'm not completely alone. I have heard from brides that they feel disrespected by guests who show up in tracksuits, or by the bereaved when their friends show up tieless and jacketless at the funeral home.

This holds true when we are guests abroad. Europeans are aghast at the shorts, fanny packs, and ill-fitting graphic T-shirts we wear into their glorious cathedrals when on vacation. The "ugly American" stereotype is not far from the truth. Our insistence on wearing what makes us comfortable—even if it makes those around us uncomfortable—is one of our less attractive national attributes.

I would argue that most of what falls into this chapter should be kept to gyms, tennis courts, and beaches, and definitely out of the workplace, unless you're an aerobics instructor. Consider this chapter something of a manifesto. I hope realizing that so much of our daily clothes were until very recently purely athletic wear will show us the way out of the monkey house.

But maybe we still haven't hit bottom. James Laver writes, "The power of a fashion once it is launched has something extraordinary about it. It is like a force of nature—a flood, an avalanche, a forest fire. Nothing seems to be able to turn it back until it has spent itself, until it has provoked a reaction by its very excess." Let's hope we're near the apocalyptic end times when it comes to slovenliness. To this end, I will offer some thoughts about what are popularly known as sweat-suit alternatives. But first, let's clear up a common misconception about American sportswear.

There's a difference between sportswear and wear for sports. When I was teaching in Korea, I would tell my students to design sportswear, and they would come back with baseball jackets—in other words, sports-wear. Sports-wear means clothes worn for sporting events. Sportswear means daywear—mostly separates, like a polo shirt and a skirt or pants.

The sportswear category is fairly elastic, though, and can include casual dresses, even fashion denim. Think Michael Kors. He's as close as we come today to classic American sportswear. Kors's designs offer sophistication and polish. These are classic items, casual but not dowdy—simple but not sloppy.

Edward, Prince of Wales, epitome of the British sportsman, was wearing oarsman tank tops out in his rowboat way back in 1920,[2] but the international explosion in sportswear is very American. As early as 1938 retailers started to notice that Americans took short trips all year round and so needed casual vacation clothes for every season.[3]

Time magazine's 1955 cover story on one of my all-time favorite designers, Claire McCardell, suggested that her rise mirrored the rise of leisure sports in America. She saw what she called "playclothes" as the future.[4] In fact, casual sportswear became known in the 1930s and '40s as the American Look. And yet, these early "play" garments managed to be as well made and attractive as they were comfortable and fun.

And they were never worn in the business world. They were clothes for playtime. Traditionally, vacation means an exemption from the usual rules. Alison Lurie writes that this often means tourists dress like children: "They wear styles identical with those sold in the baby departments of stores: elastic-waistband skirts and shorts and slacks, polo and T-shirts with easy-off open necks and snap closings, and rompers or crawlers (now called 'jump suits').

"These simple garments are constructed of the traditional materials of infant wear—cotton jersey, seersucker and polyester—and come in the traditional colors: pale pink, pale yellow, baby blue, lime green and white. Often they are printed or appliquéd with whimsical images of birds and beasts, the penguin and the alligator being current favorites."[5]

And yet, over the past fifty or so years, America's "playclothes" have become ubiquitous, not just confined to the resort. They have gone from being clothes to wear while having drinks on the beach or road tripping with the family to being clothes you wear to the theater, church, or a business meeting.

This explosion of athletic wear and rompers is very ironic when you think about how much more sedentary we've become. As we've become less active and higher-tech, we're wearing more and more workout clothes.[6] In 1975, Adidas came out with a jogging suit made of nylon and polyester, with three stripes running along the sides of the arms and legs. Run-DMC and other rap groups popularized these tracksuits in the 1980s. They went mainstream fast. In 1984, President Ronald Reagan himself went before reporters on Air Force One wearing sweatpants—although he teamed them with a collar and tie.[7] Ever since, hip-hop artists and fans have appropriated athletic wear as streetwear. Brands like BAPE (a Bathing Ape) have created high-end versions of sports clothes.

As a cultural uniform, this kind of attire is successful. The Kangol cap or Adidas jacket signify allegiance to the world of hip-hop, the same

Bike messengers helped spawn the spandex craze of the eighties.

way lots of dark eyeliner marks you as a goth. But unless you actually are a hip-hop artist, chances are that tracksuit makes you look like you belong in a gym, not onstage at Madison Square Garden.

The 1980s were the era when athletic wear really took over. This happened in subtle ways, as with the striped rugby shirt. But it also happened garishly, as in the rise of the mesh shirt, which was derived from football uniforms.[8] Most atrociously, we saw the explosion of spandex (an anagram of the word "expands"), especially as bike shorts began being worn by people who were not often on bikes.

In 1987, a *New York Times* fashion writer named Woody Hochswender described bike messengers as "envoys of chic."[9] These messengers took their look from competitive European bicyclists, and the people of America took it from them. I think history affords us the hindsight to say we should have left those skintight nylon shorts to the people who actually made a living on their bikes (further points may be deducted because their pocketless nature brought us one of fashion's true abominations: the fanny pack).

Let me now share an anecdote that may clarify for you my dislike of 1980s fashion, especially bike shorts. For three years in the mid-1980s, I was director of the Office of Admissions at Parsons. It was a role that I was proud of and took very seriously, and I'll add that my success in that position led to my appointment as associate dean. The office was responsible for a number of publications, including the annual college catalog, along with smaller direct-mail pieces targeted to high school seniors who received high scores on both their SATs and Advanced Placement or International Baccalaureate art and design exams.

Parsons's director of publications, Janet Levy, was an extremely talented designer and also happened to be a dear friend. Janet showed me a design for one of the recruitment publications and, frankly, I was horrified by it. I asked, "Janet, what happened? You have such wonderful taste and clarity of vision. This doesn't look like you."

"It isn't me," she responded. "I contracted out for it, because I wanted a fresh perspective. I like the designer's work and believe that this is a very good piece."

Well, I actively hated it: it was a cacophony of graphic symbols and a kaleidoscope of colors and patterns; it made me feel as though I were on the verge of a seizure. While I had indefatigable confidence in Janet, I did not share Janet's confidence in this designer or her work. Janet suggested that the three of us meet.

"When you meet the designer" (we'll call her Susan), she said, "and listen to her point of view, I think you'll have a better understanding of why I'm so positive."

Fine.

Janet and I sat in my office waiting for the designer, Susan, to arrive. I couldn't stop staring at the design work in question; unbelievably, it was beginning to grow on me. But was that merely monkey house at the zoo syndrome? In any case, I was eager to meet Susan and learn more about her inspiration and motivation for this design.

Susan was late. This is never good, but it is especially problematic when the conditions of the meeting are somewhat strained at best and contentious at worst. Janet and I continued to wait. (Remember, this was in the dark days—or were they brighter?—before voice and text messages.)

Eventually, I was informed that Susan had arrived. I went to greet her in the reception area, where there was a flurry of activity—nervous applicants, admissions counselors speaking to parents, a tour about to depart, and a bike messenger—but no Susan. Perhaps she was freshening up. I stood and waited. Finally, I interrupted the receptionist to ask about her. The receptionist gestured and said, "She's right there." Where? There! Susan . . . was the person whom I had mistaken for a bicycle messenger.

"Hello," I said through gritted teeth.

Can you imagine showing up for this appointment, and showing up *late*, wearing spandex shorts and a matching jacket over a tank top? And can you imagine being amply endowed and

wearing no support of any kind under the tank? If Susan were pedaling around Central Park, this outfit would have been fine (though she would have benefited from a sports bra). But this outfit was unsuitable and inappropriate for a professional meeting. I was appalled. It's semiotics, right? What message did this outfit send about her and her feelings about meeting with us?

I led Susan into my office; Janet explained that I had concerns about the design of the direct mail piece. Susan looked at me and said, "Go fuck yourself!"

That was it. I turned to Janet and said, "This meeting is over." Susan left. Janet was embarrassed. The direct mail piece was incinerated. Lesson: never underestimate the power—sometimes profound and other times subtle—of the semiotics of clothes.

Headbands were also popular during this dark period in fashion. The 1980s headband has an interesting ancestor in the frontlet worn by women during medieval times under their veils. By the late fifteenth century, these were usually bands of black velvet. In the sixteenth and early seventeenth century, the frontlet was worn with a bonnet. In the eighteenth century, the frontlet was covered in cream to remove wrinkles. "In vain, poor nymph, to please our youthful sight / You sleep in cream and frontlets all the night," wrote Thomas Parnell in "An Elegy to an Old Beauty" in 1722. Of course, the fitness craze more than 250 years later came from a similar impulse to preserve youth.

If the 1980s brought us spandex and tracksuits, the 2000s delivered a new athletic-wear scourge: yoga pants. Inexpensive at Old Navy, costly at Lululemon, yoga pants have exploded in popularity across the country. In the last few years, they've become a default for many women going to the grocery store or getting on an airplane.

Nicollette Sheridan leaves a Beverly Hills salon in low-slung pants and a hoodie, 2008.

I can understand why they have replaced the traditional sweatpant. The traditional light gray fleece sweat suit conjures up unpleasant images of the 1980s fitness craze. By comparison, yoga pants have a cachet. Tabloids snap celebrities wearing them in parking lots—"they're just like us"! But they are not meant for the outside world.

Paired with the yoga pant, you often see the slightly more redeemable hoodie. The hoodie is an interesting fashion phenomenon. Hooded cloaks were popular in Europe until the second half of the twelfth century, when the hood became a separate garment.[10]

In the United States, the hoodie's origins are the sweatshirt and children's coats. It used to be difficult to find an adult coat with a hood built into it, but now it's a common fashion accessory. It signifies youth and hipness and can look stylish. I wonder about its timelessness. I doubt we would have seen Jackie Onassis in a hoodie. And yet it is a perfectly respectable casual garment. Following the shooting of unarmed black teenager Trayvon Martin in February 2012, protests like the Million Hoodie March showed how absurd Geraldo Rivera was when he claimed the "menace" implicit in that article of clothing was to blame for that tragic and unjust death.

Another article of sports-wear—one that you see less often on the street, although who knows what the future will bring—is the swimsuit. Evidence of the bikini appears on urns

dating from 1400 BC Greece. And there is an incredible bikini mosaic from the third or fourth century AD in a villa in Sicily, specifically a room called Chamber of the Ten Maidens. The mosaic is formally called *Coronation of the Winner*, and is known less formally as "the bikini girls." It depicts young women in what look like very modern bikinis, with strapless tube-style tops, playing such sports as discus throwing and lifting weights.

But these were workout ensembles, not swimsuits. It appears that skinny-dipping was the rule for both women and men from antiquity all the way until the seventeenth century, when women began to wear bathing costumes at spas.

The Victorian era marked the birth of the swimsuit as a fashion item. Thinking it was a healthy choice for cold-water bathing, people actually wore swimwear made of flannel or wool! The earliest women's suits had

Bathing dress, 1858.

Bathing machine, 1924.

long sleeves and a long skirt over pantaloons. The skirt was often weighted down—literally, with weights in the hems—lest it float up in the water.

Men wore full-coverage swimsuits that could have doubled as long underwear. But over time, with the exception of the Speedo, men have had it pretty easy. Now we have a wide array of shorts to choose from, none of which are as scandalous as the string bikini for women.

The history of women's swimwear features a tension between a desire to be free and a desire to preserve modesty. Architecture for a time arranged a compromise. In the eighteenth and nineteenth centuries, in the United States and Europe, bathing machines were popular. They were little changing cabanas on wheels that could be driven straight into the water, so that you could change inside and then jump right in the sea, so no one saw you in your bathing clothes, wet or dry.[11]

But as people got more serious about their athletic lives, all those little rolling cabins and all that fabric started to seem unnecessary. In 1907, swimmer Annette Kellerman was arrested on a beach in Boston for wearing a tight one-piece. But the streamlined one-piece could not be stopped, and from then it was only a matter of time before everyone was wearing one, even if they still insisted on covering up as soon as they were out of the water. Tropical beach pajamas were a popular casual-wear trend in the 1930s, and some of them are pretty adorable.[12] Typically, the pants were wide leg and the tops were halters, giving a slight bell shape.

In the 1940s, one-pieces and two-pieces existed side by side, although the two-pieces were hardly the stuff of Miami Beach today. They were sturdy and bright, and looked more like shorts or skorts with cropped tank tops.

This brings us to the famous bikini. Even women in France, whom popular culture would have us believe are topless at every opportunity, blanched when they saw the first bikini on July 5, 1946. To be fair, the suit was so small it could fit into the tiny matchbox with which the model posed.

This was four days after the first post–World War II nuclear experiment. This bomb test took place over the South Pacific atoll called Bikini, and it was something of a fiasco. According to Patrik Alac's *The Bikini: a Cultural History*,[13] "By no means all of the target

Mermaid Club, Philadelphia, c. 1920.

ships, painted bright yellow and orange for the occasion, had been sunk, and the primary target vessel, the destroyer *Nevada*, had escaped damage altogether."

Four days later, the bikini's designer, Louis Réard, debuted his scandalous new two-piece bathing suit—made from a print that resembled newspaper—at a "most beautiful swimmer" press event, and gave it the provocative name "bikini." The name "bikini" provided what Alac calls "a strange link between on the one hand, a murderous weapon and on the other, a girl wearing a sexy bathing costume."[14]

It seemed like a natural press sensation. But at first, Réard couldn't find a single model willing to debut it! Finally, he recruited the nineteen-year-old nude dancer Micheline Bernardini, for whom the scandalous two-piece was downright demure. That day at the Piscines Auteuil-Molitor in Paris, Bernardini and her string bikini were a source of fascination, but the bikini was far from an instant hit.

In fact, another two-piece from 1946 was more popular: French couturier Jacques Heim's similarly named Atome, billed as "the smallest swimsuit in the world." (Réard called his suit "the bathing costume even smaller than the smallest swimsuit in the world.")[15] Heim sensibly covered the navel, which was more compatible with forties propriety, and his was a far bigger hit, although it was the name of Réard's garment that would live on.

People got a little giddy when the bikini went mainstream, 1966.

Fabric rationing apparently played some part in the popularity of two-pieces. According to one fashion textbook, during World War II, "cloth used in women's swimwear had to be reduced by 10 percent."[16] Getting rid of the middle of one-pieces was one way to do it. Still, *Vogue* didn't show a two-piece suit in its pages until July 1948.[17] And through the forties and fifties, the bikini remained relatively chaste. Typically the waistline came to above the belly button. It wasn't until the sixties that bikinis became more revealing.

The James Bond movies helped popularize the skimpy bikini and give it back its Piscines Auteuil-Molitor ability to shock. Ursula Andress, in her role as Honey Ryder in *Dr. No* (1962), famously rises out of the Caribbean Sea wearing a white bikini. From that moment until the present day, with its

Micheline Bernardini models Louis Réard's new bikini, 1946. The little box she's holding is the container for the bikini when it's not being worn.

Sports Illustrated Swimsuit Edition and weekly tabloids' "Best Bikini Bodies!" headlines, the tiny bikini has dominated the public's sense of the ideal bathing look.

Never mind that it looks terrible on nearly everyone except models. Many of us in this age of the bikini can understand the impulse the Victorians had with their bathing machines. Unless you have a "bikini body," it can be difficult to find flattering bathing wear that doesn't ride up or fall off with the first strong wave.

The widespread acceptance of the bikini belies many women's anxiety about the garment—and I hear them. There's no reason not to split the difference between Ursula Andress and those weighted-down wool skirts: a bikini top or tankini with a skirted or shorted bottom is usually more flattering than a string bikini. And if that's not enough coverage, let's lobby our designers to bring back beach pajamas!

Swimwear has played another significant part in the way athletic wear is worn on the streets today: it helped start the craze for prominent logos on clothing. Jantzen Swimwear was founded in 1910 in Portland as the Portland Knitting Company. An image of a diving girl in a red bathing suit decorated the cover of the 1920 catalog, and this logo went on to become, for a time, one of the best-known in the world.[18]

Now logos are everywhere. Walk down any street in America and you are sure to see at least a couple of Nike swooshes (designed in 1971).

So, why are logos so popular? I believe it has something to do with the cachet of heraldic crests and their American descendent: lettermen jackets and varsity sweaters. The *H* of the Harvard baseball team emerged even before Jantzen's diving girl, probably in the late nineteenth century.

To this day, wearing a school crest or letter is a symbol of prestige. That must have filtered down into our subconscious somehow, such that we desire little embroidered badges on our clothes.

According to one scholar,[19] "the logo is the modern equivalent of the maker's stamp; the hallmark or trademark that indicates the authenticity of a product." Beginning in the 1940s, that trademark, originally used to prevent piracy, moved to the outside of garments. The tennis star Fred Perry spawned a brand of sportswear that made use of a club crest displayed on the front of shirts and sweaters.

Another popular logo is the Lacoste alligator, which has come to epitomize preppiness. Tennis champion René Lacoste invented a new kind of tennis shirt in 1926 at the age of twenty-one. His nickname was "le Crocodile," because of how aggressive he was on the court, so he put the symbol of a crocodile on his white tennis shirts, which entered the market in 1933.[20] In 1977, Le Tigre introduced a tiger that rivaled Lacoste's alligator for animal-brand chic.

In the 1980s and 1990s, international sporting goods companies like Nike became omnipresent, and so did their logos. Starting in the 1980s, designers like Tommy Hilfiger made their logos increasingly prominent, and corporate logos became status symbols.

From 1995 to 2000, collections by designers including Gucci, Fendi, Dior, and Louis Vuitton saw the fanatical repeat of logos on clothing, such that the fashion press called it "logomania."[21] Nothing screams "fashion victim" to me more than someone covered head to toe in brand names.

At this point, we should talk about sneakers, as sneaker companies like Nike are arguably the most popular brand logos in the world right now. The first sneaker was a high-top canvas shoe with a rubber sole, invented in 1892 by Keds, but starting in the 1950s, the sneaker left the sports arena and was worn in public. Elvis Presley helped make them cool, as did Andy Warhol.[22] By the 1980s, the craze for jogging had put leather running shoes in closets across the country.

We know that this ubiquity is largely due to an American move to a more casual menswear appearance, but it is also due to the aggressive marketing of companies like Nike and Adidas. Since the mid-1970s, athletic shoes have outsold fashion shoes every given year. I have a confession to make: other than two pairs of John Varvatos for Converse "no strings," a slip-on version of the classic Converse sneaker made popular in the middle of the twentieth century, I did not own a pair of sneakers until we had our Heidi Klum for New Balance challenge in Episode 5 of *Project Runway* Season 9.

I do all that I can to support our sponsors (we couldn't have a show without them!) and wanted to be on-brand for the challenge. In this case, I ran out to one of those mega sporting goods stores in Times Square on a mission for New Balance shoes, size 10.5/11. I was successful, but I'm not used to wearing "real" athletic shoes. Those of you who own them and wear them know that they are engineered for buoyancy, and, in some cases, sport-

Keds from the 1950s.

specific applications such as tennis, basketball, or running. So, we launched our *Project Runway* challenge at the Armory, an Olympic and college training facility next to Columbia University.

I arrived with the producers and crew before Heidi and the designers. One of the producers called to me from across the indoor track, so I went running to see what she needed. I had no idea that the huge expanse within the track was a series of concave and convex shapes, painted to be an optical illusion of flatness.

Ha! The joke was on me. I ran and went flying twenty feet, landing on my wrists and fearful that I had broken one or both. No, I survived, but within seconds I realized that my right foot was aching, the foot on which I'd had surgery the December before. Just then, Heidi arrived and wanted me to run the track with her.

"Run the track?" I said. "I can barely walk."

Heidi looked at me as if to say, *Have a backbone!*

I find it very hard to ever say no to Heidi. So I ran.

At the end of a long and painful day, I returned to my apartment and had to cut the laces off the shoe in order to get it off my foot, because it was terribly swollen and I was in awful pain. When I finally went to the doctor five weeks later (yes, he yelled at me for waiting so long, but we were shooting!), I learned that I had broken three bones in my foot and they had incorrectly healed. To make a long story shorter, the proper wearing of athletic shoes requires a certain deftness of experience; make no assumptions that by simply trying them on, you will become an instant Olympian.

That reminds me of the new craze for running shoes in which the toes are articulated. These have been around since 2007 and are called glove shoes or barefoot shoes. One of the most popular brands is Vibram FiveFingers. The marketing behind them is that they mimic the barefoot running experience of successful marathon runners from Africa. But these marathoners have grown up running that way; we haven't. Also, aesthetically, they are just so *creepy*. They look like an alien foot. The only nice thing I can say about them is they make Crocs look slightly less awful by comparison. (Watch, now their value will skyrocket. Every time I say something bad about Crocs, it seems their stock rises.) If I ever find myself in need of a running shoe, I'll stick with sneakers. But I hope that won't be for a long, long time.

Now for a bit of fascinating—and surprising—history of the sneaker: Henry VIII (who ruled England from 1509–1547) delivered ideas related to athletic footwear during his reign, clearly a very early reference to the subject. The king was overweight and believed that tennis would help him slim down. However, he had no suitable footwear for the activity. Accordingly, he ordered the royal footwear maker to create a shoe that would help him be nimble

Michael J. Fox in *Back to the Future Part II*, 1989.

while playing tennis. What was created for him (in six pairs, no less!) was a light, canvas shoe with a felt bottom. While this is hardly the precursor of today's sneaker, it is a prime example of early footwear with an athletic function.

One of the more memorable sneakers to appear in pop culture in recent decades is the glowing Nike sneaker in the 1989 movie *Back to the Future Part II*. Trading on nostalgia for the shoe in the film, in 2011 Nike issued the Nike Mag, a limited-edition reproduction to benefit the Michael J. Fox Foundation for Parkinson's research. Alas, unlike the film shoe, the Nike Mag does not lace itself.

Sneakers can be objects of genuine obsession, much like Hermès scarves or Chanel purses. It was distressing in the 1990s to see news reports of teenagers beating each other up for their Air Jordans. Basketball hero Stephon Marbury, who grew up in New York City projects near Coney Island, responded to this sad state of affairs in a generous and creative way. In 2006, he created a stylish sneaker—the Starbury One—that cost just $14.98. The Starbury is a nice-looking sneaker with a celebrity spokesman, and it is accessible in price to pretty much every family.

Now, even though there are great sneakers out there, I put this shoe in the athletic-wear chapter rather than in the shoe chapter to drive home the point that they, like yoga pants and sweat suits, belong primarily on the playing field rather than in every facet of American public life.

At this point, as this athletic-wear chapter comes to a close, you may be asking, "If you're so smart, what *should* people wear while running errands?"

I'm so glad you asked! When I do wardrobe makeovers and encourage people to lose their ratty athletic grab, one of the first things they profess a need for is a so-called sweat-suit alternative. It becomes a matter of finding a garment that has all the ease and comfort of the sweat suit without being a sweat suit.

Now, first, I'd like to make the argument that you should look and feel good even at places you may feel don't count. Specifically, the question I hear from makeover subjects robbed of their sweat suits is: "What will I wear to the *grocery store?*"

Grocery shopping is a public activity. If you're not moved by respect and enthusiasm for your fellow humans, imagine running into someone who you do want to impress, like an ex-boyfriend or girlfriend. Won't you feel better in that scenario if you aren't completely rumpled?

Besides the vanity factor, there is the matter of ease. Anyone claiming that a sweat suit is the "easiest" garment has clearly never worn a soft dress. The dress is one piece instead of two, and all you have to do is throw it over your head rather than step into legs. If you get a wrap dress, that's just putting arms through holes and tying a knot. If the fit is correct and the proportions are right, you'll be just as comfortable as you would be in a sweat suit, but you'll look so much better.

This is not a new problem. In 1942, Claire McCardell came up with the adorable $6.95 Popover dress (see page 79). The simple gray dress came with a matching pot holder, which fit neatly into a big pocket on the skirt. The idea behind it was that you could "pop it over" your body to clean the house, then throw on a string of pearls and be ready for a cocktail party. It was the original sweat-suit alternative. The dresses sold like hotcakes; an example is now in the collection of the Metropolitan Museum of Art—and on page 79.

It depends on your lifestyle and your taste but, generally speaking, the modern sweat-suit alternative for women would be an item with some stretch. If you don't want to wear a dress—because, for example, you're going to be climbing jungle gyms in the playground with your children—consider pants and a top or a T-shirt and jeans. And have on hand a cardigan or a jacket in case you need to dress it up quickly (see: ex-boyfriend encounter, above). There are plenty of easy, unfussy clothes out there that speak to your lifestyle but don't make you look as though you belong in a spin class.

When I deliver this speech to people in mall events I host, I often hear a lot of defensiveness.

"Everyone does it!" people will say of wearing yoga pants around the town.

"So, lead!" is my unsympathetic response.

When my friend's young son says, pointing at a playmate, *"He* started it!" his parents' response is not: "Okay, then." It's: "So, *you* end it."

Let's end it together. Let's invest in comfortable, attractive, all-American sportswear, and leave the sports-wear to the world of sports.

131

1326

1273

170

9016

350

141

2092

2058

16.
SWEATERS
Knights, Fishermen, and Sweater Girls

Jerseys, knits, crochets . . . The cavalry has arrived—wearing cardigans.

NOW THAT WE'VE put on our underwear, our dresses, or our pants or skirts with tops, we can start adjusting for temperature. If we're in a chilly part of the country, we now also need a barrier between our bodies and the cold. The best way to do that is with a knit sweater, a garment as romantic as it is practical.

One of my favorite parts of one of my favorite movies is the "cerulean sweater" scene of *The Devil Wears Prada*. Miranda, the editor in chief of *Runway*, lectures young Andy about her condescending attitude toward fashion. And as loath as I am to agree with Miranda on anything, she is right to point out that fashion is neither shallow nor inconsequential.

"What you don't know is that that sweater is not just blue," Miranda says of Andy's lumpy sweater. "It's not turquoise. It's not lapis. It's actually cerulean. And you're also blithely unaware of the fact that, in 2002, Oscar de la Renta did a collection of cerulean gowns. And then I think it was Yves Saint Laurent—wasn't it—who showed cerulean military jackets. And then cerulean quickly showed up in the collections of eight different designers. And then it filtered down through the department stores, and then trickled on down to some tragic Casual Corner—where you, no doubt, fished it out of some clearance bin."

Now, I don't love the dripping disdain with which Miranda treats her underling. But I do love that scene, because it reminds us how much history there is in every garment we own. The color, the shape, and the texture—none of it is accidental. Every item we wear has a glorious (or sometimes not so glorious) history, and that history extends back years—centuries, even—before Oscar de la Renta's 2002 collection.

Whether they come from Brooks Brothers or a thrift store, the sweaters we wear have a magnificent ancestry. Their history spans the worlds of Irish fishermen, French knights, World War I soldiers, busty Hollywood "sweater girls," and the television saint Mr. Rogers. That history lives in each garment. By being aware of it, we can better appreciate what we

Anne Hathaway and Stanley Tucci in *The Devil Wears Prada*, 2006.

have. Rather than lecture people about what items they have to have in their wardrobes, I prefer to help people appreciate what they already have at their disposal and to make those things work.

Of course, even this lofty garment has its perversions. May I direct your attention to the Santa-bedecked Christmas sweater? Holiday sweaters—much like Bill Cosby's hideous repertoire, which I will describe in greater detail in the unfortunate 1980s section of this chapter—have always given me heart palpitations. My family loves those knitted reindeer-and-holly atrocities.

This kind of history helps us appreciate the innovations of modern-day designers, and, more important, to better enjoy the contents of our own dressers. When I see Liz Claiborne's vibrant fall 2010 patchwork sweaters, Michelle Obama's elegant beaded cardigans, or the latest resort color-block from Proenza Schouler, I immediately flash back on the thousands of years that got us there. Knowing the history helps me enjoy the garments more than if I just saw them as so many hunks of anonymous fabric.

Still, the ancient past is often the least fun part of history books, for me, anyway. The information is always so *sketchy*. And it is just so hard to wrap my head around the few fragments of data that exist or to trust all the experts' conclusions about those scraps.

I've spent a long time trying to figure out the earliest example of the sweater, and the earliest example of knitting. Alas, I'm left with far more questions than answers. Did you know that knitting is believed to be a fairly recent invention? Everyone says so. But I don't believe it. Wouldn't taking two pieces of fiber and weaving them by hand strike you as being the most natural way of making something? Far in advance of a *loom*, for goodness sake. That's such a sophisticated process. You'd think that aside from an animal skin, the earliest garment would have been knitted. Well, *I* would think that. No one else does.

Just to clarify: I want to make a distinction between weaving and knitting, because I found myself getting lost while attempting to defend knitting's lineage. Here's the basic distinction: a woven fabric possesses no "give"; that is, it's a static textile that doesn't stretch. Knits, by definition, stretch and move. When tight around the body, knits assume the shape of that body. When loose, knits have an organic, cascading effect.

When we refer to any woven garment (made of yarns, threads, or even reeds or grasses), we mean a textile that possesses two distinct sets of components: the warp and the weft. The warp pieces run lengthways on the textiles, and the weft components run perpendicular in an in-and-out weaving manner. In fact, "weft" is an Old English term meaning "that which is woven."

Now, on to knits. Knitting requires that one take two rows (sometimes more) of thread or yarn and, using a needle, stitch them together in a series of consecutive loops. Each stitch requires that a new loop be passed through with the next loop in order to make a bond. Once done, the process continues with the next loop, always on the needle or needles. The act of knitting generally produces the final garment, whereas weaving does not. The fact that knitting's structure of loops possesses less density than weaving's warp and weft is what is responsible for the resulting stretch.

I have an unsupported speculation to make, that is, that knitting may sit alongside weaving as being our earliest form of garment making. Detractors say that early knitting would require more sophisticated (i.e., man-made) knitting components than reeds or grasses, which could easily be used in weaving. I counter that in ancient times there were, and there still are, myriad flora with which one could knit: vines, bamboo, and papyrus being among the more obvious. In fact, being presented with a vine, for instance, it strikes me as being much more intuitive to braid them in order to build volume rather than to overlap them vertically and horizontally.

Owing to the ephemeral nature of textiles, the history of knitting in general is full of mystery and unanswered questions, because there are precious few ancient fragments available in museums. What I wouldn't give for the finding of a Mesolithic bog person dressed in knitwear, similar to the Iron Age one found in a sphagnum bog in Northern Europe wearing preserved leather shoes. What may, indeed, be found at archaeological sites are ancient sharpened sticks used for knitting. They may be in museums today, mislabeled as shallow-water fish spears or small roasting skewers.

In Julie Theaker's essay "History of Knitting 101," she writes: "Linguistically, all evidence implies that knitting is a fairly recent invention. There are no ancient legends of knitting like there are legends of spinning or weaving. . . . There are no ancient gods or goddesses who knit, no legend of how it was invented or given by the gods.

"That lack implies that it is a recent skill, developed after mythologies were established around the world." Theaker goes on to write: "A quick cruise of the Oxford Unabridged English Dictionary also reveals that the term 'to knit' wasn't added to English until the 1400s. . . . It's pretty obvious; knitting hasn't been around that long." (Once added, it was evidently popular: Shakespeare used the term thirty-eight times in plays written between 1590 and 1620.)

I'm in no position to challenge or impugn Julie Theaker's words. However, I'm a big believer in nomenclature; that is, the terms that we use to describe a person, object, activity, or event can change. So, while "to knit" and "knitting" may be relatively new terms, it doesn't necessarily mean that the activity is new. Did the renaming of Constantinople to Istanbul wipe out the history of that great city? Do we really believe that what we call a fork today was always called such?

In fact, there is evidence that even in 4200 BC, in what is now Denmark, they did what's called "needle binding" or "twined weave" with plant matter. It seems to me that this physical act of braiding is just a baby step away from the slightly more complex knitting. But apparently it took more than five thousand years for someone to pick up a second stick and invent what we now know as knitwear.

I marvel at lapses like that. It always makes me wonder what we're missing now that will seem so simple in a few thousand years. Perhaps teleportation is totally obvious, and when we figure it out we will feel just as silly as I hope all those generations of needle binders felt when knitting needles came into vogue.

In any case, there's no doubt that there was real knitting by the end of the Middle Ages, which is practically yesterday afternoon from a historical perspective. Starting around this time, you even see paintings of the Virgin Mary knitting. In one by Lorenzetti from circa 1345, the Madonna is sitting on the floor knitting with two needles while Jesus leans on her shoulder. When I look at it, I can't help wondering: Is she making him a sweater?

If it's hard to know the precise origin of knitting, it's also hard to pinpoint the very first sweater (which I'm defining as shirtlike outerwear made of something that resembles knitting, even if it's not technically made by the two-needle process).

Knitting Madonna, detail from the Buxtehude Altar, 1400–10, by Meister Bertram von Minden.

Looking through museum collections, you see some very sweaterlike things in the Bronze Age, such as a women's top from an oak coffin grave in Egtved, Denmark, from about 1370 BC. It was paired with a string skirt and a belt and is quite fashion-forward, in addition to being warm and functional. There are some beautiful Greek and Roman sculptures where the subjects are wearing something that looks a bit like an H&M tunic sweater.

But what *I* like to think of as the very first sweater is a knight's chain mail. You start to see these garments in Europe made from links of steel around 300 BC, but they really got going in the thirteenth century. Chain mail covered the chest and arms, and the process by which it was made was, essentially, protoknitting. The word "mail" even comes from the French word *maille*, which basically means "knitting."

Chain mail was what protected soldiers' bodies for hundreds of years and would have kept on doing so, too, if it hadn't been for improvements made to the crossbow in the fourteenth century. According to the Metropolitan Museum of Art's beautiful *Arms and Armor* book (a must-have for every knight-obsessed twelve-year-old), the new crossbow made it easy to pierce mail. That meant the armor makers had to develop plate armor to go over the chain mail. A bonus of this innovation was that soldiers no longer needed to hold shields, because they were wearing small shields all over their bodies.

Can you imagine being a soldier and suddenly having the use of both your hands? It must have seemed like a miracle, not unlike the epiphany Diana Vreeland had in the thirties when she discovered the liberating impact of pockets for the modern woman. Unfortunately, she was prevented from leading this particular revolution. Her superior informed her just how many millions in revenue handbag advertisers brought to the magazine, and that was the end of that. Thank goodness there was no shield-makers lobby back in the 1300s.

I also think of the sweater's origins as a symbol of patriotism and freedom from oppression. When the Pilgrims left England for America in 1620, fleeing religious persecution, they were at sea for more than two months, their futures uncertain. So what did the women do? There was no room for a spinning wheel, so the author of the great knitting history book *No Idle Hands* suggests they likely knitted their way to the New World.

We sometimes think of knitting as something domestic and insignificant, but throughout history, the craft has had a very political role. In our country, it symbolized our self-sufficiency. During the French Revolution, it symbolized fate. Madame Defarge sits quietly knitting in Charles Dickens's *A Tale of Two Cities,* but what she's really doing is knitting the names of those condemned to die in the revolution. It makes you look differently at that sweet grandmother innocently clicking away in her rocking chair, doesn't it?

One of the great lines from the 1985 movie *Pee-wee's Big Adventure* that I've always related to is: "The mind plays tricks on you. You play tricks back! It's like you're unraveling a big cable-knit sweater that someone keeps knitting and knitting and knitting and knitting and knitting and knitting. . . ."

That always reminds me of the fact that my mother told me every year for forty years that she was knitting me a fisherman's cable sweater, but the sweater never did materialize. Most grandmothers worth their salt have at least a few half-finished sweaters in their closets. But I'd bet that even they don't realize how full of symbolism those one-button gansey and jersey sweaters from the mid-1700s were. Officers wore solid colors. Sailors wor stripes. The ship's name was often embroidered on the chest.

According to *Cables, Diamonds, Herringbone: Secrets of Knitting Traditional Fishermen's Sweaters*, every sweater motif had a symbolic meaning. Every shape made by the yarn represents something: luck at sea, a happy marriage, religious fervor. Cables were ropes on ships. Diamonds were fishing nets. Herringbone was the success of the catch. Zigzags were lightning or paths through the cliffs. Hearts were love. The cross was God. Anchors were a safe journey. My favorite: zigzags were "marriage lines," referring to the ups and downs of married life. In addition, villages in Ireland had their own sweater patterns, and each sailor had his initials knitted into his sweater. How convenient, considering the rate of shipwrecks back then! If a fisherman washed ashore, everyone would know from looking at his sweater exactly where to send the body.

What's especially amazing to me about these early sweaters is that there were no pattern books. With her mother's help, a girl would begin knitting her first sweater when she met a man she was interested in marrying. Amusingly, knitters today talk on online message boards about the "sweater curse," which suggests that giving a hand-knit sweater to a loved one dooms the relationship. Those garments are so much work, I can imagine it would put a lot of pressure on both the knitter and the knit-ee to make and give one as a gift. It was probably good that men who wore the original fishermen's sweaters vanished for months or years at a time.

In fact, it's notable that the sweater was originally conceived as the garment of a man who did heavy work: jousting, fishing, and fighting wars. Even the cardigan, which now seems so ladylike, comes to us from the battlefield—in fact, from one of the toughest battles of them all.

If you had to memorize any poetry in grade school, odds are among the verses you learned was Lord Tennyson's 1870 poem "The Charge of the Light Brigade" about the infamously bloody 1854 battle of Balaclava. Here's a bit of it:

Cannon to right of them,
Cannon to left of them,
Cannon in front of them
Volley'd and thunder'd;
Storm'd at with shot and shell,
Boldly they rode and well,
Into the jaws of Death,
Into the mouth of Hell
Rode the six hundred.

But did you know they did all that *wearing cardigans*?

Their commander, Lord Cardigan, led his regiments of hussars dressed up as Hungarians with large fur caps and collarless, open-front jackets. Cardigan sweaters soon became all the rage.

Around this time, another officer named Lord Raglan gave us the raglan sleeve, because he lost his arm in the battle of Waterloo and needed loose-fitting sleeves that were easier to get in and out of.

The Saint James Company (which is still around) made its name in 1889 by creating what was known as "the genuine pure new knitted woolen Breton seaman's sweater" for deep-sea fishermen. It had the sailor's black-and-white stripes, and it quickly became a cult item in France. In one photo of Picasso, he is sitting at a kitchen table in his Breton sweater, his lower arms hidden behind the table, and fake hands made of bread appearing to emerge from his elbows. He looks mischievous and yet still very elegant.

The fall 2010 collections were *full* of black and white stripes similar to the original Breton. No one *needs* to know that those stripes were originally created to help sailors spot

Pablo Picasso at lunch, 1952.

their drowning crewmates bobbing in the ocean, but doesn't that information make a trip to Style.com that much more fun?

If the sweater started out as a man's garment, women started to adopt it when they became more physically active. Victorian women became very sporty at the end of the 1800s, and like men, they needed something to wear biking, rowing, or playing tennis. The long, voluminous dresses they were used to wouldn't work, so they started wearing knitted wool.

Victorian sweaters, as their name suggests, encouraged and absorbed sweating and allowed a full range of movement. Oddly, if you look at the pictures of sweater-clad women from this time, you see that they still had these tiny-waisted, huge-chested silhouettes. That's because they often still wore insanely restrictive corsets under their workout clothes.

Back to the sweater. Alice Maynard had a yarn shop on Madison Avenue, and a popular book: *What to Knit and How to Do It* (1903). The Maynard sweater, a turtleneck cable knit, became the sweater of the decade. Aside from the ridiculously emphasized hourglass shape underneath it, these sweaters wouldn't be out of place today.

The same cannot be said of the mutton-sleeved bicycle sweaters that predated them. Imagine, if you will, a tight neck, tight waist, and huge, poufy shoulders. These sweaters look fantastically silly, and it's hard to believe all those Victorian women didn't fall off their bicycles laughing at themselves.

Meanwhile, at all-male Princeton, freshmen at the turn of the last century were only allowed to wear black turtleneck sweaters for their full first year. Seniors could wear a white canvas suit "perfect for protecting Brooks Brothers jackets from leaky keg taps," according to *The Places and Spaces of Fashion,* but as part of their hazing rituals, the freshmen were stuck with black sweaters. You can imagine how grateful they were for a little color in their closets once they finished their first year. Of course, many young men didn't spend much time on campuses. They were shipped off to war, and the sweater followed them there.

When the United States entered World War I, American women wanted to help the soldiers overseas. The Red Cross was quick to tell them what they could do: knit. Red Cross knitting pamphlets abounded, such as 1918's "Uncle Sam Wants You to Knit to Protect His Boys—Over There." Slogans encouraged women to knit "for Sammy," to "Knit for Victory!" (A World War II British slogan was: "Make Do and Mend.")

This wartime knitting phenomenon resurfaced for subsequent wars, as well. "He's the one who's trying to make a better world for you and me," *Smart Knitting* magazine told its readership during the Korean War. "Here's the G.I. turtle-neck sweater. For this one he'll be grateful to you forevermore."

One of the all-time most creative designers, Elsa Schiaparelli burst on the scene in 1927 with, yes, a sweater. She had Armenian knitters use a traditional three-needle knitting process to make her a black-and-white sweater with a trompe l'oeil knotted bow around the neck. The graphic made it look like a real bow, but it was actually two-dimensional. I associate Schiaparelli's work with wit and whimsy and a bit of a wink, and the trompe l'oeil bow is the epitome of that. The sweater was illustrated in *Vogue* and became a huge hit, paving the way for such innovations as her famous lobster dress collaboration with Salvador Dalí.

By the 1930s, women were wearing sweaters all the time, not just for exercising. During the day, they wore jersey dresses, thanks to Coco Chanel's innovations. At night, they wore sweaters embroidered with jewels and sometimes trimmed with fancy materials, such as chiffon.

At lunch the other day with friends, I couldn't take my eyes off a woman across the restaurant from us. She had the largest breasts I'd ever seen. It's not that I was attracted to her, God knows. But she kept gesturing to them and holding them. It was hard to look away.

Maybe she just got a breast augmentation and she's celebrating? I thought. She seemed very proud. But honestly, I don't think that overabundance of cleavage is flattering. It's often matronly, which I think is the opposite of the effect that is intended. Breasts pouring out of a top tend to make a woman look like a past-her-prime Mae West type rather than the voluptuous vixen she's trying to emulate.

Girls knit for the troops in their spare time, 1943.

Sweater girl Lana Turner with Linda Perry in *They Won't Forget*, 1937.

If only this woman took as her mentor not Pamela Anderson but the sweater girls of the 1940s. The first sweater girl was Lana Turner (who, it must be said, loathed being called that). She got the nickname from wearing stretchy sweaters that showed off her curves. But that's all they did: show off her shape, not copious amounts of heaving flesh. That way she was able to play the girl next door and be sexy at the same time. The famous "sweater girl bra," so popular in the 1950s, helped. These used padding and circular stitching to create a dramatic, sculptural effect. (I almost recommended to my busty restaurant neighbor that she consider renting Lana Turner's film *They Won't Forget* to see what a sweater can do for a woman while preserving some shred of modesty, but I held my tongue.)

During this era, some teenage girls went with the Sloppy Joe style of the 1940s: men's shirts with cardigans and rolled-up jeans. Meanwhile, boys were all about varsity sweaters. The June 28, 1954 issue of *Life* magazine promoted "Sweater Girl Bathing Suits," wool-knit swimwear shaped like one-pieces with short sleeves and boy shorts. They are totally adorable and seem wholly impractical.

Sweaters have always been tied to athletics in various ways. They have been used as workout wear since the turn of the last century. They are also associated with hockey players. Isn't that amazing, that they can be so versatile? Change the athletic sweater to black and make it a turtleneck rather than a crew and suddenly it epitomizes bohemianism. Audrey Hepburn wears such a sweater in *Funny Face* (1957), paired with ballet flats and horn-rimmed glasses.

Soft sweaters have been an enduring symbol of femininity, at least since they were used in the Z-grade Ed Wood movie from 1953, *Glen or Glenda,* in which a man longs to wear his wife's white angora sweater.

This era shows how slight modifications to the same garment can change it from a symbol of female sexual power to a guard against flying hockey sticks. The more I look into these cultural shifts, the less patience I have for *Project Runway* designers who say there's no way to save a garment they're working on. The 1940s and '50s taught us that, with just a few little alterations, you can take a model from Joe College to Audrey Hepburn.

The faux innocence of the sweater girl is mocked in the notorious "cashmere sweater club" plot of the utterly bizarre 1966 black comedy *Lord Love a Duck.* In one particularly insane scene, Tuesday Weld gets *very* excited by a table full of cashmere sweaters.

"What color is that, baby?" she is asked.

"Lemon meringue!" she shrieks, biting her lip in ecstasy. "Pink put-on! Yes!" She becomes increasingly orgasmic in the store and ends up writhing in a mountain of cashmere. I always wonder what impact that film had on the sale of those sweaters.

The truth is, by the time the Kennedys were in the White House, you were seeing a lot more sweater sets, popcorn knits, and varsity sweaters than tight angora numbers. Everyone wanted to look like Jackie Kennedy during the early sixties, and she inspired generations of preppy young people to tie sweaters jauntily over their shoulders.

It's always amazing to me how one costume choice in a popular film can affect a whole generation of fashion. Faye Dunaway's turn in the 1966 film *Bonnie and Clyde* cast her as a 1930s bank robber with a penchant for cardigan sweaters. Suddenly thirties cardigans were back in.

But in general, the sweater girl went out of fashion by the end of the 1960s, because the idea of sexiness had changed. Girl-next-door wholesomeness was out. Sophistication was in. The popular skinny-rib sweaters were flattering to the newly in vogue slim body type.

Around this time, designers became more creative with knitwear. Beginning with their 1967 debut, Rosita and Ottavio Missoni turned knitting into an art form, making stylish zigzag sweaters using a weft knitting, in which one thread intertwines in horizontal rows, a technique that before that had been mostly used for home furnishings.

Sonia Rykiel was called the queen of knitwear for her vibrant striped sweaters.

Paco Rabanne brought it all back to the knights with a line of chain mail dresses and separates in 1969.

By the midsixties, the sweater girls were far too curvy for magazines. In 1966, Twiggy, aka the Cockney Kid, was dubbed "The Face of '66" by London's *Daily Express*. She wore a sweater and pants to play up how androgynous she looked.

Isn't that incredible, that in the course of ten years, the same garment could go from being the most feminine to the most masculine item at a woman's disposal? And that a single garment can at once represent debauchery and dowdiness? Such versatility!

Just a few weeks after being inaugurated in 1977, Jimmy Carter gave his first TV address on the country's energy policy. Instead of wearing a suit, he wore a cardigan. His message: wear one of these and turn down the thermostat. It kicked off an era in which the sweater was identified with frumpiness and practicality.

Also, with gentleness: according to CNN, many of the cardigans worn by the wonderful Mr. Rogers on his children's program were hand knit by his mother. A craft revival brought us innumerable sweater vests. Sweaters were soft, soothing—and a little bit boring.

Until, that is, Halston, Liza Minelli's personal designer, created asymmetrical sweaters that were certainly a long way from PBS. They screamed style, disco, and late-night parties.

The black turtleneck also became a kind of counterculture uniform, now for beatniks and the Black Panthers—amazing how just fifty years before, it had been the symbol of the cowed Princeton freshman.

By the end of this schizophrenic era, sweaters represented both fuddy-duddy-ness and edginess, safety and danger. We should all keep that in mind when doing a

At a Black Panther Party meeting, a poster criticizes the arrest of Panther leader Bobby Seale, who wears a black turtleneck.

top: Mr. Rogers, the ultimate cardigan wearer.

closet purge. Think: is your sweater more Jimmy Carter or more Halston? Sometimes it just takes changing up your icons to change your whole outlook.

Speaking of misbegotten icons: we can't forget *The Cosby Show* and its nefarious impact on American outerwear. For all the good Bill Cosby has done in the world, it must be said: as Heathcliff Huxtable, he had the most awful sweaters in world history.

One time when I was doing makeovers on *Oprah*, I was asked to help dress a man who wore nothing but hideous sweaters in offensive colors and textures. I knew those combinations of yellow, purple, brown, turquoise, and orange reminded me of something, but I couldn't quite place it at first.

Bill Cosby made Coogi sweaters famous on *The Cosby Show*, which ran from 1984 to 1992.

opposite: President Jimmy Carter wears a cardigan in the White House library during a televised fireside chat about energy conservation. April 18, 1977.

The makeover subject eventually confessed that his style icon was Bill Cosby. He'd fallen in love with the look in the 1980s and never updated it. You would think he would have trouble finding them in today's department stores. In fact, the still-thriving Australian company Coogi created the Cosby sweaters. (The Notorious B.I.G. helped popularize Coogi sweaters, as well as Kangol caps.) Would you believe, Coogi still makes Cosby sweaters? And they still cost upward of $300 each.

If you are tacky but also frugal, there are also various sites online that sell replicas of the Cosby sweaters for less than Coogi charges. In any case, I had to pry these puce-and-gold monstrosities out of the arms of this man on *Oprah*.

I sometimes see young people wearing similar sweaters ironically, but irony is no excuse. Those colors and patterns are an affront to nature and should be left in the 1980s, where they belong.

The next phase in sweaters was even more aggressively antifashion, but it was infinitely more pleasing to the eye. When the music of the Pacific Northwest became popular in

Nirvana's Kurt Cobain wore the vintage sweaters that helped define the 1990s grunge look.

opposite: Michelle Obama in a sweater set, 2010.

the nineties, cardigan sweaters became all the rage across the country, even in warm climates. Soon after Nirvana became popular, you saw young men and women dressing in these thrift-store sweaters—even in Texas in summer.

This look had an androgynous, of-the-people appeal, and it was wonderful how this era brought vintage clothing to the masses. People don't remember this now, but there was once a stigma against wearing secondhand clothes. Now you even see celebrities bragging on the red carpet that they are wearing vintage Chanel or vintage Count Sarmi.

In the early 2000s, there was a backlash against the 1990s, and suddenly lightweight knits were more formfitting. Pamela Anderson and the Pussycat Dolls ushered in a sweater girl–like body ideal, but they showed a lot more skin.

Luckily, by the end of the 2000s, the pendulum had swung back, and we had Michelle Obama wearing fashionable, but also accessible, J.Crew sweaters, even to 10 Downing Street to see the prime minister.

The era in which we're living is a wonderful time for the sweater. There are a million different styles that are flattering to various women's body types. At no time in history have we had so many options, and yet we're still developing new shapes and fabrics with which to create outerwear. I can't wait to see what the future holds.

So, what might that be?

According to a 2003 article in the *New York Times Magazine*, a class called Weaving Material and Habitation at Harvard's Graduate School of Design "has been experimenting with Lycra-spandex type materials that can stretch out to four times their original size. A poncho or sweater might expand into a 7-foot-by-4-foot tarp."

Will we need to sleep in our sweaters in the future? I certainly hope we are not visited by such an apocalypse. But I am glad the designers of America are working on the sweater-as-bomb-shelter option, just in case.

17.
COATS AND JACKETS

From Cavemen to Real Housewives

**Pelisses, trenches, peacoats . . .
Why fur belongs in the dustbin of history**

WALKING DOWN Madison Avenue on a January afternoon in 2011, you could look into the Dolce & Gabbana window and see leather jackets hanging on a rack in the window alongside a T-shirt with a photograph of a young Marlon Brando on it. This shirt from the spring/summer collection made it clear that the Brandolike motorcycle jackets on display were no accident. They were deliberately referencing the bad boy of fifties film.

Humans have worn animal skins since our earliest beginnings on the earth, when animal skins were chewed to make them soft enough for clothing. There is evidence from the Bronze Age of a man wearing a sheepskin jacket. Furrier tools were found in the first Bulgarian kingdom dating back to the seventh century AD.[1]

Even in the north, in the coldest of climates, we only need to worry about warm outerwear for a few months out of the year, and those of us who work inside and drive everywhere can get away with not being entirely serious about cold-weather clothing. In fact, as we've seen, a great deal of showing off one's class is wearing ridiculous, weather-inappropriate garb. Thorstein Veblen wrote in *The Theory of the Leisure Class,* "It is by no means an uncommon occurrence, in an inclement climate, for people to go ill clad in order to appear well dressed."[2] Nietzsche wrote that a pretty woman who feels she looks her best never catches cold even in the skimpiest dress. (Of course, have you seen his massive mustache? That's not necessarily someone from whom you want to take fashion advice.)

Friedrich Nietzsche, 1887.

In New York and L.A., I've noticed that some women who have a car and driver don't wear coats at all. They simply step from their limo right into the party. In those cases, not wearing a coat is a status symbol. It says to the world: "Who needs a coat? I'm never exposed to the elements."

The former *Vogue* editor in chief Grace Mirabella once said to a woman wafting to the lobby in her evening dress, "Don't you need a coat? You might wind up waiting on the corner for your car!"

"No," the woman said, unconcerned. "I wouldn't exit the lobby until I saw the car was there."

I find that to be really obnoxious! At least *pretend* you don't lead that rarefied a life.

Let's assume, though, that you do actually need to be out in inclement weather and so require something in the way of a jacket or coat.

Outerwear's history is pretty opaque. The Greeks and Romans wore mantles over their togas. These Greek and Roman cloaks were indispensable.[3] People were very fussy about how the mantle hung from their shoulders, with every fold signifying something about their station in life. But unless you time travel back into that era, you probably don't need to know all the details.

In medieval times, when everyone was wearing robes that looked more or less like opera coats, there were sumptuous coats called cotehardies. Or was it houppelandes? Pourpoints? I'm not sure! There are so many names for coat variants back then. It's like keeping track of all the characters in Russian literature! In the twenty-first century, we can't take it too seriously. How much do the various differences really matter to us today?

But there are a few interesting footnotes. Sir Walter Raleigh probably never did lay his cloak on a mud puddle so that the queen could walk over it, as legend has it. But he *did* wear a rather strange jacket called a mandilion or mandeville. This was worn sideways; one sleeve hung down in front and the other in back. What I find fascinating is that eventually they stopped making working sleeves, and so these pieces of fabric hanging down became merely decorative.

This reminds me of the 1990s teen habit of tying one's sweatshirt around one's waist, which became so prevalent that an inventor named Kathy Kramer came out with the BootyWrap, basically a discreet fanny pack shaped like a sweatshirt tied by the arms. Once you've gone that far down the road of commodifying a trend, it seems to me the look loses its cool factor. (Perhaps someone should start making jeans with fake underwear sticking out from the back to finally put an end to that one!)

Then along came Marlon Brando wearing a leather jacket in *The Wild One*. He kicked off a trend in which young people dressed like workingmen as a way of rebelling against the gray-flannel-suit–wearing establishment. It was the first time dressing down was used as a way of rebelling. Yes, Chanel and McCardell used workingmen's fabrics on their high-end women's garments, but they didn't have overtly political motivations in doing so. Of course, you would have thought they'd stormed the Bastille, the way people responded!

Sir Walter Raleigh, 1588.

Michael Jackson
on tour in 1984.

Here they were in their wool car coats and swing coats, and suddenly here are these rebels wearing *leather* and *denim*. Everyday coats had been relatively consistent since the end of the eighteenth century, when cloaks and coats—such as the redingote and pelisse—replaced mantles and capes. Fabrics, lengths, and detailing may vary, but the general look of the coat was a midlength or long garment with set-in sleeves.

There have been interesting variations based on the needs of each region and era. The car coat of the suburban 1950s was shorter (hip length to three-quarter length) and looser to make traveling easier. The swing coat of the 1960s was cut in a loose way so that it would swing away from the body.

Until the end of the 1700s, outerwear often hung over the shoulders rather than having set-in sleeves. Capes returned in the 1970s, and they are back now. What I love about a cape is that you can dress it up or dress it down. You can wear it with a pair of jeans or with an evening gown. If it's simple and streamlined, it has a lot of versatility; if it's complicated—covered, say, with Western fringe—it's more limiting. There are as many fabric and pattern options with a cape as with any garment, but by definition a cape has volume, so you need to be a bit more conscious of not overwhelming the rest of your outfit. Ideally, to keep the proportions right, you should pair it with something slim.

But jackets are still, as of this writing, far more common than capes. I think that's in part because jackets are more practical—it's hard to carry an over-the-shoulder bag when you're wearing a cape! And there are so many significant jackets in fashion history. In the 1980s, Michael Jackson created a frenzy for the zippered red leather jacket designed by Claude Montana for the music video "Beat It." Stadium Management Corp. trademarked the jacket and mass-produced it in 1984. In 2011, the original was auctioned off by his costume designers, Dennis Tompkins and Michael Bush, and sold for $1.8 million. For me, that look defines the 1980s. All that excess, all the flamboyance and exaggerated silhouette were rolled into one garment. And it was unisex! Of course, if you wear it now, it looks like you stepped directly out of that decade.

In the 1990s, Triple F.A.T. Goose and other down jackets were all the rage. The puffy coat isn't usually very flattering. Warm it may be, and it certainly has a history in the hip-hop community, but unless it fits very well, it's better suited to ski slopes than city streets.

While puffy coats came to us from outdoorsmen, most other coats we see on streets today owe their look to soldiers and seamen. "Uniforms are the sportswear of the twentieth century," the wise former *Vogue* editor Diana Vreeland once said.[4] That's especially true of military uniforms—"the first ready-to-wear garments," according to fashion historian Stefano Tonchi. Need proof? British sailors gave us the peacoat, derived from an early sailor's canvas coat tarred to make it waterproof (thus, tarpaulin). That's why sailors to this day are sometimes called "tars."

Fighter pilots gave us the bomber jacket. Epaulettes (shoulder boards) were originally intended to protect the shoulders from swords. Women's dresses have for centuries often featured some variation on a lancer's breastplate. Whether it's called a stomacher, plastron, gilet, or placard, you can't help but see the influence of knight's armor.

The Napoleonic Wars (1793–1815) seized the popular imagination, and the elaborate military costumes of the time found their way into everyday clothing. One woman of the period wrote in her memoirs of how much attention she received when she "walked out like a hussar in a dark cloth pelisse trimmed with fur and braided like the coat of a staff-officer, boots to match, and a fur cap set on one side, and kept on the head by means of a cord with long tassels."[5] In their military inspiration, some English walking ensembles from the early nineteenth century look eerily like the red leather Michael Jackson jacket of the 1980s.

Epaulette-wearing soldiers at West Point, 2009.

A century later, British World War II soldiers gave us the wide-bodied, narrow-waisted Eisenhower jacket. Originally called Wool Field Jacket M1944, the short coat was supposed to conserve fabric. The future president General Dwight D. Eisenhower was a fan and took to wearing one himself. The buttons are now typically zippers, but variations of this field jacket are now in many American men's closets. One fashion historian says variations on this jacket are actually "the most common piece of sportswear in the male wardrobe."[6]

Military wear has influenced fashion for centuries, but the trench coat is an example of civilian dress influencing the military. The belted trench was invented in England, probably by Burberry, for "shepherds, farmers, and country gentlemen for protection from wind and rain."[7] In World War I, soldiers wore the civilian garment into the muddy trenches, and so it became named a "trench coat" even before being officially adopted by armies. Movies like 1942's *Casablanca* made the trench

Dwight D. Eisenhower and Winston Churchill, 1945.

coat the de facto costume of smart tough guys and spies, and then it entered the fashion arena.

And, of course, we can't discuss outerwear without mentioning fur. Fur was so desired in Europe a few hundred years ago that there had to be laws about who could have it. From the fourteenth through seventeenth century, English kings and queens passed sumptuary laws regulating the best kinds of fur so that only the upper classes would have access to it. That way you could tell the classes apart by looking at their coats. If it was gray squirrel or ermine, the owner was probably an aristocrat. If it was a lesser fur, such as otter or hare, the owner was probably in the middle class. The poor wore wolf, goat, or sheepskin.[8]

Coats of the finest fur still connote status today. But not everyone is as impressed. When I see the women on the *Real Housewives* shows

Humphrey Bogart in *Casablanca*, 1942.

with their fur coats, it makes me sick. And I'm not alone. When Kelly Bensimon of the New York show bought a fur vest, she said, "It's amazing to have an organization like PETA, but I've always been a great fur wearer. . . . Do I wear fur? Yes. Do I support the abuse of animals? Absolutely not."

"Really?" Chelsea Handler responded on her show "You don't abuse animals? I think the chinchilla who just had his hide ripped off might disagree."

Vanessa Williams once defended her fur coat by saying, "I didn't kill it!"

Well, maybe you should have! Then you'd have some connection to what fur is about.

For years, I have spoken out against the cruelty of the modern fur industry. Before there was indoor heating, I can understand needing fur to keep warm. Besides, back then there weren't the same mass-production facilities, although, even hundreds of years ago, the fur trade had a real impact on nature. Beau Brummell reportedly almost decimated the beaver population because of his proclivity for beaver hats.

I once believed that it would be very difficult to have a luxury brand without fur in it. When I joined Liz Claiborne Inc., Dan Mathews from PETA came to meet with the company. We had a very serious conversation about the forty-six Liz brands going fur free. I said we could have the conversation, but that in the case of Narciso Rodriguez, one of the company's

A U.K. ad for fake fur, 1960s.

brands at that time, I believed it to be an impossible task. Fur is inextricable from his brand, so I said we needed to leave Narciso alone.

But over time, I became convinced that fur was unnecessary and even immoral. If you go to the videos at the PETA or Humane Society websites, you can see how much brutality is involved in putting together a single fur coat. There was resistance at first to eliminating fur, especially from our Juicy Couture and Kate Spade brands. But they came around. Today their faux-fur coats are adorable, and they are accessible to more people because they don't cost nearly as much as a real fur would. When we eventually parted with Narciso, we were fur free.

Now, my bile rises when I see fur on someone in this day and age. A fur coat today is the grossest form of conspicuous consumption, with only the possible exception of Kim Kardashian's $2 million engagement ring. Is it really necessary? Just because you can afford it, that doesn't mean you need to have it. It's gross. And I seldom use the word "gross." Few items of apparel to me are as gut-wrenching and repugnant as a full-length fur coat. It begs the question: why? We no longer need fur for warmth and protection. There are plenty of textiles that provide that today. It's pure whim and vanity to choose to wear fur. It shows a level of ignorance or lack of concern that reflects poorly on the wearer.

For me, leather is different. Animal rights purists see no distinction, but I see it from a fashion perspective. There are plenty of superb fake furs out there, which for me obviate the reason to wear fur at all. I even prefer fake fur that looks fake. But with leather, there aren't good synthetic options. When there are, I will wear fake leather, but I still haven't encountered a reliable leather alternative. Real leather breathes, which is important in shoes, boots, and jackets. Aesthetically, too, there's quite a difference between real and synthetic leather.

Certainly, though, if you don't like leather, while there are fewer alternatives in the shoe department, there are still plenty of good jacket options. For both women and men, I consider a cotton twill trench coat one of the essential items. It can be lined or not, so it transcends climates, unlike a topcoat. You can wear it in Florida or in Wisconsin. It doesn't have to be the classic Burberry military-inspired trench in tan. It should just be a coated cotton with a lining that can come out. That means it can transition between seasons. You can wear it to the grocery store or to the opera. It can be very fitted or it can be loose. It can be any color. A great red patent leather trench is always fun. Kate Spade has a great black one with a pink lining.

If you have a burning desire to spend thousands of dollars on a coat, you don't have to buy a fur. Take to eBay and go after something genuinely special, like a Poiret opera coat or a Pucci cape or a Trigère car coat. You will own a part of fashion history, and you won't be contributing to animal cruelty or fashion victimhood. Most important, you'll never be mistaken for a Real Housewife.

18.
HATS
Crowning Glory

Baseball caps, fedoras, berets . . .
The lost etiquette surrounding hats indoors

ONE PERK of covering the 2011 Royal Wedding for ABC was the opportunity to visit the atelier of Philip Treacy, arguably the greatest hat designer in the world. When I arrived at Treacy's London showroom the week of the wedding, it was bustling. Hats and U.K. fashion are inextricable. For the wedding, the royals and the upper crust of London society were sparing no expense when it came to their accessories.

Princess Beatrice arrived and greeted me. "I haven't seen the hat yet!" she confided. "I wonder what it will be like!"

"I'm sure it will be memorable!" I said enthusiastically.

Was it ever! There was no missing the princesses Beatrice and Eugenie, who were so done up with frippery that they looked a bit like—please forgive me, princesses—Ewoks. (The costume-y makeup didn't help.) Most of all, I was struck by Beatrice's hat. It was about the size of her head, pink, and rather resembled a toilet seat tied with a bow. The hat was a major source of conversation the next day, and it was later auctioned for some six figures to benefit a charity. I was right: it certainly was memorable.

But: back to Treacy's studio. After the *ABC News* cameras went off, Treacy said to me and to my ABC colleague Cynthia McFadden: "Now I can show you the lineup."

Princess Eugenie of York and Princess Beatrice of York, both in Philip Treacy hats, arriving at Westminster Abbey for the wedding of Prince William, 2011.

He turned around three six-foot-long blocks of foam core. They contained photographs of probably eighty women attending the Royal Wedding alongside their hats. When it came to designers for that event, people talked most about Alexander McQueen, because his house created the exquisite wedding dress, but Treacy was the most represented designer at that wedding, bar none. His hats and fascinators—lighter-weight headpieces of lace, feathers, or ribbons—were everywhere.

As we looked through the hat pictures, Cynthia, bless her heart, asked Treacy what I was wondering: "Aren't they a little, um, over-the-top?" she ventured. "I can't imagine wearing one of these."

Treacy was matter-of-fact: "This is perfectly acceptable in this culture," he told us.

It's true: over-the-top hats are the British way. Of course, so are dowdy hats. There's not much in between those two extremes in the U.K. In Britain, women are always either dressed in the most somber outfits, or they're floats in a parade.

We learned from Treacy that the queen has a hat made for every outfit. Actually, she has two hats made—and this made me laugh: one spare, *in case of wind*. Non-royals love their hats, too. In London, you can buy a Philip Treacy for hundreds, or you can go to Marks & Spencer and get a nice-looking everyday hat for the equivalent of $20.

"I guess we just aren't hat wearers in America," I said, shrugging. "You see fedoras on men sometimes, but they tend to be ironic."

Treacy corrected me: "Who in America isn't wearing a baseball cap?"

That's exactly right. We're not antihat. We're just against *dressing up*.

We can't throw a stone without hitting someone in a baseball cap. These have been around in America since the earliest days of baseball in the mid-1800s. They were originally soft but have become more structured with time. The dome of the cap now usually has air holes and there are sometimes Velcro, snap, or plastic fastenings. Since the 1980s, they have been part of young people's standard clothing repertoire.

I don't object to a baseball hat. A baseball cap brim can be shaped. It can enhance your face. I do object to

Jay-Z in a Yankees cap, 2010.

trucker hats, because they don't conform to the shape of your head. The trucker hat is an immobile structure that protrudes from your head—very unflattering. But caps generally have a long history in the West, particularly as country or athletic wear. Stiff visors came into vogue as early as the 1880s. The 1890s saw the creation of the "hook-down cap" for tennis and golf. Caps without brims are traditionally infantilizing: from the 1890s to the mid-1950s at many colleges, freshmen were made to wear beanies or "dinks" or "ducs" as a kind of hazing.[1]

Baseball caps can proclaim your allegiance to various teams or subcultures, especially hip-hop. Jay-Z raps in his New York City anthem "Empire State of Mind": "I made the Yankee hat more famous than a Yankee can." Indeed, the baseball cap is separate from sports in many people's minds. The culture around the baseball hat is such that every company, church, or theme park has its own baseball hat. You can instantly proclaim yourself to be on any "team" just by putting on the appropriate hat.

And yet, few people observe the etiquette of hats, which is that men shouldn't wear hats indoors, period. People often wear them to cover up a bad hair day even in the office, but it's not technically proper. One of the more traditional and mature faculty members in my department at Parsons always insisted that her students remove their baseball caps in her classroom. She was of an era when it was considered insulting to wear a hat in the presence of a teacher, and I respected that. Well, students rebelled!

Liza Minnelli wears a bowler in *Cabaret*, 1972.

top: Charlie Chaplin wears the same hat somewhat less sexily, 1910.

"Having to take my hat off compromises who I am as a fashion person," one student told me.

"Get over it," I said. If this were a question of religious observance and a student needed to wear a veil or yarmulke as part of her or his practice, then that is something else entirely—but if it's just a matter of wanting to accessorize your outfit with a White Sox cap? Come on. If you're a real "fashion person," you can find something to wear that can accommodate both your sensibility and an authority figure's reasonable request.

Even before the baseball cap came around, there has been a distinction made in the West between the "cap," which is less formal, and the "hat," which is more formal. Newsboys wear caps. Businessmen wear hats. In America, certainly, we tend to associate the non-baseball-cap hat with formality or uptightness, or with America before the 1960s. In noir movies, men like Humphrey Bogart are never seen outside without a hat. The men of *Mad Men*, too, are always in fedoras, soft felt hats with a brim and a crease in the top that runs front to back.

Though it's identified with the 1940s and '50s, the popularity of the fedora dates to Paris in 1882, when Sarah Bernhardt wore a variation on such a hat in Victorien Sardou's play *Fédora*. When the play came to America a few years later, the *New York Times* called it "the strongest drama written in recent years" and called her performance, "not likely to be equaled on the stage within the knowledge of playgoers now living." The fedora caught on as a fashion for women until the 1920s, when it became an affordable men's hat, good for all weathers.

A hard felt hat with a rounded top and a rolled-up brim has been around since the 1820s, but it took the name "bowler" around 1860 from the hat maker William Bowler. Though it's a very traditional hat, known in the United States also as a derby, for many of us it is associated with capital-*S* Showbiz thanks to performers like Charlie

Chaplin, and to legendary choreographer-director Bob Fosse, who used the hat as part of his choreography. Liza Minnelli seductively dons one in his *Cabaret* (1972) along with thigh-high tights and a revealing top and pair of shorts.

Another popular hat in recent history is the trilby, named after the Parisian artist's model in the 1894 George du Maurier novel and subsequent play, *Trilby*. A subculture of Jamaican-British men in the 1960s, who called themselves Rude Boys and went to dance halls, wore the trilby or the porkpie (similar, but with a flat top) along with thin ties and flashy suits. Their hat choice was inspired by American gangster movies. Later ska music revivals in the late 1970s, and then in the '80s into the '90s, brought back the porkpie hat.

The homburg hat looks to the untrained eye more or less indistinguishable from the trilby and fedora, but it has a set crown that can't be manipulated. It's the epitome of the stuffy British hat, and quite formal, although nothing's as formal as the top hat, which like most hats has more or less fallen out of favor in America outside of Halloween. In the middle of the nineteenth century, the chimneylike top hat could be up to eight inches tall! For many people, it's linked with the great dancer Fred Astaire, because of his 1935 movie *Top Hat* and because he always wore the hat so elegantly. Or, if you're of a slightly younger demographic: the

Fred Astaire wears a top hat in *Silk Stockings*, 1957.

Slash of Guns N' Roses wears a top hat on stage, 2005.

former Guns N' Roses guitarist Slash. It's also a mainstay of the steampunk subculture, whose members often sport neo-Victorian attire.

Men and women in the South still wear cowboy hats, which appear to have originated, like so much of supposedly all-American cowboy culture, with Mexican ranchers as early as the 1830s,[2] and are originally from Spain.

In recent years men like Michael Jackson and characters like Indiana Jones have created frenzies for one kind of hat or another, but men in America are far more enamored with baseball caps than felt hats. American women, too, are more likely to wear baseball caps, despite the incredible history of women's hats.

Women of recent centuries have worn such a dazzling number of different kinds of hats and caps, even just

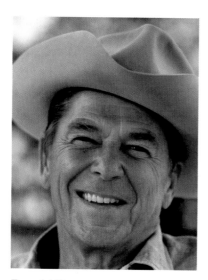

Ronald Reagan wears a cowboy hat at Rancho del Cielo, 1976.

right: Sitting Bull and Buffalo Bill in a headdress and cowboy hat, 1885.

since the 1500s, that it boggles the mind. Among the variations: the caul, fontange, round-eared cap, pultney cap, mob cap, butterfly cap, Marie Stuart cap, babet bonnet, and the Charlotte Corday cap. During the medieval period alone, there were so many different kinds of headgear—many outrageous, with cones and such—that it can make your head spin.

Some of these hats had veils. This started when the Crusaders returned from the East around the 1200s and brought with them a variation on the Islamic veil. (Fascinatingly, they also adopted the Eastern habit of buttoning dresses down the side, allowing for a snugger fit across the bust.) Veils were popular at various points in the 1800s. In the 1870s, they were long enough to cover the face and to be worn around the neck as a scarf. There were some beautiful veiled hats in the first half of the twentieth century, but unless they're deliberately evoking a bygone era, like the burlesque star Dita Von Teese, most women now only wear one on their wedding day, if at all.

From medieval times on, "bonnet" was the term for a soft cap that fit the head closely and had a crown and usually a brim. Bonnets were what women wore in the nineteenth century, usually tied with a ribbon under the chin. Irving Berlin's 1940 song, "Easter Bonnet," most famously sung by Judy Garland, celebrates the holiday's spirit of new beginnings as epitomized by the brand-new, shiny hats so many women still wear on Easter: "In your Easter bonnet / With all the frills upon it."

Wanting to wear a flashy structure on top of our heads is nothing new. In ancient Crete, women wore elaborate headdresses that were likely "the first 'smart hats' in the history of costume."[3] In America today, African-American women are keeping the tradition of the

church hat alive. The book *Crowns: Portraits of Black Women in Church Hats* (2000) says that many black women "would rather attend church naked than hatless." The hat in this case represents piety and inner strength—the church hat is not called a "crown" in the black community for nothing!

Speaking of crowns, they date back thousands of years. Rulers have worn them since antiquity as a physical manifestation of their power. In ancient Egypt, pharaohs wore two crowns: the crown of the North and the crown of the South, one circular and one conical.[4] In ancient Greece, those in power wore on their head the *korone*, a gold wreath. The laurel wreath was a symbol of the god Apollo, Olympic victors, and then of Roman emperors. Christian kings starting with Charlemagne signified the divine nature of their rule with a cross on their crown.

Witches in the popular imagination wear something rather like a crown. There are many theories about where this originated. One of the most fun is that they were derived from the dunce's hat, which was originally supposed to siphon power and wisdom into the brain. But I would like to throw out a new one: our modern conception of the witch's hat looks an awful lot like what men were wearing in Puritan New England when

top: Ad for the 1948 movie *Easter Parade*, Easter being a favorite excuse for wearing outrageous hats.

left: Gospel singer Willie May Ford Smith sports a church lady hat in the documentary *Say Amen, Somebody*, 1982.

Margaret Hamilton models the wicked witch hat, with Judy Garland in 1939's *The Wizard of Oz.*

the Salem witch trials happened, just with some added point. In any case, that pointy hat has been the defining look for witches and wizards for hundreds of years.

The structured witch's hat's opposite is the soft wool winter hat, worn either for warmth or, at other times, by hacky-sack players or followers of the grunge movement of the 1990s Pacific Northwest. From what I can tell, we can thank the Persians for this look. They took on much of the costume of the Babylonian civilization they conquered in the sixth century, but they kept their traditional hat: a soft felt cap. The Greeks called this a "Phrygian cap" and considered it a symbol of Eastern barbarism. But for the Romans, this same hat became associated with the concept of liberty.

That association stuck. Two thousand years later, the Phrygian cap became the "red cap of Liberty" during the French Revolution.[5] The hat has shown up in various revolutions since then as a symbol of rebellion or adventure. Jacques Cousteau is often pictured wearing a Phrygian cap. Bill Murray wears one in 2004's *The Life Aquatic with Steve Zissou.* So do the mice in Disney's *Cinderella*! Variations on the theme are called pixie or elf hats; they, along with the "gnome hat"—the less floppy equivalent—show up on college campuses every year.

The beret is a descendant of the Phrygian cap. It appeared in velvet as an element of evening wear from around 1820 to 1850, then returned in the twentieth century as

the quintessential French hat, although it was probably originally Basque, imported to the U.K. by Kangol in 1918. The 1967 film *Bonnie and Clyde* made it popular with American women, and Samuel L. Jackson was one of its mainstream ambassadors to men. But after beret-wearer Monica Lewinsky hit the papers, few people would wear one. For at least a few years, she did to the beret what Clark Gable did to the T-shirt: killed it.

left: A Mary Quant ad from the 1960s illustrates the beret craze.

below: Jacques Cousteau wears a Phrygian cap to work in the Greek isles.

Hats shape an overall look and can completely alter the silhouette of an outfit. In the 1910s, the basic structure of a woman's look was an upside-down triangle, with a slender body and a huge hat (by 1913, hats were as big as wagon wheels). In the 1960s, a woman sought to create the opposite shape—a right-side-up triangle—with cropped hair and an A-line skirt.

I hope now when you put on a hat you'll think of which of these traditions you're referencing, and what overall shape your hat gives your silhouette. You may even decide to take the queen's advice and consider keeping a spare on hand, in case of wind.

left: Samuel Jackson in a Kangol cap.

below: Sheet music, 1911.

QUEEN of FASHION
WALTZES

By
Chas. L. Johnson

5

PUBLISHED BY
JOHNSON PUB. CO.
KANSAS CITY MO.

19.
GLOVES
The Long-Lost Love Token

Mittens, gauntlets, fingerless . . .
Why gloves went the way of the crinoline

GLOVES. You know, I considered not even including this chapter. After all, who even wears non-winter gloves anymore, aside from race-car drivers, boxers, and baseball players?

Ultimately, I decided that gloves are worth including, if for no other reason than because they symbolize how rapidly a garment can go from an essential and everyday piece of clothing to a remnant of the past.

Few young people today realize just how necessary gloves were even sixty years ago. My mother and grandmother always wore gloves. They would never go *anywhere* without wearing gloves. That was the 1950s into the 1960s. Back then, propriety was very important, and clothing was a manifestation of that uprightness.

My family was very proper, and so was I—at times infuriatingly so. One day when I was in sixth grade, my teacher decided he was going to make me rebel. He called to me to come stand in front of the class, where he handed me an eraser.

"Tim, throw this eraser across the room," he said.

"No!" I said in horror. It was humiliating to be called up to the front of the room, and here he was telling me to act out, too.

"Throw it!" he insisted.

I would not. Finally he took the eraser back and let me return to my seat.

The 1960s hippie movement was one big "throw the eraser!" moment. The hippies challenged traditional values and, for better and for worse, caused us to jettison a lot of fashion. The girdle is one item we discussed in the underwear chapter. But the glove is even more poignant, because it has such a romantic and symbolic history.

One of the earliest images of people wearing gloves is a fresco from the island of Thera (now Santorini), circa 1550–1500 BC. Two hundred years later, King Tut was buried in Egypt with linen gloves in his tomb. In the eighth century BC, Homer mentions gloves as a means of barter.[1]

Gloves are also historically a symbol of love. Knights wore a glove from their lady on their helmet or shield to give them strength as they rode into battle.[2] Romeo says of Juliet, "O, that I were a glove upon that hand, that I might touch that cheek." They were given as love tokens in the sixteenth century, rather like an engagement ring.

In the seventeenth century, a woman would sleep with a glove under her pillow in the hope of meeting her true love.[3] Gloves back then would often be very strongly perfumed, which added to their allure, even though this practice had a less than romantic reason behind it: "The early tannage of leather had a most objectionable odour and perfumes were extravagantly used to camouflage."[4]

A man might give one of his gloves to his future father-in-law to signal his honor. (Swearing by one's glove back in the 1700s was like swearing by one's honor now.) Gloves were often worn by brides in wedding ceremonies, with the glove's ring finger removable to allow for the placing of the ring.

Gloves symbolized passion in other ways, too: throwing down a glove or hitting someone with one is an invitation to duel. Think of all the *Looney Tunes* cartoons where Bugs Bunny slaps someone with a glove, and violence ensues. Knights really did that. "Throwing down the gauntlet" (gauntlets being long, thick gloves suitable for battle and falconry) was an invitation to fight.

The thick leather gauntlet worn by men who trained birds of prey was a symbol of potency and it has since been popular with many men and women who have never even stood close to a pigeon. Gauntlet-style gloves, popular with pop stars like Rihanna, appeared in the 2009 collections of Karl Lagerfeld and Proenza Schouler.

Over time gloves, like so many garments, moved from functionality to decoration. I can't recall a single portrait of a lady from the Renaissance through the Enlightenment in which she wasn't wearing gloves. (The Virgin Mary is the only exception, but she's exceptional!) They were a symbol of status. Catherine de' Medici (1519–1589) is credited with making gloves a must-have accessory for elegant women. The gloves were supposedly so fine they could fit into a nutshell, which their owners would then carry or wear on gold chains.[5] Queen Elizabeth I loved gloves. When she died, she had more than two thousand pairs.[6]

They carried over into American life and remained a symbol of wealth for hundreds of years. When nineteenth-century fashion plate Lillian Russell rode up and down Fifth Avenue, "She would nonchalantly wave her hand, gloved in white, sparkling with simulated jewels."[7]

This Ambrogio Lorenzetti fresco from 1338–40 shows a gauntlet.

That brings us to America in the first half of the twentieth century, when gloves were essential for respectable people. C. Cody Collins, the author of a 1945 book called *Love of a Glove*, recalls preparing for church every Sunday morning: "All six sisters and three brothers impatiently grouped in the hallway as Father looked us over for perfectly clean ears, slick hair and shined shoes. Everyone proudly wore his most treasured possession, his very own gloves, neatly smooth, very tight and certainly snapped securely at the wrist and, not to be taken off until we had returned home again!"[8]

As late as the 1940s and 1950s, proper women wore gloves whenever they left the house. Claire McCardell says in her otherwise quite contemporary book, *What Shall I Wear?*, "A woman without gloves is a marked woman. It's like going barefoot to be without them."[9] But the glove was already on its way out, and by the end of the sixties, most women in America weren't wearing them. Philip Roth's Pulitzer-winning *American Pastoral* chronicles (among many other things) the demise of the glove industry in America, a collapse the book attributes in part to unions.

Perhaps we wouldn't even think twice about gloves now if it hadn't been for pop stars of the 1980s. Michael Jackson kicked off a craze among young people for wearing a single sparkly glove. How he struck upon the idea for his sequined glove was a mystery until 2009, when John Kehe wrote a story for *The Christian Science Monitor*. In 1980, Kehe was in charge of developing a music video for the Jackson Five. He gave Jackson a tour of the film production company, Robert Abel & Associates.

Kehe writes: "As we walked through the facility's maze of hallways, camera rooms, and special-effects labs, we encountered the chief film editor, Rick Ross, who was cutting and splicing a TV commercial. Rick was wearing a short white cotton glove on his left hand as he ran the film through his fingers. . . . Michael, who hadn't shown any particular enthusiasm for the tour so far, seemed suddenly transfixed by the glove and politely asked a number of questions about it, concluding with, 'Could you spare one?'" Jackson's single white glove, by then covered in sequins, first appeared on TV in 1983, when he performed "Billie Jean" for Motown's anniversary special, *Motown 25: Yesterday, Today, Forever*.

Two women in tasteful medium-length gloves study racing forms in Brisbane, 1940.

opposite: Lillian Russell, American singer and actress, wears elegant white gloves in the 1890s.

In recent years, gloves have also held sinister connotations. In old Hollywood, movie plots sometimes hinged on a woman's glove being left behind after an illicit affair. Cinematic cat burglars often wore black leather gloves to avoid leaving fingerprints and so escape detection. The black glove more famously in recent times turned up in the O. J. Simpson murder trial. In 1995, defense attorney Johnnie Cochran insisted the glove in evidence didn't fit Simpson, and that, "If it doesn't fit, you must acquit."

Today we mostly wear gloves or mittens in the winter for protection from the cold. Mittens are typically considered the more childish hand-covering option, because they are less articulated and so seem less elegant. But in the 1700s, women wore elbow-length mittens made of kid, cotton, or silk, and with decorative linings. In the 1870s, black mittens were part of evening wear!

President Ronald Reagan, First Lady Nancy Reagan, and Michael Jackson at the White House to launch the campaign against drunk driving, 1984. Even here, he wears his signature white glove.

Fingerless gloves are an interesting phenomenon. In nearly every Hollywood movie about hobos, you can tell who's down on his luck by his fingerless gloves. For this, they're nicknamed "hobo gloves." They still have an aura of poverty and toughness. Billy Idol and Madonna wore them in the 1980s. Judd Nelson's tough-guy character wears them in the 1985 movie *The Breakfast Club*. The phrase "hand in glove" is immortalized for our era by the 1983 Smiths song about a kind of doomed happiness ("Hand in glove / We can go wherever we please").

Ironically, the original cut-fingered gloves had the opposite connotation of today's fingerless gloves. They were developed at the end of the sixteenth century so that the wearer's flashy rings wouldn't be concealed. In the first half of the eighteenth century, women sometimes wore gloves with just the fingertips exposed—a trend that you can see coming back now among women who want to show off their elaborate manicures even in

Judd Nelson wears fingerless gloves in *The Breakfast Club*, 1985.

winter. They're coming back now, too, because of touch-screen phones and texting.

A young girl named Kathryn Gregory invented another variation on the fingerless glove in 1994. Wristies are pieces of polar fleece that cover the space between the glove and cuff, and I'm told they are a lifesaver in northern climates when that little extra bit of fabric can protect delicate wrists from thirty-below temperatures. One etiquette note: it is typically considered good manners to remove your glove when shaking hands, although if it's that cold, I think you should get a pass.

Today when I wear gloves, even if it's just for the practical purpose of staying warm while walking around New York City in January, I like to think of the falconer, the jewel thief, and the lovesick ladies waving their love tokens. And when a speeding car covers me in slush, I wish it were still the age of the duel.

R.I.P. GLOVES

Where you would have worn gloves one hundred years ago: to the theater, to church, to work, shopping . . . pretty much everywhere.

20.
HANDBAGS
Enemy of the Pocket

Purses, clutches, messengers . . . Size matters!

"I'VE GOT THE BEST IDEA!" Diana Vreeland announced one day to her staff at *Vogue*. "We're going to eliminate all handbags!"[1] She had become enchanted by the allure of pockets on women's clothes and envisioned a future utopia in which every woman's hands and shoulders were free of bags.

Vreeland was persuaded to give up on this flash of genius, because a vast amount of ad revenue came into *Vogue* from the handbag industry, but she did hit on a truth about fashion history: the pocket and the purse are locked in a struggle for supremacy.

For men, in the fifteenth century to the mid-sixteenth century, your "pocket" was a little pouch you used for carrying money. It was separate from your clothes. From the midsixteenth century to the late seventeenth century, it became a pouch built into hose or breeches, like a proto-cargo pant, and then into coats. Starting in 1690, pockets developed protective flaps, and starting in the eighteenth century, they appeared in waistcoats. Starting in the 1900s, there has been a wide range of pockets located in various parts of different garments.

Women for centuries had "pockets"—what we would call a little needlework-decorated purse—tied around the waist under the dress and reached through the placket hole, like a reverse fanny pack. From around 1800 to 1820, women instead had an "indispensible" or "reticule" carried in the hand for every day, and a waist-tied pair of pockets only for traveling. The "railway pocket" had the same basic form and function as today's backpacker-friendly money belt. In 1840 or so, women's skirts gained a built-in-pocket and the bodice developed a watch pocket. In 1876, women started wearing patch pockets low on the back of their dresses. (Pickpockets loved this trend.) From the twentieth century until now, pockets typically are avoided if they will spoil the line of a garment, as in a tight dress, but frequently appear in fuller skirts and outerwear.

Cut to today, when women carry many more personal items, from makeup to laptops, diapers to business reports. A woman is dependent on her purse to help her through the day, and so it often looms large when they think about major purchases.

The culture has taken this a bit too far, however. When I see young women walking around with $10,000 purses, and acting like they're a must-have status symbol, I cringe. One woman recently told me she bought a vintage Kelly bag (the famous purse made by Hermès and named after Grace Kelly) for $8,000. She was thrilled. "It came with its original felt case!" she said brightly.

There's a fashion cult around the idea of the designer handbag. To me, it seems like branding run amok. So, where did this branded-handbag frenzy come from? For me, the mid-1950s marks the threshold between bags as functional and bags as status symbols. In 1956, you had the Kelly bag from Hermès. This same bag had been around since 1892 as a saddle carrier and was turned into a day purse in the 1930s. Then in 1956, Princess Grace was photographed holding the

Francesco Terzio's portrait of Archduke Ferdinand II (1529–95) shows the pouch pocket, among other things.

oppposite: Prince Rainier III of Monaco with Grace Kelly. She holds the Hermès bag that later was named in her honor.

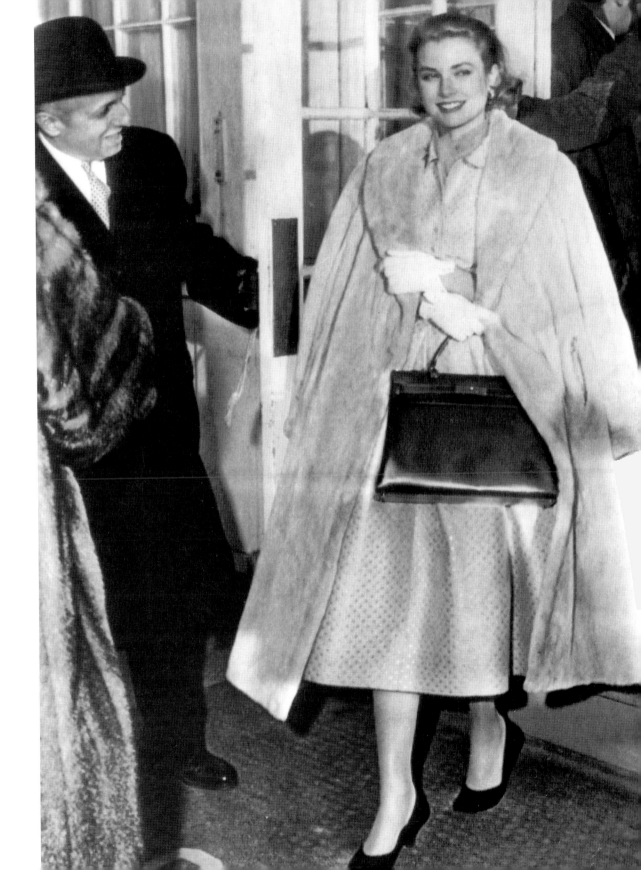

QUESTIONS TO ASK WHEN BUYING AN EVERYDAY PURSE

» Is it big enough to hold everything, but not so big that it looks like you're going away for the weekend?

» Is it sturdy enough to hold up to daily wear?

» Is it a color that will go with most of what you may find yourself wearing?

» Will it stay on your shoulder? Is the strap too short or too slippery? Put it on and then try running around a little to see what happens (but not toward the door, lest the guard thinks you're trying to shoplift!).

» Is it bigger in the interior than the opening, so that it's like digging around in a fishbowl to find your keys?

» Can you zip or snap the purse closed for security when around small, curious children or in big, potentially pickpocket-obscuring crowds?

» Are there enough pockets for the things you access regularly, or will you need some kind of insert to organize the contents?

» Is this a purse you can see yourself living with day in and day out?

purse in front of her stomach—supposedly to conceal her pregnancy. Hermès renamed the purse the Kelly bag, and a cult was born.

Hermès created another cult in 1981, when the British actress and singer Jane Birkin spilled the contents of her Kelly purse on an airplane. As legend has it, nearby was Jean-Louis Dumas-Hermès, who (inspired by the airplane incident) had a larger bag made for her three years later. The new bag was called the Birkin, and it's since become a huge status symbol. (When Martha Stewart carried her pricey Birkin to court for her 2004 trial, it may have made her less sympathetic to the jury.) Ironically, in 2006 Jane Birkin said in an interview that she doesn't carry her Birkin anymore because it gave her tendinitis.[2]

In 1955, Chanel presented the quilted 2.55 bag. I like Chanel's scientific way of naming things. Chanel No. 5 was the name of the fifth perfume sample she tested. The 2.55 bag was named after the month and year she created it: February 1955. There is symbolism in every aspect of the 2.55. The lining is the color of the uniforms of the convent where she grew up, and the chain was modeled after the caretakers' key chains. A zippered compartment was for the stashing of secret love letters such as Chanel had cause to hide. The chain was significant, because until then only working women put bags over their shoulders. The 2.55 bag brought the shoulder strap to the leisure class.

From the 1950s on, there was a rush to create expensive, branded bags. The bag-crazy characters on *Sex and the City* fueled the fire for such purses, especially the 1997 Fendi baguette. This purse is an even more extreme example of conspicuous consumption than the Kelly or Birkin, because it's almost too small to hold anything!

Prior to the 1950s, the bag may have been exquisitely beautiful, but you didn't have the same branding frenzy. The term "purse" has been used since medieval times to describe a pouch or, from the fourteenth century on, a small bag for carrying money. Men were therefore the first to carry purses, because they controlled the money—literally, the purse strings! This money purse could be cut free, similar to how muggers will break the straps of a woman's purse today.

But the elegant embroidered purses we see sometimes in museums didn't always carry money. Decorative purses of the seventeenth century were just that, because their owners were so rich that they didn't typically engage directly in cash exchanges. These purses sometimes did serve, though, as sewing bags, holding needle and thread, or a mirror for grooming on the go. Starting in the eighteenth century, the stocking purse, which was knitted, became popular. Some of these were framed using pinchbeck (faux gold) and heavily embroidered designs.

Speaking of decorative purses, let's talk about Elizabeth II. You never see her without a travel-kennel size handbag draped over her arm. What's in it? We know she's not carrying money. A compact? Lipstick? Couldn't one of her ladies-in-waiting carry the bag? But if that were to happen we'd all be disappointed, wouldn't we?

In the 1800s, purses began to show metal fastenings, and by the middle of the century there came about the "sovereign purse." This was, according to the *Berg Encyclopedia*, "a metal, tubular container with internal springs, holding sovereigns at one end and half-sovereigns at the

Martha Stewart with her Birkin bag.

A tam-o'-shanter coin purse, so called because it resembles the traditional Scottish hat.

top: A decorated purse, circa 1825.

other." Holding coins separate from the rest of the purse has always been an issue, because metal can stain. In the early twentieth century, the beaded tam-o'-shanter coin purse came into vogue, and making these at home was a popular craft project.

In modern times, women have carried purses of all sizes and materials, often with compartments. The term "handbag" has been in use roughly since the nineteenth century for a small travel bag, and since the late nineteenth century, it's been the British name for a woman's bag held by the handles or, later, hung from the shoulder.

Men today often won't carry a bag at all but will instead cram their pockets full of wallets, phones, keys, and so on, completely ruining the line of their pants. To avoid this problem, some will create a much bigger fashion problem by wearing a fanny pack. The fanny pack is the ultimate anti-fashion accessory. (Hippies were antifashion, but of course nearly every antifashion trend has had a big impact on fashion. You could say the same thing about grunge, punk, and hip-hop. Luckily, the fanny pack revolt has been for the most part suppressed.)

The fanny pack is unflattering and makes you look deformed at the waist. It is so utilitarian that it's the day-to-day equivalent of a tool belt, which has yet to enter the fashion world, for good reason. In this spirit, there was, for a time, a push for the "man purse," which looked rather like a binocular case without the binoculars. To me, it usually seemed silly and dandyish.

Why not carry a messenger bag instead, especially if you're not wearing a suit? I used to carry one all the time, but they were so heavy that they would pull at the shoulder of my suits. Now I carry in my hand a black leather tote with short handles. If I need my hands free, as when I was recently on crutches, I will break out the messenger bag instead. And if I'm dressing up, I'll just stick some cash, a single credit card, and my key in the breast pocket of my jacket.

For women, the day bag is utilitarian. It should accommodate your needs and your lifestyle. We shouldn't rule out aesthetics, obviously, but there's such a difference in the day-purse needs of a woman who has a baby versus a lady who lunches versus someone with grown children and a place of work.

For night, women need a clutch. Generally speaking, the smaller the handbag, the more evening it becomes. The bigger it is, the more daytime. For daytime one also wants a textile that is easy to clean, such as leather.

When it comes to colors, I'm always telling women who aren't comfortable with bold colors in their clothes to take a chance with their accessories. And when it comes to cost, there is no reason to go into debt over a handbag. I avoid the *New York Times* page with the ads for zillion-dollar handbags. They make me mad! Who wants to be this kind of fashion victim?

Zach Galifianakis wears a man purse in 2009's *The Hangover*.

WHAT PURSE GOES WITH THAT LOOK?

» Formal event: tiny clutch

» Business meeting: leather briefcase or carryall

» Dinner date: smallish leather or metallic bag

» To the playground: cloth or leather shoulder bag with accessible pockets for diapers/toys/tissues

» Running errands: everyday purse (see page 274)

First off: these purses are not as special as you think they are. In an exposé called *Bringing Home the Birkin,* Michael Tonello travels the globe buying and then reselling these top-shelf handbags, only to discover that in 2005, he alone has purchased more than the company claims to have made: "I have to laugh," Tonello writes, "when I read articles that claim Hermès makes 'about 100 Birkins a year.' If that were truly the case it would mean that I bought the entire annual production that year—and then some!"[3]

You can get a sturdy, fashionable, long-lasting day purse or briefcase for $200 to $400. This is an area of fashion where having to make do with less is a good thing. If you're budget minded, you're forced to look harder for things, and you can discover a whole world that you never would have found otherwise.

My recommendation: don't be branded. Brand yourself! If you do more research and find something you're really excited about, like embroidered waistcoats from the nineteenth century or tam-o'-shanter coin purses, you'll have a lot less competition from other collectors, and you'll be making a much more exciting fashion statement.

HOW TO SHOP WITH THE PAST, PRESENT, AND FUTURE IN MIND

"To choose clothes, either in a store or at home, is to define and describe ourselves."

—*The Language of Clothes*[1]

THROUGHOUT HISTORY, you see dozens or even hundreds of years roll by with only one look at people's disposal. You couldn't find a poufy party skirt in ancient Egypt. There were no slinky sequin dresses during the Regency period. But these days, more than at any other time in history, we have an almost infinite number of choices when it comes to our clothes' shape, material, and style.

Throughout the Western world—and anywhere else you can find a computer—you can buy a sack dress or a bustier, an oversize T-shirt or a skin-tight tube dress. Trends come and go, but the stores of today are packed with every imaginable silhouette.

This should be liberating, but often it is overwhelming. With an increase in options, our expectations of what a garment can or should do for us have exploded. Alison Lurie writes: "The man who goes to buy a winter coat may simultaneously want it to shelter him from bad weather, look expensive and fashionable, announce that he is sophisticated and rugged, attract a certain sort of sexual partner and magically infect him with the qualities of Robert Redford."[2] Good luck on *that* shopping trip!

What's more, even though *theoretically* you can get any size or shape you want, stores often have a glut or a dearth of certain merchandise. If you try to shop at a department store in December for holiday wear, you may be told it is actually time for cruise wear. If you try to buy a swimsuit for an end-of-summer vacation, you may be told only fall clothes are available. It's outrageous.

And yet, if you can imagine: it's better than it was even fifty years ago. It used to be that if you went to a department store and wanted to buy a pair of pants, you went to the pants department. If you wanted a skirt, you went to the skirts department. Clothes were sorted by garment, across all brands.

In 1976, Liz Claiborne said that the power of the Liz Claiborne brand was that you could mix and match, so she brought all her clothes to one place on the retail floor. It created a lot of controversy, and quite a revolution. As we know, that's how we shop today. We should take our hat off to her for that.

This makes it easier to pick a few brands that appeal to you and try on everything they have, even things that don't look like "you" at first. You need to experiment. Try shapes and colors you wouldn't think to try. Hanger appeal is a big issue. I hold things up to women I'm shopping with and hear: "I'm not wearing that!"

"Just put it on!" I say. "Don't dismiss it by making assumptions." You don't always know from what it looks like on the hanger.

One time when I went shopping at a department store in Chicago with some makeover subjects, every rack was crammed with product. We couldn't even disentangle the clothes, much less flip through the rack and look at the range of items available.

"Why do you have so much out here?" I asked a floor manager. "It's making it hard to shop."

"We don't want to have to go to the back for sizes," he said.

Well, he certainly didn't need to do that for us. We went shopping somewhere else!

Bad shopping experiences can happen even at the highest end. I was recently at a well-known New York store, intent upon buying a particular brand of suit. I found the suit, but it wasn't in my size. I spoke to a very aloof salesperson. I presented him with my card and asked if they would let me know if they found the suit in my size. He seemed uninterested, so I wasn't altogether surprised when one week, two weeks, four weeks went by without my hearing from him. I went to another store, Saks Fifth Avenue, and bought the suit. Mr. Solomon of Saks even e-mails me personally when something special comes in that he thinks I might like. I haven't been back to the other store's suit department since.

You should never shop anywhere that doesn't seem to have your interests at heart or that makes you feel bad. Shopping is always at least in part about gathering information. Salespeople should help you learn about yourself and what you like. It should not be an exercise in frustration or demoralization. Go someplace with knowledgeable salespeople. Department stores' lingerie floor staff will usually measure you and give you advice on which styles to try. Jeans store staff should measure you and help you figure out what style looks best. Seek out these safe harbors and avoid the sand traps of bad salespeople and poorly organized sales floors. We should be learning all the time from those who know more than we do.

(Speaking of education, when I hear that a designer is "self-taught," I bristle. "Isn't that fantastic?" people will ask me after saying the designer has had no formal training.

"No!" I respond. "That isn't fantastic at all."

On *Project Runway,* those self-taught designers are usually the ones who give us the most trouble. If designers haven't been through school, they haven't experienced a critique. They aren't used to listening to feedback, and they often take any criticism as a personal attack. I believe in education.)

We certainly need to educate ourselves about fit if we hope to keep up with the clothing industry's constantly changing sizing systems. Vanity sizing is an epidemic today, and it makes it hard to know what your size is. I often see clothes clearly marked on the tag as a size 4 when they're really a 6, or as a 12 when they're a 14. This is supposed to make women feel better about buying those clothes, but it often just serves to confuse.

"I'm a twelve in this brand but a fourteen in this one, and a ten in this one?" women will say in shock in the dressing room. "So what am I *really?*"

The truth is, we live in a ready-made world, and that means we buy the garments off the rack that are closest to us in fit. If they fit us like a glove without any tailoring, it is a miracle. More often than not, the waist of a pair of jeans will fit perfectly, but the thighs won't. Or the bust of a shirt will fit but the shoulders won't.

The best thing to do is to stop thinking of yourself as a certain size, forever and always. Before you have a baby you may be a 34B, and after you may be a 36DD. Two years later, you may be a 34C. You should be remeasured every year or two to know where you are on the spectrum. Even in the same brand, you may be a 16 in one cut of jeans and a 14 in another. The only solution is to gather as much information as possible about what styles you like and what sizes usually fit you best.

If you have access to a good tailor, you should by all means make use of him! I find it tragic that we in the United States are losing our knowledge of how to construct and repair clothes. We live in an increasingly disposable culture, whereby we buy cheap clothes at the Gap or Old Navy and then toss them when they grow worn (which is often quickly, because modern mass-market quality is not exactly up to couture standards). The solution to this is to spend more money on higher quality garments and to have them repaired rather than throwing them out.

As recently as the 1960s, the vast majority of clothes bought in America were made in America—specifically in New York City's garment district. Today only about 5 percent of the clothes we buy are made here. There's a wonderful documentary called *Schmatta: Rags to Riches to Rags* that explores this steep decline in American-made clothing. (Sewing machines, incidentally, entered mass production in America in the 1850s, later making possible the ready-to-wear uniforms for the Civil War. There should be one in every neighborhood at the local tailor's, but unfortunately the seamstress in the corner storefront is going the way of the Made in America label.)

I'm always fascinated by who made clothes during which periods. In Roman times, the textile industry shifted from homemade garments to public production on large estates called *gynaeceum*. Female slaves worked there and made togas. Outsourcing was the rule for hundreds of years. A major shift took place in Europe around 1300 when men started weaving and women focused on spinning.[3] In the Renaissance, women made clothes for the family, unless the family was rich; professional men made clothes for the upper classes.

If you aren't handy with a needle or sewing machine yourself, a good tailor can basically be a therapist for your fashion life. Give him or her all the items you love but that drive you crazy: "This one is too tight in the hips." "This one is too short." "This button keeps popping off." When the clothes return, with any alterations made for typically just a few dollars each, your clothes will be just as you like them and you will have expanded your wardrobe without having spent a fortune. Having a tailor will also make it easier to shop for vintage clothes: you can buy things you love and then have them altered to fit you.

But back to sizing and fit: America increasingly demands plus sizes, and designers have been slow to catch up to this demand. In many regards, the high-end fashion world can feel disconnected from the world most of us live in. Often when I see a collection come out, I wonder, *Who is the woman these clothes are made for?* I sure don't know her.

There's an active lack of interest in fitting a real shape. One prominent designer whom I will not shame in these pages (especially because she is far from alone) told me, "I'm not interested in dressing anyone larger than a size twelve."

"Maybe you should be!" I replied.

Last I heard, something like 64 percent of Americans were significantly beyond the weight most designers are "interested in dressing." I am told the median size for American women is a 14P (*p* for petite). Are you as stunned by this revelation as I was? It's true.

Fashion models today are so different from the women buying the clothes. That has not always been the case. If you look at issues of *Vogue* or other fashion magazines from the 1950s, you'll see models in possession of womanly (albeit spectacular) bodies and expressive, mature faces. Star models typically were over thirty, and they had curves. They just looked like extraglamorous versions of the women buying the dresses.

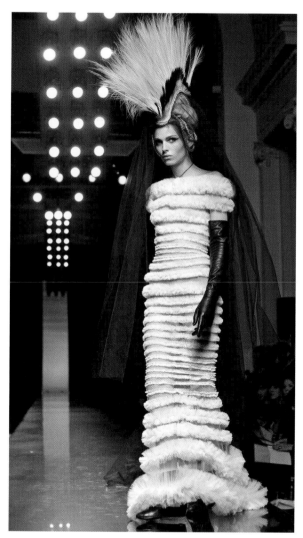

Andrej Pejic on the runway for Jean Paul Gaultier's spring/summer 2011 Paris fashion week show.

It almost seems shocking now, when models are all in their teens and look as though they're playing dress up. In 2011 there was a cover of French *Vogue* featuring a ten-year-old model. Ten years old! Did she look ten? No, she looked twenty-five! What does that say to young people? I worry about the pressure this puts on our teenagers and tweens. Limb-lengthening surgery is extremely popular in Russia. Girls have their legs broken apart and lengthened with bone fills to make them taller.

Having children modeling high fashion is bad enough, but Gaultier's 2011 fashion show took things one step further. It featured a stick-thin, androgynous-looking male model named Andrej Pejic modeling women's clothes, including the bridal gown. I have nothing against androgynous looks or men wearing dresses. (As we've seen in this book, men wore robes for centuries.)

But men and women just have different bodies. A woman with hips will never be able to fit into clothes tailored to a thin young man. Therefore, to me, selling women's clothes using a teenage boy's body is the ultimate cynicism. It's as if the fashion industry is saying, "Here is the perfect woman for our clothes: a boy!"

Models were once mature women. What I love about these older models is that they had so much sophistication. They were stunning, and you could believe they would wear those clothes. The fifties models photographed by Richard Avedon were relatable but inspiring at the same time. You had the feeling that if they could look that fantastic in these dresses, so could you. The movie *Funny Face* came out in 1957, and it was perhaps the last time we saw sophisticated women with experience of the world as icons of fashion and beauty. In 1964, when the fashion film *Blow-Up* came out, you have the model Veruschka as the epitome of the fashionable woman. She was all arms and legs and vacant stare. Models ever since then have been getting thinner and younger.

Kay Thompson in *Funny Face*, 1957.

If you see a fourteen-year-old, size-0 model looking incredible in a gown, it's hard to know if you will be able to pull it off unless you are a size 0 and fourteen! It's enough to make a woman feel terrible for not being a wisp of a teenager. I have a reverence for fashion and the industry, but I also recognize the ridiculousness of so much of it. The part of fashion that I find bewildering and peculiar is the considerable part of it that's a freak show.

What really irks me is that women are so often made to feel bad for how they look while at the same time being made to feel bad that they care! Linda Grant writes in *The Thoughtful Dresser* that the "great misogynist trick" is to "judge and condemn women for the various failures of our appearance while simultaneously barking that only feeble shallow creatures such as women would pay any attention to how they look."[4] So true!

We should feel proud if we care about our appearance. I know vanity is supposedly one of the seven deadly sins, but I don't agree. I consider it a virtue.

Veruschka in *Blow-Up*, 1966.

Isaiah was neither the first nor last to complain about women paying too much attention to how they looked, but here's what he says in the Bible about fashionable ladies: "In that day the Lord will take away the bravery of their tinkling ornaments about their feet, and their cauls, and their round tires like the moon, the chains, and the bracelets, and the mufflers, the bonnets, and the ornaments of the legs, and the headbands, and the tablets, and the earrings, the rings, and nose jewels, the changeable suits of apparel, and the mantles, and the wimples, and the crisping pins, the glasses, and the fine linen, and the hoods, and the veils. And it shall come to pass, that instead of sweet smell there shall be stink; and instead of a girdle a rent; and instead of well set hair baldness; and instead of a stomacher a girding of sackcloth; and burning instead of beauty."[5]

Well. That may well be true. But for the purposes of life in the here and now, there is no harm in wanting to look good. Dress philosophers like Quentin Bell would say that a kind of "sartorial morality" demands that we dress well for one another's sake as well as our own, that what we wear is a very extension of our personhood, even our soul! I think we owe it to ourselves and to each other to be a little bit vain. Pride may goeth before a fall, but it also goeth before a good social life and career advancement.

Given the pressure to look good but not care about it, and the other difficulties I've listed, it's no wonder people fail to enjoy clothes shopping. Is it a surprise that so many people I meet say they feel defeated by the whole prospect? The two most common attitudes I see among the unhappy-in-clothes are the Giver-Uppers and the Fashion Victims. These are two perfectly reasonable, but ultimately self-defeating, responses to the problems I've detailed above. Let's examine how these issues manifest themselves, and determine what can be done about them.

First of all: the Giver-Uppers. Throughout history there have been attempts to create a utilitarian uniform. The British designer John Cavanagh, for example, came up with his Basic jumpsuit in 1963.[6] He believed this look would become "automatic for work, travel and all active life." It looks rather like a white garbage bag tied at the knees. In a way, he was a visionary: this is where a lot of women in this country are today. Of course, the "Basic" today is a pair of baggy capri pants or shorts tied at the knees, paired with an oversize once-white T-shirt.

Most women I meet on makeover shows are stuck in a rut and have thrown in the towel. I am here to say: don't do it! I understand how daunting it can feel to reclaim a sense of pride in our bodies and in our appearance. But the only way to get it back is to make an effort. Set aside time and money to look through your closet, then go to a store to try on some things that aren't "you" as you know yourself now.

If you can't find anything you like in department stores, go vintage! Before the 1990s, shopping in thrift stores connoted poverty. But the grunge era made it popular. In 2001,

Julia Roberts even wore a vintage Valentino dress to the Oscars. Michelle Obama has worn vintage, too. Shopping at thrift stores is good for the environment, and it rewards creativity. Most clothes were also better made fifty years ago. Back in the fifties, you had couture and then everything else. You didn't have so many tiers of quality. The number of stitches per inch on what would be considered a cheap dress in 1960 was far greater than what you'd get from H&M today. Vintage shopping also connects us in a very direct way to the rich history of clothing.

Wherever you shop, try to think outside the box. Your clothes reflect how broad your life is. If your closet only has sweatpants, how big is your life? Get out there! Try on a million different styles if you have to and find something that makes you feel the way you want to be!

On the other extreme, there are the Fashion Victims, who put way too much time, energy, and money into their looks. I disagree with the Duchess of Windsor: I think you *can* be too thin or too rich. Wit-

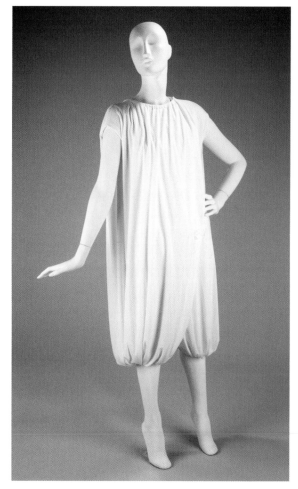

John Cavanagh's 1963 "Basic" jumpsuit.

ness the $4,000 pair of jeans, and the more skeletal models.

Watching fashion shows, I often feel like designers are trying too hard. They will show, say, a fur-trimmed parka with an asymmetrical A-line dress, a lumpy sweater, and snakeskin stockings. It's likely that even *they* never meant those looks to leave the runway together. But you see wealthy shoppers wearing those clothes exactly like that, as though they are paying homage to the designer's strictest vision, when in fact they are more likely paying homage to a feverish stylist's last-minute backstage pile on.

Designers these days frequently have stylists who decide how to present the designer's clothes in a show. I'm so glad we don't have stylists on *Project Runway*, because making the designer do his or her own styling is the only way you can know exactly what the designer had in mind. Otherwise, it begs the question: What is the designer's vision? Did the designer even intend for those pieces to go together?

If you look at the "Who Got It Right?" monthly feature in *People StyleWatch*'s poll, the don'ts are usually the ones going too far, doing too much. The Fashion Victims don't have any more integrity than the Giver-Uppers, and they're not having any more fun. Wearing flip-flops every single day may be sad, but you can just as easily go shopping at Neiman Marcus with unlimited credit and end up feeling defeated. Both sets of people are panicking when they should be learning about their bodies, educating themselves about what's out there, and enjoying the adventure of dressing in a way that suits them.

So, how do you get out of whichever rut you're in and start enjoying your closet more? I encourage everyone to do some soul-searching, to think through all the eras and styles we've discussed and ask yourself honestly: What kind of clothes do I like best?

Do I like the draped clothes of ancient Greece or the tailored clothes of ancient Egypt? Am I a Cleopatra or a Helen?

Do I like the boxy, easy silhouette of the 1920s, the hyperfeminine look of the 1950s, or the late-Victorian focus on structure?

Do I prefer the over-the-top trends of the French, or the various attempts by the British to provide sober alternatives?

Do I wear athletic wear when there are no athletics in my vicinity?

Am I dressing old for my age, as in dirndls, or young for my age, as in graphic tees?

Look in your closet, too, before the next time you go clothes shopping and think about what's missing. To what degree is your closet timeless? Are there a lot of trendy items? How much variety does it have? Do you have something to wear to a wedding? To the beach? For a hot date?

These questions I hope will serve as a kind of mantra that can replace the agony I often hear from women when they talk about heading into shops, hoping to find "something that I won't hate."

Remember: if getting your fashion right were easy, everyone would have looked fabulous throughout history. And as we now know, it's never been easy and probably never will be. But that doesn't mean it can't be fascinating and a whole lot of fun.

APPENDIX
Your Closet Work Sheet

Now that we've taken a tour of the last few thousand years in clothes, let's take a look at your closet. I have a lot of experience in closets. Aside from being my go-to hiding place as a child, I spent a lot of time in them when I was taping the two seasons of *Tim Gunn's Guide to Style*, a makeover show on Bravo.

My cohost and I (supermodel Veronica Webb in Season 1 and the divine Gretta Monahan in Season 2) would begin the makeover journey with an overview of what was in the closet of the person with whom we were working that week. We found everything from the sublime to the ridiculous. I'm talking about apparel *and* organization.

The most common closet affliction was *cramming*. Yes, we taped all of our shows in the New York area, where space is at a premium and closets are painfully small, but I suspect that this issue extends beyond our geographic area. A clothes closet, in my opinion, should be everyone's number one priority for organization. Why? Two reasons: 1) You'll know what's where, and 2) You'll end up taking better care of what you own.

Another common affliction was poor clothing maintenance. Why purchase the item at all if you're going to roll it into a ball and stuff it on a top shelf out of reach? I always demanded a stepladder in order to exhume whatever was hiding in those out-of-reach places. Sometimes I'd find some really good pieces. ("Oh, that's were that was!" our subject would exclaim.) At other times, I'd find things that would cause me to ask whether it wouldn't have been less trouble to seek out a garbage bin rather than a closet crevice.

The content of the average American closet was the catalyst for this history of fashion. I've wanted to write a fashion history book for more than a decade, because the topic fascinates me, as it provides a special lens with which to view the development of our societies and cultures. And I have to add that the older I get, the hungrier I am for historical information, because it enlarges the context for everything in our lives.

In this case, the closet is the context: *your* closet. I presume to know what's in it, and the book addresses the closet content of both genders: ergo, the indispensible value of my dear friend, colleague, and cowriter, Ada Calhoun. Between us, our closets cover all of the bases. We each performed a closet inventory and quality assessment for the other, and it was fascinating. At Ada's apartment and deep into her closet excavation, I was struck by a refrain that I frequently invoke: "Thank god I'm a man! It's so much easier to be a man!"

Ada is superbly organized, thankfully for her, because women have myriad items of apparel, and let us not forget about accessories. I can't even recall how many categories Ada's closet is organized by: dresses, skirts, shirts, jackets, sweaters, jeans. . . . In my case it's merely five: suits, shirts, pants, sweaters, and outerwear. Period. And accessories? How about a little box containing cuff links? Oh, and then there are neckties . . . and shoes . . . and undergarments . . . pajamas . . . I guess I have more categories of items than I initially thought. Neither Ada nor I have very much in the category of athletic wear. Urban nerds are we!

So, let's look at that closet and see if we can't figure out what to cherish and what to leave in the past. . . . I recommend grabbing a tape measure and a pen and carving out a couple of hours.

First, let's talk about YOU.

What is your life like? Do you need clothes that are . . .

☐ Casual (housework, playground, grocery shopping)?

☐ Athletic (yoga, running, mountain climbing)?

☐ Party ready (cocktails, dates, dinner parties)?

☐ Business appropriate (office work, client meetings, job interviews)?

☐ Formal occasions (we all need clothes for weddings and funerals!)?

Describe your style. Are you: Frumpy? Classic? Preppy? Polished? Formal? Casual?_____

Are you happy this way, or do you want to make some kind of change?_____

How has your style evolved over the years? If you're a grown-up, are you still wearing the same clothes you wore in high school or college? _____

Who is your style icon? (Mine is Cary Grant—or George Clooney for people who don't watch old movies! Ada's is Debbie Harry of the band Blondie.) _____

What's the most beautiful garment you've ever owned? _____

What's something you look back on and regret wearing? _____

Time to do a physical self-inventory and figure out how to accentuate the positive!

We want you to feel good and confident! That means being realistic. Look in a full-length mirror (everyone should have a full-length mirror), and be honest about what you see.

At my age now, I am battling the bulge. You have to fight it through proper eating, exercise, and posture. In the course of my work, I encounter a lot of people who have completely let themselves go. When does that moment happen when you say, "I don't give a damn"? None of us can afford to let that happen! Staying fit and happy with our bodies can be hard. But it's worthwhile.

Take every required measurement and put them in the spaces provided in the following diagram. Then refer to the chart and find your sizes in each garment.

Now, ask yourself some questions: _____

What parts of your body are you most proud of? _____

Do you have what you consider trouble areas? _____

Do you have a high waist or a low waist? _____

Do you have broad or narrow shoulders? _____

Do you have long legs or short legs? _____

How busty are you? _____

Do you have slender hips or wide hips? _____

Measurements & Sizes

WOMEN'S DRESS SIZES

Standard sizing is far from an exact science. You may be a 4 in one brand and a 6 in another. Vanity sizing makes it more complicated by calling a 12 a 10 and so on. So don't feel wedded to your number, but below are some charts in case you aren't sure of your size and want a range. Many online sellers, like eBay, have good charts to use as a frame of reference.

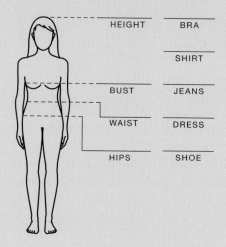

	HEIGHT	BRA
		SHIRT
	BUST	JEANS
	WAIST	DRESS
	HIPS	SHOE

Bust (inches)	Waist (inches)	Hips (inches)	U.S. letter size	U.S. number size	European size
26–28	23	33.5	XXS	0	30
28–30	24	35	XS	2	32
30–32	25–26	36–37	S	4–6	34–36
32–34	27–28	38–39	M	8–10	38–40
36–38	29.5–31	40.5–42	L	12–14	42–44
40–42	32.5	43.5	XL	14–16	44–46

PLUS SIZES

Bust (inches)	Waist (inches)	Hips (inches)	U.S. letter size	U.S. number size
42–45	34–37	44–46	1X	14W–16W
45–49	37–42	47–52	2X	18W–20W
49–53	41–47	51–56	3X	22W–24W
53–57	45–52	55–60	4X	26WE–28WE
58–59	52–54	60–62	5X	32WE

MEN'S DRESS SHIRTS / SUITS

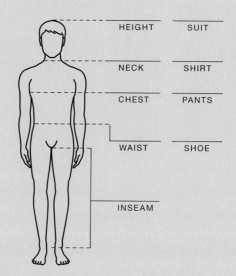

HEIGHT — SUIT

NECK — SHIRT

CHEST — PANTS

WAIST — SHOE

INSEAM

SUIT HEIGHT

5'7" or under ....S (short)
5'8" to 6' ....R (regular)
6' or taller.............................L (long)

SUIT SIZES

Neck (inches)	U.S. size (inches)	European size
14–14.5	34–36	48
15–15.5	38–40	50
16–16.5	42–44	52
17–17.5	46–48	54

JACKET/COAT SIZES

Chest (inches)	U.S. letter size	European size
34–36	XS	46
38–40	S	48
40–42	M	50
42–44	L	52
44–46	XL	54

PANTS SIZES
(inseam of 30/32/34 inches available for all sizes)

Waist (inches)	U.S. letter size
28	XS
30	S
32	M
34	L
36	XL

MEN'S SHIRTS

CASUAL

Chest (inches)	U.S size	European size
32–35	XS	40
35–38	S	42
38–41	M	44
42–45	L	46
46–49	XL	48
50–53	XXL	50

DRESS, BUTTON DOWN

Neck (inches)	U.S. size	European size
14–14.5	S	37
15–15.5	M	38
16–16.5	L	39
17–17.5	XL	40
18–18.5	XXL	41

Remember: body types go in and out of fashion. Sometimes large bodies are in vogue; sometimes slender ones are. You just need to determine which you are and dress for yourself, not for what's *in* right that second. Think of the larger women in the 1920s, trying to put on Chanel's boyish dresses, or more athletic women in the 1950s, when everyone wanted an hourglass figure. We're lucky enough to live in an era when there are clothes out there for every body type. Make use of them!

Now let's look at your CLOSET.

Does anything in your closet need to be cleaned, ironed, or mended? If so, take it off the hanger and put it in a pile to launder or tend to. No use keeping it in plain sight until it's actually something you can wear!

Is there anything in your closet that you haven't worn in ages? Why not just put it in storage or give it away?

Do you have shoes, underwear, hosiery, and bags to pair with everything in your closet?

Do you have enough clothes for each season? Do you have a coat for winter? A jacket for spring and fall? Light clothes for summer?

Now, let's be specific:

1. Underwear
First, throw out all the ratty, stretched-out, riding-up underwear. Now how many pairs do you have? Do you have some really nice underwear for special occasions? Do you have shapewear? Do all your bras actually fit? What size are you really? If you're not sure, go get measured—it's free!—in the lingerie department of a boutique or department store.

2. T-Shirts
Throw away all the T-shirts you have that are falling apart or stained. If it's really special to you, put it in storage. Of the remaining shirts, which ones fit you well in the shoulders, bust, and waist? What size are you? What is the best neckline on you? What is the best length? Get some simple cotton T-shirts of whatever style looks best on you and consider wearing them as undershirts (under jackets or button-down shirts) more often than on their own.

3. Jeans
Get rid of all the jeans that don't fit you. What do all your jeans look like on? Do they show off too much when you bend over? If so, could this be fixed by a belt or by a leotard-like undershirt? Consider investing in some flattering dark-wash jeans if you don't already have some.

4. Dresses

Is your favorite dress a Helen or a Cleopatra? Which of those two dress types do you have more of? Do you have a dress to wear to a funeral? To a wedding? To a business interview? Do you have shoes and purses to match every dress? Do you have anything on a hanger that is getting stretched out? Jersey dresses need to be folded. Which of your dresses are day? Night? Day into night?

5. Capri Pants and Shorts

Throw them away. Just kidding. No, really: if we're talking about cargo capris, take a good hard look at them and see if they are doing anything for you. Look at all the shorts you have and determine if they're the right length for you. If not, what length might be better?

6. Skirts

What length are most of your skirts? Is that the best length for you? Do you have skirts for day and for night? For work and for play? Do you have shoes that match all your skirts?

7. Belts

Do you have belts that match all your shoes, men? Women, do you have a range of belts to go with various dresses, skirts, and pants? It's good to have a range of fabrics, widths, and colors. Metallics are a valuable option to have.

8. Dress Shirts

Get rid of anything that's worn or yellowing. Examine your collars. Are all the plastic stays still in there? If not, consider getting some metal collar stays. Do you have button-down shirts for casual wear? Do you have dress shirts to match your suits and pants?

9. Ties and Scarves

Do you have at least one tie? Think of funerals! Even if you don't want to consider the possibility that you might have to attend one at some point, you have to be sartorially prepared for these things. Have you considered a pocket square?

10. Vests

Do you have any vests? Do you have vests to go under any three-piece suits? Consider getting a vest to liven up a pair of jeans and a shirt.

11. Suits

Do you have a suit to wear to a wedding? To a business interview? To a funeral? Is everything in good working order?

12. Pants

Do you have pants for all your suits? Do you prefer cuffs or no cuffs, pleats or no pleats? Does the waistline fall in the right place for you? Does anything need to be let out or taken in?

13. Hosiery

Throw out or mend all your ratty, pilled, holey socks and tights. Do you have socks or tights that match all your shoes? Meaning: white socks for white sneakers, black socks for black dress shoes, black tights for black heels to be worn with dresses?

14. Shoes

Do you have shoes to match every dress or suit in your closet? If you have a brown dress and no brown or other matching shoes, why do you still have that brown dress?

15. Athletic Wear

Is all your athletic wear actually for athletics? If not, why not? Consider retiring workout clothes as everyday wear.

16. Sweaters

How are your sweaters doing? Are any of them stretched out? Never put a knit on a hanger. That's a quick way to ruin a sweater. Do you have enough sweaters for the winter? Cardigans? Pullovers? What could you use more of?

17. Coats and Jackets

You know I am not a fan of fur, so we won't talk about that here. Do you have a trench with a removable lining? That's really all you need, unless you live in a cold climate, in which case, do you have a warm-enough coat?

18. Hats

Are your hats in good shape? Do you have winter hats if you need them? Do you have a hat for dressing up? Baseball caps? Do you have a trucker hat? (If so, why?)

19. Gloves

As we've discussed in the gloves chapter, this is a garment that's pretty much out of fashion except for winter wear. Do you have some warms ones if you need them? And now a moment of silence for all the gloves that didn't make it out of the 1960s. Okay, moving on . . .

20. Handbags

Are you a handbag cultist? You do know that you don't need to spend tons of money on a purse, right? Good. Now, do you have a large bag for day that meets all your needs and a small bag for night for keys, lipstick, and whatever else you need? Men, do you have a messenger bag, tote, or briefcase? Then you're all set.

Congratulations! You now know what you have, what you don't have, and what size you are in every garment. You know the history of your clothes, and I hope you have been inspired by some of the glorious and shocking fashions of past centuries. We can now head forward into what is always the most fascinating era of fashion: the future.

NOTES

Introduction: Why a History of Western Fashion?

1. Patricia Rieff Anawalt, *The Worldwide History of Dress* (New York: Thames & Hudson, 2007), 101.

1. Underwear: Security vs. Freedom

1. Akiko Fukai, ed. *Fashion: A History from the 18th to the 20th Century,* vol. II (Cologne: Taschen, 2006), 338–39.
2. www.staylace.com/textarea/newspaperarticles/star_tribune020900.html.
3. Grace Evans, "Underwear," in *Berg Encyclopedia of World Dress and Fashion,* vol. 8, *West Europe.*
4. James Laver, *Taste and Fashion: From the French Revolution Until To-day* (London: G. G. Harrap, 1937), 49–50.
5. Colleen Gau, "Brassiere," in *A–Z of Fashion.*
6. Vintageadsandstuff.com/maidenform.
7. "Maidenform Blushes," *Time,* April 25, 1983, www.time.com/time/magazine/article/0,9171,923573,00.html.
8. Leigh Summers, "'Elegance, Comfort, and Durability!' Class, Countours, and Corsetry," chapter 3 of *Bound to Please: A History of the Victorian Corset* (London: Berg, 2001).
9. Marianne Thesander, *The Feminine Ideal,* trans. Nicholas Hills (London: Reaktion Books, 1997), 26.
10. Ibid., 43.
11. David Kunzle, quoted in Thesander, ibid., 43.
12. Sara Pendergast and Tom Pendergast, *Fashion, Costume, and Culture: Clothing, Headwear, Body Decorations, and Footwear Through the Ages,* vol. 5 (Detroit: UXL, 2004), 978.
13. Alison Lurie, *The Language of Clothes* (New York: Henry Holt, 2000), 249.
14. Naomi E. A. Tarrant, "England," in *Berg Encyclopedia,* vol. 8, *West Europe.*
15. Elizabeth Hawes, *It's Still Spinach* (Boston: Little, Brown, 1954), 137.
16. Phyllis G. Tortora, "Types and Properties of Fashionable Dress," in *Berg Encyclopedia of World Dress and Fashion,* vol. 3, *The United States and Canada.*
17. Susan M. Watkins, "Fashion, Health, and Disease," in *A—Z of Fashion,* quoting Bernard W. H. Rudofsky, *Are Clothes Modern?.*
18. Tarrant, "England."
19. Mireille M. Lee, "Ancient Greek Dress," in *Berg Encyclopedia,* vol. 9, *East Europe, Russia, and the Caucasus.*
20. James Laver, *Costume and Fashion: A Concise History* (New York: Thames & Hudson, 2002), 50.
21. Ibid., 58.
22. Rodney Bennett-England, *Dress Optional: The Revolution in Menswear* (London: Peter Owen, 1967), 40.
23. Ibid.
24. Charlotte Mankey Calasibetta and Phyllis Tortora,

eds., *The Fairchild Dictionary of Fashion*, 3rd ed. (New York: Fairchild Publications, 2003), 462.

25. Jan Glier Reeder, *High Style: Masterworks from the Brooklyn Museum Costume Collection at the Metropolitan Museum of Art* (New York: Metropolitan Museum of Art, 2010), 197.

2. T-Shirts: From Underwear to Everywhere

1. www.scribd.com/doc/33873413/1892-Dr-Jaeger-s -Sanitary-Woolen-System-Company-Catalogue.
2. Alice Harris, *The White T* (New York: HarperCollins, 1996), 16.
3. Dennita Sewell, "T-Shirt," in *A–Z of Fashion*.
4. Ed Branigan, "The Evolution of Garment Printing," *SGIA Journal* (second quarter, 2010), 24.
5. Sewell, "T-Shirt."
6. Branigan, "The Evolution of Garment Printing," 24.
7. Harris, *The White T*, 20.
8. Sewell, "T-Shirt."
9. Branigan, "The Evolution of Garment Printing," 25.
10. Harris, *The White T*, 34–35, photo.
11. Harris, *The White T*, 47, photo.
12. Tommy Hilfiger, *All-American* (New York: Universe, 1997), 60.
13. Branigan, "The Evolution of Garment Printing," 25.
14. www.sojones.com/news/1465-the-most-famous -statement-t-shirts/.
15. Amber Easby and Henry Oliver, *The Art of the Band T-Shirt* (New York: Gallery, 2007), 3.
16. Ibid.
17. Ibid., 33.
18. Kendra Nordin, "Smiley Face: How an In-House Campaign Became a Global Icon," *The Christian Science Monitor*, October 4, 2006, 1, www.csmonitor .com/2006/1004/p15s01-algn.html.
19. Charlotte Brunel, *The T-Shirt Book*, foreword by Bruno Collin (New York: Assouline, 2002), 14.
20. Imani Perry, "'Malcolm X,' by Manning Marable," *San Francisco Chronicle* (April 24, 2011), www .sfgate.com/cgi-bin/article.cgi?f=/c/a/2011/04/23/ RV611J2B0B.DTL.
21. Harris, *The White T*, 13.
22. Michiko Kakutani, "Brand Che: Revolutionary as Marketer's Dream," *The New York Times*, April 20, 2009, www.nytimes.com/2009/04/21/books/21kaku .html?scp=1sq=&st=nyt.
23. Ibid.
24. www.condenaststore.com/-sp/Che-Guevara -wearing-a-Bart-Simpson-T-shirt-New-Yorker- Cartoon-Prints_i8544414_.htm.
25. Brunel, *The T-Shirt Book*, 9.

3. Jeans: The Italian, French, German, English, Indian, All-American Garment

1. James Sullivan, *Jeans: The Cultural History of an American Icon* (New York: Gotham Books, 2006), 14.
2. Clare Sauro, "Jeans," in *A–Z of Fashion*.
3. Ibid.
4. http://blog.urbanoutfitters.com/features/the_levis_ archives?cm_mmc=broadcast-_-Q32010-_-100812l evisBuyers-_-banner&cm_lm=ashleyelizabethk@ gmail.com.
5. Robert Selbie, *The Anatomy of Costume* (New York: Crescent Books, 1977), 4.
6. Sullivan, *Jeans*, 13.
7. Carl Sandburg, *Abraham Lincoln: The Prairie Years and the War Years*, ed. Edward C. Goodman (Boston: Mariner Books, 2002), 27.
8. www.forbes.com/2005/11/29/most-expensive-jeans -cx_sy_1130feat_ls.html.

4. Dresses: From the Toga to the Wrap Dress

1. Phyllis Tortora, "Toga" in *A–Z of Fashion*.
2. Robert Selbie, *The Anatomy of Costume* (New York: Crescent Books, 1977), 18.
3. Ibid., 14.
4. www.stanford.edu/~plomio/history.html.
5. François Boucher, *20,000 Years of Fashion: The History of Costume and Personal Adornment*, expanded ed. (New York: Harry N. Abrams, 1987), 303.
6. Patricia A. Cunningham, "Dress Reform," in *Berg Encyclopedia of World Dress and Fashion*, vol. 3, *The United States and Canada*.
7. Rebecca Arnold, "Madeleine Vionnet," in *A–Z of Fashion*.
8. James Laver, *Taste and Fashion: From the French Revolution Until To-day* (London: G. G. Harrap, 1937), 124.
9. Hal Vaughan, *Sleeping with the Enemy: Coco Chanel's Secret War* (New York: Knopf, 2011), 142.
10. Liz Mellish, "Early History of Dress," in *Berg Encyclopedia of World Dress and Fashion*, vol. 9, *East Europe, Russia, and the Caucasus*.
11. Gillian Tineke Vogelsang-Eastwood Rooijakkers, "Egypt: Historical Dress," in *Berg Encyclopedia of World Dress and Fashion*, vol. 1, *Africa*.
12. Ibid.

13. Ibid.

14. James Laver, *Costume* (London: Cassell, 1963), 7.

15. Ibid., 32.

16. Ibid., 36.

17. Ibid., 45.

18. James Laver, *Costume and Fashion: A Concise History* (New York: Thames & Hudson, 2002), 97.

19. Ibid., 97.

20. Melissa Leventon, *What People Wore When: A Complete Illustrated History of Costume from Ancient Times to the Nineteenth Century for Every Level of Society* (New York: St. Martin's Griffin, 2008), 154–55.

21. Boucher, *20,000 Years of Fashion*, 251.

22. Ibid., 291.

23. Laver, *Costume and Fashion*, 130.

24. Alison Lurie, *The Language of Clothes* (New York: Henry Holt, 2000), 64.

25. Ibid., 69.

26. Laver, *Costume and Fashion*, 184–86.

27. *Key Moments in Fashion: From Haute Couture to Streetwear, Key Collections, Major Figures and Crucial Moments That Changed the Course of Fashion History from 1890 to the 1990s* (London: Hamlyn, 1998), 15.

28. Anne Stegemeyer, *Who's Who in Fashion*, 2nd ed. (New York: Fairchild Publications, 1988), 5.

29. Ibid., 32.

30. "Carmen Says: A Couture Veteran Discusses the Way Things Were, Are, and May Never Be Again," *Garmento*, Issue 1 (2010), 45.

31. GeoffreyBeane.com.

32. Jane Eastoe and Sarah Gristwood, *Fabulous Frocks* (London: Pavilion, 2008), 6–7.

33. Judith Watt, ed., *The Penguin Book of Twentieth-Century Fashion Writing* (New York: Viking, 1999), 175.

34. Arnold Scaasi, *Women I Have Dressed (and Undressed!)* (New York: Scribner, 2004), 111–12.

35. Caroline Evans, *Fashion at the Edge: Spectacle, Modernity and Deathliness* (New Haven, CT: Yale University Press, 2003), 71.

36. Urmee Khan, "Liz Hurley 'Safety Pin' Dress Voted the Greatest Dress," *The Telegraph* (October 9, 2008), www.telegraph.co.uk/news/celebritynews/3167702/Liz-Hurley-safety-pin-dress-voted-the-greatest-dress.html.

37. Georgina O'Hara, *The Encyclopedia of Fashion* (New York: Harry N. Abrams, 1986), 32.

5. Capri Pants and Shorts:
   The Plague on Our Nation

1. Alison Lurie, *The Language of Clothes* (New York: Henry Holt, 2000), 45.

2. Ibid., 46.

3. Joseph H. Hancock II and Edward Augustyn, "Pants, Trousers," In *Berg Encyclopedia*, vol. 10, *Global Perspectives*.

4. Richard Martin and Harold Koda, *Jocks and Nerds: Men's Style in the Twentieth Century* (New York: Rizzoli, 1989), 113.

5. Ibid., 121.

6. Skirts: Mini, Midi, Maxi, and More

1. Paul Poiret, *King of Fashion: The Autobiography of Paul Poiret*, trans. Stephen Haden Guest (London: V&A Publishing, 2009), 36.

2. Quentin Bell, *On Human Finery*, rev. ed. (London: Hogarth Press, 1976), 37.

3. James Laver, *Taste and Fashion: From the French Revolution Until To-Day* (London: G. G. Harrap, 1937), 49–50, 55.

4. Myra Walker, "Miniskirt," in *A–Z of Fashion*.

5. Ibid.

6. Sara Pendergast and Tom Pendergast, *Fashion, Costume, and Culture: Clothing, Headwear, Body Decorations, and Footwear Through the Ages*, ed. Sarah Hermsen, vol. 5 (Detroit: UXL, 2004), 908–9.

7. Ralph Graves, ed., "The Midi Muscles In," *Life*, August 21, 1970.

8. Valerie Steele, *Encyclopedia of Clothing and Fashion*, vol. 2 (Farmington Hills, MI: Charles Scribner's Sons, 2005), 9.

9. Andrew Bolton, *Bravehearts: Men in Skirts* (London: V&A Publications, 2003), 26–27.

7. Belts: Friend to Soldiers and Vixens

1. www.iceman.it.

2. James Laver, *Costume* (New York: Hawthorn Books, 1964), 2.

3. Ibid.

4. Valerie Cumming, C. W. Cunnington, and P. E. Cunnington, *The Dictionary of Fashion History* (Oxford: Berg, 2010), 11.

5. Berg Fashion Library, image of embroidered canvas suspenders, c. 1840.

8. Dress Shirts: Prudery and Puffery

1. Ester Juhasz, "Jewish Dress in Central and Southwest Asia and the Diaspora," in *Berg Encyclopedia of World Dress and Fashion*, vol. 5, *Central and Southwest Asia*.

2. James Laver, *Costume and Fashion: A Concise History*

(New York: Thames & Hudson, 2002), 97.

3. Ibid., 76 (image).

4. Ibid., 79.

5. Richard Martin and Harold Koda, *Jocks and Nerds: Men's Style in the Twentieth Century* (New York: Rizzoli, 1989), 15.

6. Ibid., 16–17.

9. Ties and Scarves: *Color Me Beautiful,* Hermès, and Other Cults

1. Jean-Louis Dumas-Hermès, *How to Wear Your Hermès Scarf* (Paris: Editions Hermès, 1986), 1.

2. Nadine Coleno, *The Hermès Scarf: History and Mystique* (London: Thames & Hudson, 2009), 29.

3. Andrew Baseman, ed., *The Scarf* (New York: Stewart, Tabori and Chang, 1989), 50.

4. Coleno, *The Hermès Scarf,* 18.

5. Baseman, *The Scarf,* 50.

6. Jan Glier Reeder, *High Style: Masterworks from the Brooklyn Museum Costume Collection at the Metropolitan Museum of Art* (New York: Metropolitan Museum of Art, 2010), 198.

7. James Laver, *Taste and Fashion: From the French Revolution Until To-day* (London: G. G. Harrap, 1937), 22.

8. Simon Doonan, "Bring Back Nancy Red!" *The New York Observer,* January 8, 2001, www.observer.com/2001/01/bring-back-nancy-red/.

9. Nina Lalli, "Checkered Past: Arafat's Trademark Scarf Is Now Military Chic," *Village Voice,* February 15, 2005, www.villagevoice.com/2005–02–15/nyc life/checkered-past/.

10. Anna König, "Neckties and Neckwear," in *A–Z of Fashion.*

11. Ibid.

12. Avril Hart, *Ties* (New York: Costume & Fashion Press, 1998), 68.

13. Richard Martin and Harold Koda, *Jocks and Nerds: Men's Style in the Twentieth Century* (New York: Rizzoli, 1989), 9.

10. Vests: Take That, France!

1. James Laver, *Costume and Fashion: A Concise History* (New York: Thames & Hudson, 2002), 54.

2. Valerie Cumming, C. W. Cunnington, and P. E. Cunnington, *The Dictionary of Fashion History* (Oxford: Berg, 2010), 218.

3. *Memoirs and Interesting Adventures of an Embroidered Waistcoat* (London: printed for and sold by J. Brooke,

at the Golden Head, under St. Dunstan's Church, Fleet-Street, 1751), 12.

4. Ibid., 13.

5. Sara Pendergast and Tom Pendergast, *Fashion, Costume, and Culture: Clothing, Headwear, Body Decorations, and Footwear Through the Ages,* ed. Sarah Hermsen, vol. 5 (Detroit: UXL, 2004), 907–8.

11. Suits: All Hail Beau Brummell!

1. Ian Kelly, *Beau Brummell: The Ultimate Man of Style* (New York: Free Press, 2006), 5.

2. Colleen Gau, "Conventional Work Dress and Casual Work Dress," in *Berg Encyclopedia of World Dress and Fashion,* vol. 3, *The United States and Canada.*

3. Bernhard Roetzel, *Gentlemen* (Cambridge: Könemann, 2004), 92–93.

4. Richard Martin and Harold Koda, *Jocks and Nerds: Men's Style in the Twentieth Century* (New York: Rizzoli, 1989), 113.

5. Ibid., 114–15.

6. Ibid., 115.

7. Nik Cohn, *Today There Are No Gentlemen: The Changes in Englishmen's Clothes Since the War* (London: Weidenfeld and Nicolson, 1971), 29–30.

8. Sara Pendergast and Tom Pendergast, *Fashion, Costume, and Culture: Clothing, Headwear, Body Decorations, and Footwear Through the Ages,* ed. Sarah Hermsen, vol. 5 (Detroit: UXL, 2004), 896.

9. James Laver, *Taste and Fashion: From the French Revolution Until Today* (London: G. G. Harrap, 1937), 20–21.

10. Colleen R. Callahan, "Children's Clothing," in *A–Z of Fashion.*

11. *Women's Wear Daily,* "Moment 11: Women Embrace Menswear," November 1, 2010, www.wwd.com/eye/fashion/moment-11-women-embrace-menswear-3344600?navSection=issues.

12. Melissa Leventon, *What People Wore When: A Complete Illustrated History of Costume from Ancient Times to the Nineteenth Century for Every Level of Society* (New York: St. Martin's Griffin, 2008), 154–55.

12. Pants: The Truth About Dress Reform

1. By the aptly named designer Amy Sly, www.buzzfeed.com/sly/am-i-wearing-pants.

2. James Laver, *Costume and Fashion: A Concise History* (New York: Thames & Hudson, 2002), 15.

3. Quentin Bell, *On Human Finery,* rev. ed. (London: Hogarth Press, 1976), 64–65.

4. Rosalie Kolodny, *Fashion Design for Moderns* (New York: Fairchild, 1968), 103.

5. Judith Thurman, "Closet Encounters: Charting the Rise of the Fashionable American Woman," *The New Yorker* (May 10, 2010), www.newyorker.com/arts /critics/artworld/2010/05/10/100510craw_artworld _thurman.

6. Joseph H. Hancock II and Edward Augustyn, "Pants, Trousers," in *Berg Encyclopedia of World Dress and Fashion*, vol. 10, *Global Perspectives*.

7. *Key Moments in Fashion: From Haute Couture to Streetwear, Key Collections, Major Figures and Crucial Moments That Changed the Course of Fashion History from 1890 to the 1990s* (London: Hamlyn, 1998), 101.

8. Shaun Cole, "Lesbian and Gay Dress," in *Berg Encyclopedia of World Dress and Fashion*, vol. 8, *West Europe*.

13. Hosiery: From the *Mayflower* to the Bedroom Floor

1. Nan H. Mutnick, "Snapshot: Hosiery," in *Berg Encyclopedia of World Dress and Fashion*, vol. 3, *The United States and Canada.*

2. Ibid.

3. Sara Pendergast and Tom Pendergast, *Fashion, Costume, and Culture: Clothing, Headwear, Body Decorations, and Footwear Through the Ages*, ed. Sarah Hermsen, vol. 5 (Detroit: UXL, 2004), 927.

4. James Laver, *Costume and Fashion: A Concise History* (New York: Thames & Hudson, 2002), 58.

5. Anne L. Macdonald, *No Idle Hands: The Social History of American Knitting* (New York: Ballantine Books, 1988), 3.

6. American Red Cross. *The War-Time Manual: Describing the Organization, History, Works and Reliefs of the American Red Cross Society* (Chicago: Service Publishers, 1917), 66.

7. Nan H. Mutnick, "Snapshot: Hosiery."

8. http://ask.metafilter.com/15115/What-color-socks -should-I-wear-with-brown-shoes-and-blue-jeans.

14. Shoes: The World at Your Feet

1. Andrew Bolton, *Alexander McQueen: Savage Beauty* (New York: Metropolitan Museum of Art, 2011). Three examples: Eclect Dissect (autumn/winter, 1997–98), red and black leather; La Dame Bleue (spring/summer, 2008), carved wood, leather, and silver beading; precollection (autumn/winter, 2006– 2007) red silk embroidered with black and white silk thread.

2. Jan Glier Reeder, *High Style: Masterworks from the Brooklyn Museum Costume Collection at the Metropolitan Museum of Art* (New York: Metropolitan Museum of Art, 2010), 227.

3. *Illuminating Fashion*, exhibit at the Pierpont Morgan Library.

4. Quentin Bell, *On Human Finery*, rev. ed. (London: Hogarth Press, 1976), 37.

5. Ibid.

6. James Laver, *Costume and Fashion: A Concise History* (New York: Thames & Hudson, 2002), 33.

7. Robert Selbie, *The Anatomy of Costume* (New York: Crescent Books, 1977), 20.

15. Athletic Wear: Attack of the Playclothes

1. Sara Pendergast and Tom Pendergast, *Fashion, Costume, and Culture: Clothing, Headwear, Body Decorations, and Footwear Through the Ages*, ed. Sarah Hermsen, vol. 5 (Detroit: UXL, 2004), 983.

2. Richard Martin and Harold Koda, *Jocks and Nerds: Men's Style in the Twentieth Century* (New York: Rizzoli, 1989), 23.

3. Rebecca Arnold, *The American Look: Fashion, Sportswear and the Image of Women in 1930s and 1940s New York* (London: I. B. Tauris, 2009), 199; also "Dress Trade More Attentive to Resort Wear," *Women's Wear Daily*, November 11, 1938.

4. Judith Thurman, "Closet Encounters: Charting the Rise of the Fashionable American Woman," *The New Yorker* (May 10, 2010), www.newyorker.com/arts /critics/artworld/2010/05/10/100510craw_artworld_ thurman.

5. Alison Lurie, *The Language of Clothes* (New York: Henry Holt, 2000), 58.

6. Bradley Quinn, "Sportswear," in *A–Z of Fashion*.

7. Martin and Koda, *Jocks and Nerds*, 30.

8. Ibid., 28.

9. Ibid., 27.

10. James Laver, *Costume and Fashion: A Concise History* (New York: Thames & Hudson, 2002), 60.

11. "History of the Bikini," Time.com, http://www.time .com/time/photogallery/0,29307,1908353,00.html.

12. Marybelle S. Bigelow, *Fashion in History: Apparel in the Western World* (Minneapolis: Burgess, 1979), 295.

13. Patrik Alac, *The Bikini: A Cultural History* (London and New York: Parkstone Press, 2002), 21.

14. Ibid., 29.

15. Ibid., 31.

16. Sara Pendergast and Tom Pendergast, *Fashion, Costume, and Culture: Clothing, Headwear, Body Decorations, and Footwear Through the Ages,* ed. Sarah Hermsen, vol. 5 (Detroit: UXL, 2004), 854.

17. Alac, *The Bikini*, 32.

18. Jantzenswim.com.

19. Jane Pavitt, "Logos," in *A–Z of Fashion*.

20. Martin and Koda, *Jocks and Nerds*, 121.

21. Pavitt, "Logos."

22. Martin and Koda, *Jocks and Nerds*, 30.

17. Coats and Jackets: From Cavemen to *Real Housewives*

1. Liz Mellish, "Early History of Dress," in *Berg Encyclopedia of World Dress and Fashion*, vol. 9, *East Europe, Russia, and the Caucasus*.

2. Quentin Bell quotes his hero Veblen, in *On Human Finery*, rev. ed. (London: Hogarth Press, 1976), 15.

3. Robert Selbie, *The Anatomy of Costume* (New York: Crescent Books, 1977), 15.

4. Stefano Tonchi, "Military Style," in *The Berg Companion to Fashion*, ed. Valerie Steele (Oxford: Berg, 2010), 507.

5. Walking dress ensemble (1817–1820) image caption of white silk dress with bands and braiding, Berg Fashion Library.

6. Stefano Tonchi, "Military Style," in *The Berg Companion to Fashion*, 507.

7. Ibid.

8. Julia Emberley, "Fur," in *A–Z of Fashion*.

18. Hats: Crowning Glory

1. John Potvin, ed., *The Places and Spaces of Fashion, 1800–2007* (New York: Routledge, 2009), 117.

2. Laurel Wilson, "Western Wear," in *Berg Encyclopedia of World Dress and Fashion*, vol. 3, *The United States and Canada*.

3. James Laver, *Costume and Fashion: A Concise History* (New York: Thames & Hudson, 2002), 23.

4. Ibid., 18–19.

5. Ibid., 15.

19. Gloves: The Long-Lost Love Token

1. C. Cody Collins, *Love of a Glove: The Romance, Legends and Fashion History of Gloves and How They Are Made* (New York: Fairchild, 1945), 10.

2. Ibid., 15.

3. Ibid., 13.

4. Ibid., 16.

5. Ibid., 24.

6. Ibid., 29.

7. Ibid., 76.

8. Ibid., 4.

9. Claire McCardell, *What Shall I Wear? The What, Where, When and How Much of Fashion* (New York: Simon & Schuster, 1956), 57.

20. Handbags: Enemy of the Pocket

1. Diana Vreeland, *D.V.* (1984), ed. George Plimpton and Christopher Hemphil (New York: Da Capo Press, 1997), 89.

2. Annie Groer, "Hermès v. Hermès," *The Washington Post*, June 28, 2006, quoting March 2006, *Scotland on Sunday* interview with Jane Birkin, www.washington post.com/wp-dyn/content/article/2006/06/28/AR2006062801276.html.

3. Michael Tonello, *Bringing Home the Birkin: My Life in Hot Pursuit of the World's Most Coveted Handbag* (New York: William Morrow, 2008), 152.

Conclusion: How to Shop with the Past, Present, and Future in Mind

1. Alison Lurie, *The Language of Clothes* (New York: Henry Holt, 2000), 5.

2. Ibid., 34.

3. Leopoldina Fortunati, "Wearable Technology," in *Berg Encyclopedia of World Dress and Fashion*, vol. 10, *Global Perspectives*.

4. Linda Grant, *The Thoughtful Dresser: The Art of Adornment, the Pleasures of Shopping, and Why Clothes Matter* (New York: Scribner, 2010), 10.

5. Quentin Bell, *On Human Finery*, rev. ed. (London: Hogarth Press, 1976), 21–22, quoting Isaiah 3:16–24.

6. Jan Glier Reeder, *High Style: Masterworks from the Brooklyn Museum Costume Collection at the Metropolitan Museum of Art* (New York: Metropolitan Museum of Art, 2010), 220.

BIBLIOGRAPHY

Our favorite resource was the massive *Berg Encyclopedia of World Dress and Fashion*, which came out in 2010 from Oxford University Press, just as we were beginning our research. We extensively consulted the *Berg* (which has collected many of the best print, online, and photographic resources into its database) both in print at the New York Public Library and online at BergFashionLibrary.com. Online materials are available only by subscription, but interested readers should see if their local public library subscribes. Here is a list of specific authored Berg articles:

Bye, Elizabeth K. "Nautical Style." In *A–Z of Fashion*.

Chico, Beverly. "Headdress." In *A–Z of Fashion*.

Cole, Shaun. "Lesbian and Gay Dress." In *Berg Encyclopedia*. Vol. 8, *West Europe*.

Cox, Caroline. "Lingerie." In *A–Z of Fashion*.

Emberley, Julia. "Fur." In *A–Z of Fashion*.

Evans, Grace. "Underwear." In *Berg Encyclopedia*. Vol. 8, *West Europe*.

Friedel, Robert. "Zipper." In *A–Z of Fashion*.

Gau, Colleen. "Brassiere." In *A–Z of Fashion*.

Gau, Colleen, and Valerie Steele. "Corset." In *A–Z of Fashion*.

Greatrex, Tom. "Waistcoat." In *A–Z of Fashion*.

Hancock, Joseph H., II, and Edward Augustyn. "Pants, Trousers." In *Berg Encyclopedia*. Vol. 10, *Global Perspectives*.

Juhasz, Esther. "Jewish Dress in Central and Southwest Asia and the Diaspora." In *Berg Encyclopedia*. Vol. 5, *Central and Southwest Asia*.

König, Anna. "Neckties and Neckwear." In *A–Z of Fashion*.

Lee, Mireille M. "Ancient Greek Dress." In *Berg Encyclopedia*. Vol. 9, *East Europe, Russia, and the Caucasus*.

Mellish, Liz. "Early History of Dress." In *Berg Encyclopedia*. Vol. 9, *East Europe, Russia, and the Caucasus*.

Mutnick, Nan H. "Snapshot: Hosiery." In *Berg Encyclopedia*. Vol. 3, *The United States and Canada*.

Parsons, Jean L. "Leisure." In *Berg Encyclopedia*. Vol. 3, *The United States and Canada*.

Pavitt, Jane. "Logos." In *A–Z of Fashion*.

Quinn, Bradley. "Sportswear." In *A–Z of Fashion*.

Rooijakkers, Gillian Tineke Vogelsang-Eastwood. "Egypt: Historical Dress." In *Berg Encyclopedia*. Vol. 1, *Africa*.

Sauro, Clare. "Boots." In *A–Z of Fashion*.

Sewell, Dennita. "T-Shirt." In *A–Z of Fashion*.

Stall-Meadows, Celia. "Accessories of Dress." In *Berg Encyclopedia*. Vol. 3, *The United States and Canada*.

Tonchi, Stefano. "Military Style." In *A–Z of Fashion*.

Tortora, Phyllis G. "Types and Properties of Fashionable Dress." In *Berg Encyclopedia*. Vol. 3, *The United States and Canada*.

Walford, Jonathan. "Shoes." In *A–Z of Fashion*.

Walker, Myra. "Miniskirt." In *A–Z of Fashion*.

Watkins, Susan M. "Fashion, Health, and Disease." In *A–Z of Fashion*.

Webber-Hanchett, Tiffany. "Bikini." In *A–Z of Fashion*.

Wilson, Laurel. "Western Wear." In *Berg Encyclopedia*. Vol. 3, *The United States and Canada*.

We also looked at countless books and articles. (Our favorite scholar is the late James Laver, and we very much enjoy the *Fairchild Dictionary of Fashion*.) Here is a list of those:

Alac, Patrik. *The Bikini: A Cultural History*. London and New York: Parkstone Press, 2002.

American Red Cross. *The War-Time Manual: Describing the Organization, History, Works and Reliefs of the American Red Cross Society*. Chicago: Service Publishers, 1917.

Anawalt, Patricia Rieff. *The Worldwide History of Dress*. New York: Thames & Hudson, 2007.

Arnold, Rebecca. *The American Look: Fashion, Sportswear and the Image of Women in 1930s and 1940s New York*. London: I. B. Tauris, 2009.

Baclawski, Karen. *The Guide to Historic Costume*. London: Batsford, 1995.

Barthes, Roland. *The Language of Fashion*. Translated by Andy Stafford. New York: Berg, 2005.

Baseman, Andrew, ed. *The Scarf*. New York: Stewart, Tabori and Chang, 1989.

Batterberry, Michael, and Ariane Batterberry. *Fashion: The Mirror of History*. New York: Greenwich House, 1977.

Bell, Quentin. *On Human Finery*. Revised ed. London: Hogarth Press, 1976.

Bennett-England, Rodney. *Dress Optional: The Revolution in Menswear*. London: Peter Owen, 1967.

Berch, Bettina. *Radical by Design: The Life and Style of Elizabeth Hawes, Fashion Designer, Union Organizer, and Best-Selling Author*. New York: Dutton, 1988.

Bigelow, Marybelle S. *Fashion in History: Apparel in the Western World*. Minneapolis: Burgess, 1979.

Black, Alexandra. *The Evening Dress*. New York: Rizzoli, 2004.

Black, Sandy. *Knitwear in Fashion*. New York: Thames & Hudson, 2002.

Bolton, Andrew. *Alexander McQueen: Savage Beauty*. New York: Metropolitan Museum of Art, 2011.

———. *Bravehearts: Men in Skirts*. London: V&A Publications, 2003.

Boucher, François. *20,000 Years of Fashion: The History of Costume and Personal Adornment*. Expanded ed. New York: Harry N. Abrams, 1987.

Branigan, Ed. "The Evolution of Garment Printing." *SGIA* [Specialty Graphic Imaging Association] *Journal* (second quarter, 2010).

Breward, Christopher. *The Culture of Fashion: A New History of Fashionable Dress*. Manchester: Manchester University Press, 1995.

Breward, Christopher, and Caroline Evans, eds. *Fashion and Modernity*. Oxford: Berg, 2005.

Brooks, Amanda. *I Love Your Style: How to Define and Refine Your Personal Style*. Foreword by Diane von Furstenberg. New York: HarperCollins, It Books, 2009.

Bruhn, Wolfgang, and Max Tilke. *A Pictorial History of Costume: From Ancient Times to the Nineteenth Century*. Mineola, NY: Dover, 2004.

Brunel, Charlotte. *The T-Shirt Book*. Foreword by Bruno Collin. New York: Assouline, 2002.

Bunn, Austin. "Not Fade Away." *New York Times Magazine* (December 1, 2002), www.nytimes.com/2002/12/01/magazine/01JEANS.html?pagewanted=all.

Buxbaum, Gerda, ed. *Icons of Fashion: The Twentieth Century*. Munich: Prestel, 2005.

Calasibetta, Charlotte Mankey, and Phyllis Tortora, eds. *The Fairchild Dictionary of Fashion*, 3rd ed. New York: Fairchild Publications, 2003.

Carter, Ernestine. *Magic Names of Fashion*. Englewood Cliffs, NJ: Prentice Hall, 1980.

Chierichetti, David. *Edith Head: The Life and Times of Hollywood's Celebrated Costume Designer*. New York: HarperCollins, 2003.

Cleland, Liza, Glenys Davies, and Lloyd Llewellyn-Jones. *Greek and Roman Dress from A to Z*. London: Routledge, 2007.

Clifford, Stephanie. "One Size Fits Nobody: Seeking a Steady 4 or a 10," www.nytimes.com/2011/04/25/business/25sizing.html?_r=1&scp=1&sq=%22one%20size%20fits%20nobody%22&st=cse.

Cohn, Nik. *Today There Are No Gentlemen: The Changes in Englishmen's Clothes Since the War*. London: Weidenfeld and Nicolson, 1971.

Coleno, Nadine. *The Hermès Scarf: History and Mystique*. London: Thames & Hudson, 2009.

Collins, C. Cody. *Love of a Glove: The Romance, Legends and Fashion History of Gloves and How They Are Made*. New York: Fairchild, 1945.

Condra, Jill, ed. *The Greenwood Encyclopedia of Clothing Through World History*, 3 vols. Westport: Greenwood Press, 2008.

Contini, Mila. *Fashion: From Ancient Egypt to the Present Day.* Edited by James Laver. New York: Odyssey Press, 1965.

Cosgrave, Bronwyn. *The Complete History of Costume and Fashion from Ancient Egypt to the Present Day.* New York: Checkmark Books, 2000.

Cunningham, Michael, and Craig Marberry. *Crowns: Portraits of Black Women in Church Hats.* New York: Doubleday, 2000.

Dechter, Gadi. "XXXXXXXL: The Secret History of the Galaxy Tall Tee." *Baltimore City Paper* (August 10, 2005), www2.citypaper.com/bob/story.asp?id=10381.

Design Museum. *Fifty Shoes That Changed the World.* London: Octopus Publishing, Conran Octopus, 2009.

Domnick, Sabine. *Cables, Diamonds, Herringbone: Secrets of Knitting Traditional Fishermen's Sweaters.* Camden, ME: Down East Books, 2007.

Doonan, Simon. "Bring Back Nancy Red!" *The New York Observer* (January 8, 2001), www.observer.com/2001/01/bring-back-nancy-red/.

Drake, Alicia. *The Beautiful Fall: Lagerfeld, Saint Laurent, and the Glorious Excess in 1970s Paris.* New York: Little, Brown, 2006.

Dumas-Hermès, Jean-Louis. *How to Wear Your Hermès Scarf.* Paris: Editions Hermès, 1986.

Easby, Amber, and Henry Oliver. *The Art of the Band T-Shirt.* New York: Gallery, 2007.

Eastoe, Jane, and Sarah Gristwood. *Fabulous Frocks.* London: Pavilion, 2008.

Eicher, Joanne B., Sandra Lee Evenson, and Hazel A. Lutz. *The Visible Self: Global Perspectives on Dress, Culture, and Society*, 2nd ed. New York: Fairchild Publications, 2000.

English, Bonnie. *A Cultural History of Fashion in the Twentieth Century: From the Catwalk to the Sidewalk.* New York: Berg, 2007.

Evans, Caroline. *Fashion at the Edge: Spectacle, Modernity and Deathliness.* New Haven, CT: Yale University Press, 2003.

Falluel, Fabienne, Muriel Barbier, and Shazia Boucher. *The Story of Lingerie* (Temporis Collection). New York: Parkstone Press, 2005.

Fogarty, Anne. *Wife Dressing: The Fine Art of Being a Well-Dressed Wife.* 1959. Reprinted with an introduction by Rosemary Feitelberg. New York: Glitterati, 2007.

France, Kim, and Andrea Linett. *The Lucky Shopping Manual: Building and Improving Your Wardrobe Piece by Piece.* New York: Gotham Books, 2003.

Fraser, Kennedy. *The Fashionable Mind: Reflections on Fashion, 1970–1981.* New York: Knopf, 1981.

Fukai, Akiko, ed. *Fashion: A History from the 18th to the 20th Century.* Vol. II. Cologne: Taschen, 2006.

Garland, Madge. *The Changing Form of Fashion.* New York: Praeger, 1971.

Gorsline, Douglas. *What People Wore: 1,800 Illustrations from Ancient Times to the Early Twentieth Century.* New York: Dover, 1994.

Grant, Linda. *The Thoughtful Dresser: The Art of Adornment, the Pleasures of Shopping, and Why Clothes Matter.* New York: Scribner, 2010.

Graves, Ralph, ed. "The Midi Muscles In." *Life* (August 21, 1970).

Groer, Annie. "Hermès v. Hermès." *The Washington Post* (June 28, 2006), www.washingtonpost.com/wp-dyn/content/article/2006/06/28/AR2006062801276.html.

Harris, Alice. *The Blue Jean.* New York: PowerHouse Books, 2002.

————. *The White T.* New York: HarperCollins, HarperStyle, 1996.

Hart, Avril. *Ties.* New York: Costume & Fashion Press, 1998.

Hartley, Marie, and Joan Ingilby. *The Old Hand-Knitters of the Dales. With an Introduction to the Early History of Knitting.* Clapham (via Lancaster), Yorkshire: Dalesman, 1951.

Hawes, Elizabeth. *Anything but Love: A Complete Digest of the Rules for Feminine Behavior from Birth to Death, Given Out in Print, on Film, and Over the Air, Read, Seen, Listened to Monthly by Some 340,000,000 American Women.* New York: Rinehart, 1948.

————. *Fashion Is Spinach.* New York: Random House, 1938.

————. *It's Still Spinach.* Boston: Little Brown, 1954.

————. *Men Can Take It.* Illustrated by James Thurber. New York: Random House, 1939.

————. *Why Is a Dress?* New York: Viking, 1942.

————. *Why Women Cry: Or, Wenches with Wrenches.* New York: Reynal & Hitchcock, 1943.

Hazen, Gale Grigg. *Fantastic Fit for Every Body: How to Alter Patterns to Flatter Any Figure.* New York: Rodale, 1998.

Heimann, Jim, ed. *60s Fashion: Vintage Fashion and Beauty Ads.* Cologne: Taschen, 2007.

Heimann, Jim, and Alison A. Nieder. *20th Century Fashion: 100 Years of Apparel Ads.* Cologne: Taschen, 2009.

Hermès. *How to Wear Your Hermès Scarf.* Paris: Hermès, 1994.

Hilfiger, Tommy. *All American.* New York: Universe, 1997.

Hollander, Anne. *Sex and Suits: The Evolution of Modern Dress.* New York: Kodansha International, 1994.

Jackson, Carole. *Color Me Beautiful: Discover Your Natural Beauty Through the Colors That Make You Look Great and Feel Fabulous.* Washington, DC: Acropolis Books, 1980.

Johnson, Anna. *Handbags: The Power of the Purse.* New York: Workman, 2002.

Kakutani, Michiko. "Brand Che: Revolutionary as Marketer's Dream." *The New York Times* (April 20, 2009), www.nytimes.com/2009/04/21/books/21kaku.html?scp=1&sq=&st=nyt.

Kamitsis, Lydia. *Vionnet.* Paris: Assouline, 1996.

Kehe, John. "Michael Jackson's Famous Glove: Where It All Started." *The Christian Science Monitor* (June 26, 2009), www.csmonitor.com/USA/2009/0626/p02s19-usgn.html.

Key Moments in Fashion: From Haute Couture to Streetwear, Key Collections, Major Figures and Crucial Moments That Changed the Course of Fashion History from 1890 to the 1990s. London: Hamlyn, 1998.

Khan, Urmee. "Liz Hurley 'Safety Pin' Dress Voted the Greatest Dress." *The Telegraph* (October 9, 2008), www.telegraph.co.uk/news/celebritynews/3167702/Liz-Hurley-safety-pin-dress-voted-the-greatest-dress.html.

Kidwell, Claudia B., and Margaret C. Christman. *Suiting Everyone: The Democratization of Clothing in America.* Washington, DC: Smithsonian Institution Press, 1974.

Kiewe, Heinz Edgar. *The Sacred History of Knitting.* Oxford: Art Needlework Industries, 1967.

Kneitel, Ken, Bill Maloney, and Andrea Quinn. *The Great American T-Shirt.* New York: New American Library, 1976.

Koda, Harold, and Andrew Bolton, eds. *Chanel.* New York: Metropolitan Museum of Art, 2005.

Kolodny, Rosalie. *Fashion Design for Moderns.* New York: Fairchild, 1968.

Kunzle, David. *Fashion and Fetishism: A Social History of the Corset, Tight-Lacing, and Other Forms of Body-Sculpture in the West.* Totowa, NJ: Rowman and Littlefield, 1982.

Lalli, Nina. "Checkered Past: Arafat's Trademark Scarf Is Now Military Chic." *Village Voice* (February 15, 2005), www.villagevoice.com/2005-02-15/nyc-life/checkered-past/.

Langner, Lawrence. *The Importance of Wearing Clothes.* Introduction by James Laver. New York: Hastings House, 1959.

Laver, James. *Costume.* London: Cassell, 1963.

————. *Costume and Fashion: A Concise History.* New York: Thames & Hudson, 2002.

————. *Costume Through the Ages: 1000 Illustrations.* Illustrated by Erhard Klepper. New York: Simon & Schuster, 1963.

————. *Taste and Fashion: From the French Revolution Until To-day.* London: George G. Harrap, 1937.

Lee, Sarah Tomerlin, ed. *American Fashion: The Life and Lines of Adrian, Mainbocher, McCardell, Norell, Trigère.* New York: Quadrangle, 1975.

Leibowitz, Elissa. "The 'In' Shirt with the Outré Name." *The Washington Post* (January 29, 2009).

Lerner, Maura. "The Observatory: Study Shows How We Suffer for Fashion." *The Star-Tribune* (February 9, 2000).

Leventon, Melissa. *What People Wore When: A Complete Illustrated History of Costume from Ancient Times to the Nineteenth Century for Every Level of Society.* New York: St. Martin's Griffin, 2008.

Lewis, Jeremy, ed. *Garmento*, Issue 1 (2010).

Lurie, Alison. *The Language of Clothes.* New York: Henry Holt, 2000.

Macdonald, Anne L. *No Idle Hands: The Social History of American Knitting.* New York: Ballantine Books, 1988.

Malcolm, Trisha, ed. *Vogue Knitting: Designer Knits.* New York: Butterick, 1998.

Martin, Richard. *American Ingenuity: Sportswear, 1930s–1970s.* New York: Metropolitan Museum of Art, 1998.

Martin, Richard, and Harold Koda. *Jocks and Nerds: Men's Style in the Twentieth Century.* New York: Rizzoli, 1989.

McCardell, Claire. *What Shall I Wear? The What, Where, When and How Much of Fashion.* New York: Simon & Schuster, 1956.

McDowell, Colin. *The Literary Companion to Fashion.* London: Sinclair-Stevenson, 1995.

————. *McDowell's Directory of Twentieth Century Fashion.* Englewood Cliffs, NJ: Prentice Hall, 1985.

McNeil, Peter, ed. *Fashion: Critical and Primary Sources.* 4 vols. Oxford and New York: Berg, 2009.

Memoirs and Interesting Adventures of an Embroidered Waistcoat. London: printed for and sold by J. Brooke, at the Golden Head, under St. Dunstan's Church, Fleet-Street, 1751.

Milbank, Caroline Rennolds. *New York Fashion: The Evolution of American Style*. New York: Harry N. Abrams, 1989.

Mullin, Wendy. *Built by Wendy Dresses: The Sew U Guide to Making a Girl's Best Frock*. New York: Potter Craft, 2010.

Nickel, Helmut, ed. *Arms & Armor from the Permanent Collection*. New York: Metropolitan Museum of Art, 1991.

Nordin, Kendra. "Smiley Face: How an In-house Campaign Became a Global Icon." *The Christian Science Monitor* (October 4, 2006), www.csmonitor.com/2006/1004/p15s01-algn.html.

O'Hara, Georgina. *The Encyclopedia of Fashion*. Introduction by Carrie Donovan. New York: Harry N. Abrams, 1986.

Peacock, John. *The Chronicle of Western Fashion: From Ancient Times to the Present Day*. New York: Harry N. Abrams, 1991.

————. *Fashion Sourcebooks: The 1920s*. London: Thames & Hudson, 1998.

————. *Fashion Sourcebooks: The 1930s*. London: Thames & Hudson, 1998.

————. *Fashion Sourcebooks: The 1940s*. London: Thames & Hudson, 1998.

————. *Fashion Sourcebooks: The 1950s*. London: Thames & Hudson, 1998.

————. *Fashion Sourcebooks: The 1960s*. London: Thames & Hudson, 1998.

————. *Fashion Sourcebooks: The 1970s*. London: Thames & Hudson, 1998.

————. *Fashion Sourcebooks: The 1980s*. London: Thames & Hudson, 1998.

Pendergast, Sara, and Tom Pendergast. *Fashion, Costume, and Culture: Clothing, Headwear, Body Decorations, and Footwear Through the Ages*. Edited by Sarah Hermsen. 5 vols. Detroit: UXL, 2003–2004.

Peres, Daniel, and the Editors of *Details*. *Details Men's Style Manual: The Ultimate Guide for Making Your Clothes Work for You*. New York: Gotham Books, 2007.

Perry, Imani. "'Malcolm X,' by Manning Marable." *San Francisco Chronicle* (April 24, 2011), www.sfgate.com/cgi-bin/article.cgi?f=/c/a/2011/04/23/RV611J2B0B.DTL.

Poiret, Paul. *King of Fashion: The Autobiography of Paul Poiret*. Translated by Stephen Haden Guest. London: V&A Publishing, 2009.

Potvin, John, ed. *The Places and Spaces of Fashion, 1800–2007*. New York: Routledge, 2009.

Purdy, Daniel Leonhard, ed. *The Rise of Fashion: A Reader*. Minneapolis: University of Minnesota Press, 2004.

Reeder, Jan Glier. *High Style: Masterworks from the Brooklyn Museum Costume Collection at the Metropolitan Museum of Art*. New York: Metropolitan Museum of Art, 2010.

Roetzel, Bernhard. *Gentleman: A Timeless Fashion*. Cologne: Könemann, 2004.

Rutt, Richard. *A History of Hand Knitting*. London: Batsford, 1987.

Scaasi, Arnold. *Women I Have Dressed (and Undressed!)*. New York: Scribner, 2004.

Selbie, Robert. *The Anatomy of Costume*. New York: Crescent Books, 1977.

Steele, Valerie. "The Revolution: Liberty, Equality, and Antiquity." In *Paris Fashion: A Cultural History*. Oxford: Berg, 1998.

Steele, Valerie, ed. *The Berg Companion to Fashion*. Oxford: Berg, 2010.

————. *Encyclopedia of Clothing and Fashion*. Vol. 2: *Fads to Nylon*. Farmington Hills, MI: Thompson Gale, 2005.

————. *Fifty Years of Fashion: New Look to Now*. New Haven: Yale University Press, 1997.

————. *The Impossible Collection of Fashion*. New York: Assouline, 2011.

Stegemeyer, Anne. *Who's Who in Fashion*. New York: Fairchild Publications, 1988.

Sullivan, James. *Jeans: A Cultural History of an American Icon*. New York: Gotham Books, 2006.

Tatar, Steven, with Denise Grollmus. *The Ohio Knitting Mills Knitting Book: 26 Patterns Celebrating Four Decades of American Sweater Style*. New York: Artisan, 2010.

Tétart-Vittu, Françoise. *Auguste Racinet: The Complete Costume History*. Cologne: Taschen, 2006.

Theaker, Julie. "History 101." Knitty.com (Spring 2006), http://knitty.com/ISSUEspring06/FEAThistory101.html.

Thesander, Marianne. *The Feminine Ideal*. Translated by Nicholas Hills. London: Reaktion Books, 1997.

Thomas, Inigo. "Just Dandy: The Enduring Mystique of the White Suit." Slate.com (May 25, 2005), http://img.slate.com/id/2119498/.

Thompson, Gladys. *Patterns for Guernseys, Jerseys, and Arans: Fishermen's Sweaters from the British Isles*. New York: Dover, 1979.

Thurman, Judith. "Closet Encounters: Charting the Rise of the Fashionable American Woman." *The New Yorker*

(May 10, 2010), www.newyorker.com/arts/critics/artworld/2010/05/10/100510craw_artworld_thurman.

Time. "Fashion: The American Look." *Time* (May 2, 1955).

Tonello, Michael. *Bringing Home the Birkin: My Life in Hot Pursuit of the World's Most Coveted Handbag.* New York: William Morrow, 2008.

Tortora, Phyllis G., and Robert S. Merkel, eds. *Fairchild's Dictionary of Textiles*, 7th ed. New York: Fairchild Publications, 1996.

Tosa, Marco. *Evening Dresses 1900–1940.* Translated by Carolyn Cotchett. The Twentieth Century: Histories of Fashion. Modena, Italy: Zanfi Editori, 1988.

Trebay, Guy. "American Fashion's Coming-Out in Paris." *The New York Times: Thursday Styles* (January 12, 2011), www.nytimes.com/2011/01/13/fashion/13Costume.html?src=twt&twt=nytimesstyle.

Vaughan, Hal. *Sleeping with the Enemy: Coco Chanel's Secret War.* New York: Knopf, 2011.

Vinken, Barbara. *Fashion Zeitgeist: Trends and Cycles in the Fashion System.* Translated by Mark Hewson. Oxford: Berg, 2005

Vreeland, Diana. *D.V.* Edited by George Plimpton and Christopher Hemphil. 1984. Reprinted with a new foreword by Mary Louise Wilson. New York: Da Capo Press, 1997.

Weibel, Adèle Coulin. *Two Thousand Years of Textiles: The Figured Textiles of Europe and the Near East.* New York: Pantheon Books, 1952.

Weldon Owen. *Style Yourself: Inspired Advice from the World's Top Fashion Bloggers.* Foreword by Jane Aldridge. San Francisco: Weldon Owen, 2011.

Welters, Linda, and Patricia A. Cunningham, eds. *Twentieth-Century American Fashion.* Oxford: Berg, 2005.

Werle, Simone. *50 Fashion Designers You Should Know.* Munich: Prestel, 2010.

Willett, C., and Phillis Cunnington. *The History of Underclothes.* 1951. Reprinted with revisions by A. D. Mansfield and Valerie Mansfield. London: Faber and Faber, 1981.

Williams, Beryl. *Fashion Is Our Business.* Philadelphia: J. B. Lippincott, 1945.

———. *Young Faces in Fashion.* Philadelphia: J. B. Lippincott, 1956.

Yohannan, Kohle, and Nancy Nolf. *Claire McCardell: Redefining Modernism.* Foreword by Dorothy Twining Globus. Introduction by Valerie Steele. New York: Harry N. Abrams, 1998.

We love museums, and went to several fashion exhibits that were especially inspiring:

American Woman: Fashioning a National Identity. New York: Metropolitan Museum of Art. Visited August 2010.

Cleopatra: The Search for the Last Queen of Egypt. Philadelphia: Franklin Institute. Visited December 2010.

Illuminating Fashion. New York: Pierpont Morgan Library. Visited June 2011.

The Master of Blue Jeans. New York: Didier Aaron Gallery. Visited January 2011.

Savage Beauty: Alexander McQueen. New York: Metropolitan Museum of Art. Visited July 2011.

Sporting Life. New York: the Museum at FIT. Visited August 2011.

ACKNOWLEDGMENTS

For professional support and general wonderfulness: Peter Steinberg, Marsha Tonkins, and Jonathan Swaden. For making the publishing process so joyful: everyone at Gallery Books, including Louise Burke; Jen Bergstrom; Jen Robinson; Jean Anne Rose; Alex Lewis; Lisa Litwack; Chris Sergio; Jaime Putorti; Kris Tobiassen; and especially our brilliant editor, Trish Boczkowski; as well as Greg Kirmser for his excellent photo research. For the crash course in fashion history: everyone at the New York Public Library, especially Clayton Kirking and Jay Barksdale. The Wertheim Study was a lovely place to work—and to be shushed for whispering. Thanks especially to all the fashion experts and authors we consulted in person and in print.

ILLUSTRATION CREDITS

Page 2: Marie Antoinette by Élisabeth Vigée-Lebrun (1779)/Palace of Versailles; page 3: Apeda Studio, NYPL, isadora_0011vb; page 4: Everett Collection; page 5: PP238.11.007, courtesy of the Maryland Historical Society; page 10: Everett Collection; page 11: Mary Evans/National Magazine Company/Everett Collection; page 12: Mary Evans Picture Library/Everett Collection; page 15: Advertising Archive/Everett Collection; page 16: Everett Collection; page 17: Michael Cali/Rex Features/Everett Collection; page 24: Everett Collection; page 25: Eliot Elisofon/Time & Life Pictures/Getty Images; pages 26, 27, 28: Everett Collection; page 29: © Universal/Everett Collection; page 30: Jason Smith/Everett Collection; page 31: Matthew Diffee/The New Yorker/Condé Nast; page 33: Frank Micelotta/Getty Images Entertainment/Getty Images; page 38: Everett Collection; pages 39, 41: Advertising Archive/Everett Collection; page 42: Walker Evans/Everett Collection; pages 43, 44: Everett Collection; page 45: Advertising Archive/Everett Collection; page 50: (*left*) Bain Collection, Library of Congress; (*right*) "Grandma + My Dad" © sflovestory/CC-BY-SA-2.0; page 51: Albert Edwin Roberts, Queensland Museum; pages 53, 54, 55 (*top*): Everett Collection; page 55 (*bottom*): © Miramax/Everett Collection; page 56: (*upper left*) Mary Evans/Peter & Dawn Cope Collection/Everett Collection; (*upper right*) Mary Evans Picture Library/Everett Collection; (*bottom*): Brooklyn Museum Costume Collection/The Metropolitan Museum of Art/Gift of Diana S. Field; page 57: JACQUES DEMARTHON/AFP/Getty Images; page 58: Mary Evans/National Magazines/Everett Collection; page 59: Mirrowpix/Everett Collection; page 60: Everett Collection; page 61: © The Metropolitan Museum/Art Resource; page 62: (*left*) © The Metropolitan Museum/Art Resource; (*right*) Mary Evans/National Magazines/Everett Collection; page 63: (*top*) David Longendyke/Everett Collection; (*bottom*) Tim Boxer/Hulton Archive/Getty Images; page 64: CSU Archives/Everett Collection; page 65: Mirek Towski/DMI/Time Life Pictures/Getty Images; page 67: © 20th Century Fox/Everett Collection; page 68: (*left*) © The Metropolitan Museum/Art Resource; (*right*) Gianni Dagli Orti/The Art Archive at Art Resource; pages 69, 70 (*top*): Mary Evans Picture Library/Everett Collection; page 70 (*bottom*): AISA/Everett Collection; page 71: Marcus Gheeraerts, National Portrait Gallery; page 72: (*top*) Mary Evans Picture Library/Everett Collection; (*bottom*) Los Angeles County Museum of Art; page 73: Royal Collection, Belgium; page 74: (*left*) Images of Empire/Universal Images Group via Getty Images; (*right*) The National Archives; page 75: Prints & Photographs Division, Library of Congress, LC-USZ62–72813; page 76: Mary Evans Picture Library/Everett Collection; page 77: Everett Collection; page 79: © The Metropolitan Museum/Art Resource; page 80: Brooklyn Museum Costume Collection/Metropolitan Museum/Gift of Mrs. Emmet Whitlock; page 81: Everett Collection; page 82: (*left*) © The Metropolitan Museum/Art Resource; (*center*) Brooklyn Museum Costume Collection/Metropolitan Museum/Diana S. Field; (*right*) The Philadelphia Museum of Art/Art Resource; page 83: (*top*) Everett Collection; (*bottom*) Richard Young/Rex USA/Everett Collection; pages 84, 85: Everett Collection; page 86: © Aaron Spelling Prod./Everett Collection; page 87: © Paramount/Everett Collection; page 90: Jon Kopaloff/FilmMagic/

Getty Images; pages 91, 92: Everett Collection; page 93: (*left*) Mirrorpix/Everett Collection; (*right*) Curt Gunther/Hulton Archive/Getty Images; page 95: Warner Bros./Everett Collection; page 96: Mary Evans Picture Library/Everett Collection; pages 100, 101: Everett Collection; page 102: Advertising Archive/Everett Collection; page 104: 20th Century Fox/Everett Collection; page 105: Mirrorpix/Everett Collection; page 106: Everett Collection; page 110: Josiah Wedgwood and Sons Ltd., 18th century/Indianapolis Museum of Art; page 111: (*top*) *Uranometria* (1661), Courtesy of the United States Naval Observatory Library; (*bottom*) Horatio Hale, Musée de Séminaire, Québec; page 112: Superstock/Everett Collection; page 113: Everett Collection; page 114: Dee Cercone/Everett Collection; page 115: Jean-Marc Nattier, Former Crown collection; page 117: Brooklyn Museum Costume Collection/Metropolitan Museum/Gift of Arturo and Paul Peralta-Ramos; page 121: Higgins Armory Museum; page 122: Mary Evans Picture Library/Everett Collection; page 123: Superstock/Everett Collection; page 125: Advertising Archive/Everett Collection; page 130: *Salome Receives the Head of John the Baptist* by Caravaggio, National Gallery, London; pages 133, 134, 137: Mary Evans Picture Library/Everett Collection; page 139: Advertising Archive/Everett Collection; page 144: Mary Evans Picture Library/Everett Collection; page 148: Jeff Vespa/WireImage/Getty Images; page 152: Print by Robert Dighton, 1805; page 156: Mary Evans/APL/Everett Collection; pages 157, 158: Everett Collection; page 159: CSU Archives/Everett Collection; page 160: Everett Collection; page 161: Advertising Archive/Everett Collection; page 162: © Universal Television/Everett Collection; page 163: Mary Evans/APL/Everett Collection; page 165: Liu Weibing/© Xinhua/Photoshot/Everett Collection; pages 170, 171, 173: Everett Collection; page 174: © Illustrated London News Ltd/Everett Collection; page 180: Advertising Archive/Everett Collection; pages 181, 182: Everett Collection; page 183: David Jackson, V&A Museum; page 184: © Warner Bros./Everett Collection; page 190: (*top*) © The Metropolitan Museum/Art Resource; (*bottom*) Jean-Etienne Liotard, Musée d'Art et d'Histoire; page 191: (*left*) S Gaboury/DMI/Rex Features/Everett Collection; (*right*) BATA Shoe Museum; page 192: (*top*) Museum für Angewandte Kunst; (*bottom*) manuscript of Renaud de Montauban, 15th century; page 194: "Flip-Flops Between Baltimore and Washington" © 2006 Betsy/CC-BY-SA-2.0; page 196: Everett Collection; page 197: "Spanish Oldtimers" © 2006 David/CC-BY-SA-2.0; page 198: Everett Collection; pages 199, 202: Advertising Archive/Everett Collection; page 208: Everett Collection; page 209: "A Guy on a Bike Wearing Spandex" © 2009 Ed Yourdon/CC-BY-SA-2.0; page 211: Maximillion/Everett Collection; page 212: Harper's magazine, 1858; page 213: Everett Collection; page 214: Bain Collection, Library of Congress, LC-B2- 2801–11; page 215: Everett Collection; page 216: Keystone/Hulton Archive/Getty Images; page 218: Advertising Archive/Everett Collection; page 220: Mary Evans/ Amblin/Univeral/Ronald Grant/Everett Collection; page 224: © 20th Century Fox/Everett Collection; page 227: Bertram von Minden/Buxtehude Altar, 1400–1410; page 230: Robert Doisneau/Gamma-Rapho/Getty Images; page 232: Fox Photos/Hulton Archive/Getty Images; pages 233, 235 (*top*): Everett Collection; page 235: (*bottom*) David Fenton/ Archive Photos/Getty Images; page 236: Everett Collection; page 237: © Carsey-Werner/Everett Collection; page 238: Roger Sargent/Rex Features/Everett Collection; page 239: Stephen Boitano/Everett Collection; page 242: Everett Collection; page 243: Portrait of Sir Walter Raleigh (1554–1618) 1588 (oil on panel), English school (16th century)/private collection/The Bridgeman Art Library; page 244: Richard Young/Rex USA/Everett Collection; page 246: (*top*) John Pellino, U.S. Army; (*bottom*) Rex USA/Everett Collection; page 247: Everett Collection; page 248: Advertising Archive/ Everett Collection; page 252: Photoshot/Everett Collection; page 253: Gregorio T.Binuya/Everett Collection; pages 254, 255: Everett Collection; page 256: (*top*) Brian Rasic/Rex USA/Everett Collection; (*bottom left*) U.S. Federal Government; (*bottom right*) David F. Barry, Library of Congress, LC-USZ62–21207; pages 258, 259, 260 (*top*) 261: Everett Collection; page 261 (*bottom*): Charles L. Johnson, *Queen of Fashion Waltzes*. Kansas City, MO: Johnson Pub. Co.,1911; page 265: Fresco by Ambrogio Lorenzetti, Palazzo Pubblico; page 266: CSU Archives/Everett Collection; page 267: John Oxley Library, State Library of Queensland; page 268: U.S. Federal Government; page 269: © Universal Pictures/Everett Collection; page 272: Archduke Ferdinand II by Francesco Terzio, Kunsthistorisches Museum; page 273: Howard Sochurek/Time & Life Pictures/Getty Images; page 275: Monika Graff/Getty Images News/Getty Images; page 276: (*top*) American Folk Art Museum; (*bottom*) courtesy of the Ladybug Collection; page 277: Frank Masi/© Warner Bros./ Everett Collection; page 283: Pascal Le Segretain/Getty Images Entertainment/Getty Images; page 284: Mary Evans/ MGM/BRIDGE/Ronald Grant/Everett Collection; page 285: Everett Collection; page 287: Brooklyn Museum Costume Collection/Metropolitan Museum of Art/Joel Productions and Paramount Pictures